Ministers and
Generals

DESMOND MORTON

Ministers and Generals

Politics and the Canadian Militia

1868-1904

UNIVERSITY OF TORONTO PRESS

© University of Toronto Press 1970
Printed in Canada by
University of Toronto Press, Toronto and Buffalo
ISBN 0-8020-5228-2

TO MY FATHER
A SOLDIER AND A VERY
GENTLE MAN

Preface

So far as questions of defence have figured in the history of Canada since Confederation, they have usually been considered as illuminating a particular aspect of the relations of Great Britain with the new Dominion. Yet defence was also a problem for Canadians themselves. Developing the institutions and the expertise to manage an unexpected and unsought responsibility was a problem of self-government. It was also a problem of public opinion and of politics to find a place for military organizations and ideas in a community which had always borrowed both from elsewhere.

Of course, military institutions were only a particular feature of the development of instruments of nationality. For Canadians, nationality was more a matter of growth than of creation: the Militia Department proved to be an excellent vantage point for watching the strains of that process. In particular, it could be seen in the careers of the eight British officers who filled the appointment of General Officer Commanding the Canadian militia. It is the experience of those officers and of the Canadian politicians with whom they came in contact that provides the theme for this study.

With only one real exception, the succession of British officers who commanded the militia came to grief in Canada. One was dismissed, three resigned to avoid that fate, and two were withdrawn at the behest of the British government. The conflicts which enveloped the office of the GOC arose from different circumstances, but in their regular succession they compelled Canadians to realize that both the power and the responsibility to develop their own military policies lay with them. It was a task they accepted slowly and with evident reluctance in the years between the first Militia Act of 1868 and Sir Frederick Borden's revised act of 1904. The contrast was striking. The 1868 act created no more than a modest auxiliary for the British regular garrison which really defended Canada. Borden's Militia Act created a national army, commanded by Canadians and standing on its own in North America.

This book is about that transformation.

Acknowledgments

This work is the result of the inspiration of many minds and the help of many hands. The subject was suggested by Dr J. Mackay Hitsman and it could not have been completed without the encouragement and assistance of Professor S. F. Wise, director of history at Canadian Forces Headquarters, and of members of his staff, notably Warrant Officers Fred Azar and Paul Marshall. Inspiration and advice have also come from Colonel Charles Stacey, who made the old Army Historical Section a post-graduate school for many to whom the path of scholarship seemed prematurely blocked. Part of the research for this study was carried out while I was an officer in the Army Historical Section in Ottawa. I am indebted to the Department of National Defence for permission to use it in the present publication.

I have benefited from the kindness of staffs in libraries and archives in Canada, the United Kingdom, and the United States in the course of this study. I am particularly grateful to Professor C. Bruce Fergusson, the archivist of Nova Scotia, for allowing me to use the Sir Frederick Borden Papers when they were still in the course of being catalogued. By gracious permission of Her Majesty the Queen, I was allowed to use papers in the Royal Archives at Windsor Castle.

The basis of this study was a doctoral dissertation submitted to the University of London in 1968. In preparation for that work I had the valued advice and encouragement of my supervisors, Dr Ralph Miliband and Dr Kenneth Bourne of the London School of Economics and Political Science. I am also grateful to Professor Jean Blondel of the University of Essex who pressed on me, with too little success, the value of generalizing theory. For financial support during two years of full-time study, I am indebted to the Rhodes Trustees and to the Canada Council. For an opportunity to interrupt my career and for added support, I owe much to my former employer, the New Democratic Party of Ontario.

This book has been published with the help of a grant from the Social Science Research Council of Canada, using funds provided by the Canada Council. I am also grateful for the assistance of the Publications Fund of the University of Toronto Press. Like many other authors, I have benefited greatly from the editorial advice of the staff of the press, in particular Miss M. Jean Houston and Mr Gerald Hallowell.

Finally, for advice, support, recurrent proof-reading, and much more than a person can ever demand or repay, I thank my wife, Janet. For the mistakes, misjudgments, and wrongheadedness, I thank only myself.

Contents

Illustrations

ABBREVIATIONS

BP	Sir Frederick Borden Papers, Nova Scotia Archives
Cab.	Cabinet Papers, Public Record Office, London
CFHS	Historical Section, Canadian Forces Headquarters
CHAR	*Annual Report* of the Canadian Historical Association
CHR	*Canadian Historical Review*
CO	Colonial Office Papers, Public Record Office, London
CP	Caron Papers, Public Archives of Canada
DAG	Deputy Adjutant General
GOC	General Officer Commanding
HP	Hutton Papers, Public Archives of Canada
l.b.	Letterbook
LP	Laurier Papers, Public Archives of Canada
MD	Military District
MP	Macdonald Papers, Public Archives of Canada
NLS	National Library of Scotland
PAC	Public Archives of Canada
PRO	Public Record Office, London
RAW	Royal Archives, Windsor Castle
RG	Record Group, Public Archives of Canada
WO	War Office Papers, Public Record Office, London

Ministers and
Generals

CHAPTER ONE

Canadian Defence and Politics

1868-74

It is a commonplace of Canadian constitutional history that the British North America Act of 1867 added of itself almost nothing to the powers of self-government already enjoyed by the three colonies which made up the new Dominion. Canada remained a colony, her external affairs in British hands, her legislation subject to review and even to disallowance by British governments. The importance of Confederation lay in the added strength it gave Canada to fulfil her existing responsibilities.

One of these was defence. Since 1782, when Britain had resumed the task of defending her shrunken North American empire, the colonial contribution to security had been determined by the local governments. The achievement of responsible government meant that this contribution was, in fact as well as in theory, subject to local control. However, the local defence role was minor. The defence of British North America depended on regular army garrisons provided by the British government, paid for by British taxpayers, and commanded by British generals.[1]

In the 1860s, when much else was changing in North America, Britain was also reconsidering her defence responsibilities in the area. Twice during the decade, after the Trent Affair of 1861 and again during the Fenian raids which followed the end of the American Civil War, large reinforcements had been rushed to the British garrison in Canada. While British politicians and taxpayers began to question the cost of their

North American commitment, some British soldiers were having second thoughts about its military feasibility. Lieutenant Colonel W. F. D. Jervois of the Royal Engineers concluded a study of British defences with a report, early in 1864, that an American invasion could not successfully be resisted.[2]

The defence of British North America was a partnership in which the British were growing weary of their predominant responsibility. Canadians were also conscious of the problem. The delegates to the Quebec Conference of October 1864, where the foundations of Confederation were laid, were acutely aware that the huge American armies might turn northward when their Civil War was over. For their benefit, Colonel Jervois was on hand with a second, much more optimistic, report. Canada could be made secure, he suggested, at a cost of $8,770,000 in new fortifications and other preparations.[3]

This was welcome news for Canadians. George Brown, the Reform leader and a partner in the Confederation coalition, later acknowledged that rumours of indefensibility had been bad for business: "the capitalist is alarmed and the immigrant is afraid to come among us."[4] Of course, the estimated cost of security was high – as much as the annual public revenue for the province of Canada – but as long as the threat of American invasion remained, it had to be faced. The same session of the Canadian provincial Parliament which endorsed the Quebec resolutions on Confederation also voted an unprecedented million dollars for defence purposes.

It was in the shadow of threatened American invasion in the spring of 1865 that the cornerstone of Canadian defence policy until the end of the century was laid. Fresh from their session of Parliament, Sir John A. Macdonald and his three leading colleagues, George Etienne Cartier, George Brown, and Alexander Galt, set out for London. In terms of practical assistance the returns from their mission were small: the British consented to complete some important outpost forts at Lévis, opposite Quebec. Rather, it was the intangible assurances that the Canadians could value. A committee of senior officers under the Duke of Cambridge declared that Canada was indeed defensible in terms of Jervois' later report. Militarily, the judgment might be dubious, but it was what Canadians wanted to reassure their nervous compatriots.[5] Even more valuable was the declaration which Edward Cardwell, the colonial secretary, embodied in the report on the ministerial discussions. Having had assurances from the Canadians that "... that Province is willing to devote all her resources both in men and money to the maintenance of her connexion with the Mother Country ... the Imperial Government fully acknowledged the reciprocal obligation of defending every portion of the Empire with all the resources at its command."[6]

For the Canadians this was a precious reassurance, and it remained Canada's only formal guarantee of the only possible protection which might avail against American invasion. In the later years of the century the Cardwell commitment was to be recalled by Canadian politicians and British officials alike. At the same time, Canada preserved her own position of limited liability in the defence partnership. "All her resources" was translated into a promise to spend a million dollars a year for defence. That was three times as much as the province had ever spent before on its militia but to the Canadian delegates it seemed like a bargain. To George Brown, a man whose past record might have promised bitter resistance to military spending, the 1865 agreement seemed cause for elation. To his wife he wrote: "We have received strong assurances that all the troops at England's disposal & the whole navy of Gt. Britain will be used for the defence of every portion of Canada in the event of war. We have got quit of the burden of five million dollars for works of defence. We have choked off the cry that we will do nothing towards defence."[7]

Even if the leading Fathers of Confederation wanted only a secure and subordinate role in determining military policy, the events of their decade forced defence considerations upon them. The Fenian threat proved a valuable ally for the pro-Confederation forces. It also imposed a military effort on the provinces, particularly New Brunswick and Canada, which greatly strengthened the local militia organizations. Of course, military considerations were not always an argument for closer union. The financial burden of new fortifications was a major expense which the new Dominion could be expected to impose, while there were others, like the Rouge leader A. A. Dorion, who claimed that safety lay in disunity: "The battles of Canada cannot be fought on the frontier but on the high seas and at the great cities of the Atlantic coast; and it will be nothing but folly for us to cripple ourselves by spending fifteen or twenty millions a year to raise an army of 50,000 for the purpose of resisting an invasion of the country. The best thing that Canada can do is to keep quiet and give no cause for war."[8]

It was partly because defence was important and partly because it was highly controversial that when he formed his new cabinet on July 1,

1867, Sir John A. Macdonald entrusted the Department of Militia and Defence to his old friend and ally, George Etienne Cartier. As a provincial minister, Cartier had already been responsible for education, railway legislation, and the adoption of a civil code in Lower Canada. To create a military system for the very unmilitary Canadians was a task worthy of his stature.[9]

Cartier's task was to amalgamate the three quite different militia systems of the three provinces which entered Confederation in 1867. Although all of the provinces paid lip-service to the principle of universal obligation for militia service, in New Brunswick and Canada the compulsory aspect had fallen into abeyance. In both provinces the alarms of the Civil War and the subsequent Fenian threat had meant that small bodies of militia had been embodied for long periods of time on the frontier. It had proved politically wiser to exploit the volunteer spirit than to enforce compulsory service on a larger number. In both the lower provinces there were units of volunteer militia, mostly dating from the British volunteer movement of 1859 or the visit of the Prince of Wales in 1860, but in Nova Scotia volunteering had barely extended beyond Halifax.[10]

Understandably, Cartier based his new organization on the militia system of the province of Canada. It had been the excitement of the Crimean War, more than a decade before, which had led to a demand for militia reform in Canada. A commission visited New York, Massachusetts, and Connecticut and found that the old compulsory militia had been supplanted by enthusiastic new volunteer corps. As a result, the Canadian Militia Act of 1855 owed as much to American as to British influence, a consideration to bear in mind when considering why subsequent British commanders found it difficult to relate the Canadian system to their own Militia and Volunteers.[11]

Cartier's Militia Bill was introduced to the Dominion Parliament on March 31, 1868. It provided for an Active Militia of forty thousand men and a Reserve Militia in which nearly every other able-bodied Canadian male between the ages of sixteen and sixty could be required to serve. Apart from the extensive provisions for organizing and mustering the huge Reserve Militia, most of the legislation dealt with the Active Militia. Canada was to be divided into nine military districts, and these in turn were to be subdivided into Brigade and Regimental Divisions. Each Regimental Division was to provide a quota of Active Militia. If sufficient volunteer corps were not forthcoming, the government could raise a Regular Militia, composed of volunteers if possible, of balloted men if necessary. Men in the Regular Militia were to serve for two years but the enlistment period for the volunteers would be three years. However, if a volunteer grew tired of the service, he could resign by giving his commanding officer only six months' notice. The bill provided for training of between eight and sixteen days a year and established that volunteers, regardless of rank, would receive fifty cents a day for their services.

The bill was a substantial achievement for the aging Minister of Militia, and he defended it, in French and English, in a speech lasting five and a half hours. In its course he ranged from rhetorical justification of the role of armies in the development of nationhood to detailed explanations of obscure points. To those who claimed that Canada could not be defended at all, Cartier presented the example of the Confederate States, whose four million people had raised 400,000 soldiers for four years of resistance. His system would mobilize 700,000 men. Appealing to English-speaking MP s, he declared that his bill proved the determination of Canadians to remain under the British Crown. Indeed, he suggested, members would probably have agreed to an even more expensive military system. However, he reassured them, "the measure before you looks to economy and it is especially from that point of view that it recommends itself to the House."[12]

Cartier's bill received royal assent on May 22, 1868, and came into force on October 1. It really established two edifices. One was the imposing framework of the militia, with references to enrolments, ballots, and regimental divisions, and, above all, with its promise that in the event of war 700,000 Canadians could be called into the field. The other was the real military structure, a militia designed to survive among a people with little proven appetite for sustained military effort. Cartier was determined that his militia system would survive, but to do so it had to be saved from its own enthusiasts. The militia would survive in peacetime because it was voluntary or it would not survive at all. That shrewd realization was to govern Cartier's militia policy through his remaining years in office.

The test of the voluntary system began on October 1 when members of the old provincial militias could remuster into the new force. In the lower provinces remustering was almost a test of Confederation; a decision to join virtually signified acceptance of the new Dominion. By the end of the year Cartier could claim substantial success for his system, with a total of 37,170 enrolled of the required 40,000. The earlier weakness of the volunteer movement in Nova Scotia, as well as a residual hostility to Confederation, could explain why only 928 of the volunteers came from the eastern-most province. The first enrolment of Reserve Militia in 1869 found a total of 618,896 eligible men.*

Although Cartier was able to find volunteers to fill the ranks of his militia, other criticisms of his system proved well founded. Militia officers had complained that unless men could be compelled to serve out their enlistments, discipline could not be preserved. They soon were reporting that their men moved away without notice, sometimes taking their uniforms with them. Employers refused men leave to go to camp. Some militiamen bluntly refused to turn out. For those who did go to camp, training was too short to reach even a modest standard of efficiency. If a volunteer had received all the training the law allowed, he would have served only 192 hours in three years; in practice, training periods were much shorter. The militia pay of fifty cents a day was only half the wage of a common labourer and many volunteers were obliged by their employers to hire substitutes. To help them the practice arose of training "two days in one," an abuse made possible by a Militia Act definition that a day of training consisted of three hours of drill.[13]

The militia organization did not provide a balanced military force. The infantry numbered 27,449 out of a total strength of 37,170, and there were only ten batteries of field artillery and 1,500 cavalry. The act provided that a military train, commissariat, hospital, ambulance, and other corps might be organized "whenever the exigencies of the service may require the same,"[14] but they did not materialize as peacetime organizations until the end of the century. The absence of naval defence was even more significant. A long series of strategic appreciations, of which Colonel Jervois' was only the latest, had concluded that the successful defence of Canada depended on maintaining naval supremacy on at least Lake Ontario. The Militia Act provided for a marine militia as the third component of the Active Militia but it was never organized. The few companies of naval militia which had belonged to the old provincial militias rapidly disappeared.

These inadequacies were as apparent to Canadian politicians as they were to British generals. Even Macdonald referred to the volunteers as "Holiday soldiers" and admitted that the Fenians did not take them

* See Appendix A.

seriously.[15] The simple fact was that Canada was taking advantage of her limited liability status in the defence of British North America. Meanwhile, her militia could expect to be armed and equipped largely at British expense, her officers and non-commissioned officers would train at schools organized by British regiments, and the garrison as a whole would continue to set standards of discipline and smartness for the volunteers to emulate. The British were now building the forts at Lévis which they had promised in 1865, while Canadians too were living up to their commitments. Indeed, under the threat of Fenian invasion they had been spending considerably more than a million dollars a year on defence since 1865. The same session of the Dominion Parliament which passed the Militia Act went on to authorize a loan of $5.5 million to build the fortifications Colonel Jervois had suggested four years earlier.[16]

Yet, even as Cartier watched over the remustering of his volunteers, the defence situation in North America was being utterly transformed. The first omen of change was the British reaction to the Canadian request for a guarantee for the fortification loan. There was none. Instead, orders came to recall part of the British garrison and to withdraw the Royal Navy personnel who had been manning anti-Fenian patrols on the Great Lakes. Late in 1868, when Cartier and William McDougall, the minister of public works, arrived in London to arrange for the transfer of the territories of the Hudson's Bay Company to the Dominion, they found that Gladstone's first government had just taken office. While Cartier haggled over trifles with minor War Office officials, Edward Cardwell, now the secretary of state for war, was busy elsewhere, working out plans to eliminate the garrisons from self-governing colonies.

The new policy moved through the machinery of British government with impressive speed. A despatch of April 14, 1869, from Lord Granville, the colonial secretary, to Sir John Young, the governor general, was the first official intimation to the Canadians of British intentions. In blunt terms it announced that the garrison of sixteen thousand troops was being reduced that year to only six thousand – of whom four thousand in central Canada would remain only as a "temporary arrangement." Granville offered help for the Canadians in setting up their own defences – but entirely at Canadian expense.[17]

The new policy drew much more violent reactions from British soldiers than from Canadian politicians. The Duke of Cambridge, commander-in-chief, protested to Cardwell that the reduction of the garrisons would "lead to the ultimate and not very distant loss of our Colonial Possessions."[18] From Montreal Lieutenant General Sir Charles Windham, commanding in North America, warned that the orders to concentrate his remaining forces at Quebec and Halifax would "sound the death knell for all the militia organization of Canada."[19] Canadian ministers, on the other hand, offered little reaction. Certainly there were no steps to replace the departing British. When Windham removed a garrison of two hundred regulars from Prescott as too few to withstand a Fenian attack, a mere twenty-four local volunteers took their place.[20] After all, drastic reductions of the garrison had occurred before. If Canada assumed such British tasks as patrolling the Great Lakes or guarding key points, she would only justify the Gladstone government in its policies.

A year later a despatch from Granville to Young announced that the "temporary arrangement" was over. Henceforth only Halifax would be garrisoned as an imperial station, with fifteen hundred men. For the balance of 1870 a battalion of infantry and a battery of artillery would remain at Quebec. There were some signs of conciliation. If the Canadians still wanted to proceed with their fortification loan, the British government would provide a guarantee. The British authorities were also willing to help Canada build her own regular army, with officers and men from the departing garrison. Perhaps most important, Granville transmitted the assurance that the withdrawals were "... contingent upon a time of peace, and are in no way intended to alter or diminish the obligations which exist on both sides in case of foreign war."[21]

There were some further efforts to fill the military vacuum the British found they were leaving in North America. In February 1870 Sir Charles Windham died. His appointment of Lieutenant General Commanding in North America was given to Sir Hastings Doyle, the British commander at Halifax, but another officer, Lieutenant General the Honourable James Lindsay, was sent out to Canada to supervise the arrangements for the British withdrawal, to take charge of the joint British-Canadian expedition to the Red River colony, and to help the Canadian government to organize its own military forces. Although he was highly successful in his first two tasks, Lindsay entirely failed to persuade the Canadian government even to give serious consideration to the suggestions he advanced.[22]

To some extent, Canadian sang-froid seemed justified by the events of 1870. The long-awaited resumption of the Fenian raids took the form of a few feeble incursions across the Quebec border, countered with triumphant ease by the local militia. The expedition to the Red River proved to be a bloodless success. Canadian public opinion refused to become upset by the prospect of the British withdrawal. Post-Confederation self-confidence and a short attention span for military concerns combined to encourage peace of mind. Some members of the Liberal opposition even welcomed the British departure as a contribution to better relations with the United States. Lieutenant Colonel W. F. Coffin, a Canadian civil servant, expressed a variety of reactions:

Let England withdraw every regiment tomorrow if she so wills it, we shall miss the social qualities of the officers, and the familiar faces of the most charming of our women won from us by men whose choice approves their taste; we shall miss the welcome presence of a grave and respectable soldiery; our farmers' daughters will lose many good husbands and the country a wealth of useful settlers; we shall gain a priceless amount of self-reliance and the money now expended on the accommodation of Her Majesty's troops will be applied to promote the efficiency of our own militia.[23]

Some problems had to be faced. The British had ended their generous policy of lending arms and equipment to the Canadian militia in 1868 but they could not take their barracks and fortifications back to Britain. These were accordingly presented to Canada. The Militia Department also agreed to buy several hundred thousand dollars' worth of stores; the rest was shipped to England or Bermuda or sold to local contractors. The stock of surplus blankets was presented to the victims of the great Chicago fire of 1871. These arrangements drew some of the petulant criticism which was a common Canadian reaction to the withdrawal; the official in charge found it necessary to explain in his final report that, contrary to rumour, sentry boxes had not been shipped back to England but had been sold on the spot.[24]

Lindsay and other British observers had recognized that one of the most urgent Canadian problems would be to find qualified men to look after the fortifications and stores the Dominion had suddenly acquired. Seven militia storekeepers, with their handful of clerks and labourers, were hardly sufficient. During the winter of 1870–1, some of the Canadian troops raised for the Red River expedition were used to guard Kingston and Montreal and a small force of British regulars remained at Quebec until November 11, 1871. With Canadian public opinion strongly opposed to "standing armies," it was complicated to organize even a small military establishment to man the major fort-

resses on a more permanent basis. The solution, suggested to Cartier by
his staff, was to provide artillery schools at Kingston and Quebec. Each
school would be organized as a battery, with permanent officers and
non-commissioned officers. The rank and file would be called out from
existing militia artillery units, serve for a year, and return to their
batteries as experienced soldiers. The idea was approved by the cabinet
and money for the batteries was included in the 1871 estimates. After a
further delay the services of Captain Thomas Bland Strange of the Royal
Artillery were secured from the War Office. He and Lieutenant George
French, another British artillery officer who had become the militia's
Inspector of Artillery and Warlike Stores, were promoted to the
militia rank of lieutenant colonel, and on October 20, 1871, they were
each authorized to organize one of the batteries.[25]

Conditions of service hardly seem enticing: a soldier was entitled to
a uniform, shelter, daily rations of a pound of beef and a pound of
bread, and the standard militia pay of fifty cents a day. However, both
batteries soon had their quota of men. French, at Kingston, recruited
many of his soldiers from returned veterans of the Red River expedition, while Strange, at Quebec, found that French-Canadian loggers
soon made good, practical gunners. The last British troops had left
Quebec before Strange could take over the Citadel and the first task
for his recruits was to hoist the heavy fortress guns out of the snow and
on to their carriages.[26]

Another service of the British garrison was harder to replace. Schools
of instruction now had to be organized by the local militia staff officers
and this placed too heavy a burden on their initiative, energy, and
professional knowledge. The two embodied batteries gave the militia
gunners a significant advantage; in the infantry and cavalry, the decline in standards was soon apparent.[27]

Only a few militia enthusiasts complained. Canadians as a whole
had refused to react to the astonishing reversal in their defence system.
The changes in the Militia Department could hardly have been more
limited. The two new artillery batteries cost less than a hundred thousand dollars a year and the makeshift local schools cost half as much
as had been spent on such training before 1871.[28] One casualty of the
withdrawal was the fortification loan. In a disarmed Canada, the Jervois proposals were evidently irrelevant. The Canadian government
was delighted to be able to persuade Gladstone to transfer the British
guarantee to an equivalent loan for the construction of the Intercolonial Railway.[29] Unwillingly and without even wishing to admit it,

Canada had become the senior partner in her own defence. During the ensuing thirty years Canadians were obliged to grow into the responsibilities which had been dropped upon them. In time, Britain rediscovered a desire to control policies in which her own interests were still involved and part of the story of those years concerns the British attempt to reassert its influence.

While the British military withdrawal from central Canada was transforming the structure of authority in Canadian defence, an equally revolutionary development was transforming Canadian defence policy. Since 1782 there had been only one real problem for Canadian security: the possibility of war with the United States. Concealed among the many reasons for the withdrawal of their garrison was a British suspicion that they no longer had the military resources to cope with this problem. Admittedly, the Gladstone government was not prone to moods of military grandeur nor was the era marked, in Britain, by expansive self-confidence. Nevertheless, the facts behind the doubts were real enough. In four years of civil war the Americans had mobilized what a highly intelligent British observer described as "one of the most formidable forces the world has ever seen."[30] The fortifications proposed by Colonel Jervois were still unbuilt and in 1870 Cardwell was warned that Quebec itself, despite all the millions spent on it, was virtually indefensible.[31]

Canadians might not be privy to the memoranda exchanged between British generals and politicians but they could draw their own conclusions. Alexander Mackenzie, a leading Liberal, maintained in 1868 that the fortifications for which Canadians were urged to borrow $5.5 million were intended "to provide facilities for the escape of British troops in case of disaster." It was an ungenerous but not unreasonable interpretation of Jervois' plan.[32] The best security for Canada was, perhaps, as A. A. Dorion had suggested, "to keep quiet and give no cause for war."[33] That was the major value of the otherwise painful Treaty of Washington, finally concluded on May 8, 1871. Thereafter, the American, British, and Canadian governments refused to allow their differences to approach the threshold of armed conflict. By the end of 1871 the United States had become, relative to her population and resources, as nearly disarmed as Canada. The bulk of her small regular army was fully engaged against the Indians of the western plains. Her militia organization had returned to the careless hands of the state governments.

Canada's next best guarantee of security was the Cardwell commitment of 1865, and a persistent theme in her military policy after Confederation was to do just enough to keep that pledge alive. Alfred Gilpin Jones, a Liberal minister of militia, made the point explicitly in 1878 that "... he had always felt the amount we paid annually for military purposes was more to show the Horse Guards our willingness as far as possible to take upon ourselves a fair share of our own defence than for any other purpose."[34] At the Colonial Conference of 1887 the chief Canadian spokesman, Sir Alexander Campbell, pointed out to sceptical British ministers that Canada had spent on an average more than the promised million dollars a year for defence.[35] Even the Canadian rifle team, sent annually to Wimbledon or Bisley, was part of the military effort. In 1884, when his colleagues threatened to eliminate the government subsidy to the team, the Minister of Militia argued successfully that it would "have a bad effect in England."[36]

Before 1871 possibility of war with the United States had been the centrepiece of defence policy for Canada; after that year it was at best an ambiguous justification for any defence effort. Indeed, the ambiguity owed a good deal to British influence. It is evident that the British no longer seriously contemplated war with the United States. Her remaining strongholds in Canada, at Halifax and later at Esquimalt, were never garrisoned on a scale to resist an American attack.[37] At the same time, British officers in Canada, particularly after 1895, continued to see the Americans as their natural enemies. As late as 1910, in an inspection of the Canadian militia, General Sir John French made readiness for war with the Americans his criterion in judging the force.[38]

To most Canadians this attitude was unreal. Even those who felt strong antipathy to American institutions and values could hardly hope to persuade their countrymen to arm for war with the United States.[39] Canadians had other priorities, as David Mills, a prominent Ontario Liberal, pointed out: "... in a country situated as we were, not likely to be involved in war, and having a large demand upon our resources for ordinary public improvements, it was highly desirable to have our military affairs conducted as cheaply as possible."[40] Colonel Walker Powell, the senior Canadian-born militia officer, expressed remarkably similar sentiments: "... where the energies of the population are so largely needed in the prosecution of the ordinary pursuits, it is indispensable that any provision for the defence made by Canada should be practical, and the means for conveying instruction of such a nature as to cause the greatest good to result from the least expenditure of time and money."[41]

Being much closer to the United States than to Britain in political style and language, Canadians as a whole were prepared to dismiss even such outbursts as the Venezuela crisis of 1896 as merely pre-election jingoism. "We know perfectly well that every time a general election is drawing on in the United States," an MP commented in 1896, "they get up a war scare, and make announcements that there are going to be difficulties, and they do it all for a purpose."[42] When some Canadians a few years later proposed to build a navy to counter the naval militias established by some of the American states on the Great Lakes, the Toronto *Globe* proceeded to crush them with ridicule: alleging that a new American gunboat might one day shoot down the clocktower on its waterfront building, the paper proposed that "the staunch old stone hooker Anna Maria Susan Jane be equipped with armor, turrets, quick-firing guns and other appliances and ordered to cruise about between the Don and the Humber."[43]

If Canadians could not normally believe in preparing for war with the United States, why maintain a military organization in peacetime? Fortunately for military enthusiasts, other roles and opportunities presented themselves in surprising profusion in the years between 1871 and 1900. Men of the militia participated in four expeditions in the North West and British Columbia. A force of eight thousand men took part in the North-West campaign of 1885 and several contingents were sent to the South African War of 1899–1902. With Canadians as a whole, the militia shared two Russian war scares, the Venezuela crisis of 1895–6, and a series of confrontations on the Alaska boundary. Far more frequently, militia were called out to support the civil authority in riots and strikes. In the absence of adequate police forces outside the major cities, the militiamen became a magistrate's only resource for even such routine duties as guarding a hanging or breaking up a boxing match.

Listing the military and police functions of the militia does not, however, exhaust the number of roles the institution played in post-Confederation Canada. If the survival of the force in some form might be guaranteed by the recurrent need for its services, its structure and development were guided by more purely political considerations. The Canadian militia, in common with other institutions of Canadian government of the era, was enmeshed in a complex system of patronage and influence which transcended, when it did not displace, the norms and values of conventional administration.

Political influences pervaded the Militia Department from top to bottom. Responsibility for militia policy rested with the cabinet and, in principle, with the Minister of Militia and Defence. The constitutional model was self-consciously British but there was one essential feature which was specifically Canadian. In forming his first ministry, Macdonald felt compelled to provide a weighted representation for the interests of race, religion, province, and even district, sometimes with little regard for the talents of those appointed. It was an agonizing precedent which virtually every subsequent Canadian Prime Minister has felt obliged to follow.

Membership in a federal cabinet meant recognition of a politician's stature within his group or region. It also implied a responsibility for delivering the support of that group or region to the party in power, a task facilitated by a minister's access to the power of patronage. The representative nature of the cabinet meant that nearly all cabinet ministers had an interest in militia administration and appointments. The militia organization had unique advantages as an instrument of patronage; hardly a constituency lacked at least a drill shed and a company of volunteers. Major militia appointments involved all the representative interests of race, religion, and region, not to mention the competing claims of party loyalty.* A weak minister, or one of low prestige with his colleagues, had little chance of preserving the departmental interest, much less of pursuing an aggressively independent policy. Ministerial influence was reinforced by the practice of submitting every permanent militia appointment and even trivial decisions on expenditure to the collective authority of a Privy Council order.

Often more important than the Minister of Militia in determining

---

* The operation of the system may be illustrated by the appointment of a surgeon to the military school at London in 1888. The Minister of Agriculture, Sir John Carling, was the MP for London and also western Ontario's representative in the cabinet. His nominee for the lucrative post, a Conservative doctor from London, was opposed by a politically active doctor from Stratford, who happened to be a Roman Catholic. The Catholic members of the cabinet were mobilized on his behalf and the resulting struggle lasted for more than a year. Aided by his own heroic exertions in a crucial by-election, the Catholic doctor was eventually appointed. (CP, file 12326.)

the government's overall defence policy was the Prime Minister. As well as his pre-eminent influence in council, the Prime Minister was also the government's link with the Governor General. The Governor General, in turn, was the most direct and legitimate channel for British influence in military, as in other, spheres of Canada's public policy. Cartier's Militia Act had provided that the commander-in-chief of the militia was the Queen, acting indirectly through the Governor General. This may have diminished the direct authority that pre-Confederation Governors General had exercised in military matters, but it did not inhibit most vice-regal appointees from applying their own conception of the special royal prerogative in militia affairs.

Beyond the Governor General and the cabinet was Parliament; beyond Parliament, the electorate. There were politicians who were unalterably opposed to the militia. The elderly Reformer, Malcolm Cameron, once declared that he "would as soon think of teaching his child to drink whiskey or steal as to be a soldier." Cameron went much farther than public opinion and was rebuked by the chief organ of his own party, the Toronto *Globe*.[44] In parliament, anti-militarism was less common than a generalized objection to defence spending and a suspicion of military men. This mood could be combined with a shrewd political concern with the pay, comfort, and welfare of the individual militia volunteer.

The volunteers themselves were well represented in the House of Commons. The annual examination of the Militia Department estimates came to be known as "Colonel's Day" and other MPs tended to stay away, confident that the government's economical spirit would withstand the siege. "... [1]n a House like this," complained one MP, "with Colonels on his right, Colonels on his left, Colonels all around him and in front of him, with about every fourth man in the House a Lieut. Colonel," he found it daunting to oppose military extravagance.[45]

The "Colonels" were a cantankerous lobby,* overwhelmingly representing the rural militia and after 1878 predominantly Conservative. Their goals were not higher defence spending as much as a redistribution of the existing expenditure in favour of the rural battalions. As a result, their main target of attack was the militia staff and later the permanent corps, the chief competitors for militia money. The most

* See Appendix B.

impressive demonstration of the militia lobby's strength took place
during the debate on the 1868 Militia Bill. Militia officers had been
incensed by the provision in the bill that they would receive the same
pay as their men. Led by Major Mackenzie Bowell, a Conservative MP,
and with the gleeful support of the Liberal opposition, the militia MPs
forced through amendments cutting the salaries of the full-time staff
officers. In vain Cartier and Macdonald tried to quell the rebellion
but, after three divisions in which the majority against them rose from
one to four, the government had to give way.[46]

Beyond the parliamentary colonels lay the nebulous political influence of the "militia vote." Militiamen had votes in nearly every constituency in Canada and, as Colonel George Denison repeatedly
pointed out, their drill pay was the only form of public spending that
penetrated down every dusty concession road in the country.[47] Denison
made other claims for the militia voters. It was the volunteers, organized by himself and other aggrieved militia officers, who had beaten Sir
George Cartier in Montreal East in 1872.[48] The *Canadian Military
Gazette* later boasted that men of the militia had helped to sweep
Mackenzie's government out of power in 1878 and the Conservatives
in 1896.[49] Such assertions deserve caution. The property qualification
for federal electors would have kept many rank and file militiamen
from the polls until at least 1898. In 1904, when a deliberate attempt
was made to mobilize militia voters against the Laurier government,
even the organizers of the campaign confessed that the results were
imperceptible.[50]

However, in the calculations of politicians, belief can be as influential as knowledge. A keen practical politician like Adolphe Caron was
conscientious about his responsibility for the militia vote. "I believe the
volunteers will give us a big lift in 1883," the newly appointed Minister
of Militia reported to Macdonald, "That is what I am trying to
work."[51] At least some militia voters were expected to be faithful to
the government. In 1886, at the request of the Conservative candidate
in a by-election in Winnipeg, Caron wired the local permanent force
commander to allow his men to vote, adding: "I trust to your usual
tact and judgement to see that our friends have a fair show."[52] The
Conservative won by twelve votes.

The "militia vote" mattered less because of numbers than because of
the prominence of militia officers in their communities. When the
rural militia battalions were formed in the mid-1860s, local prominence

was as likely to earn a man the command of his county battalion as the nomination for member of parliament. Once adopted, the joint roles complemented each other. In Parliament, the "Colonels" could express their hostility to unpopular staff officers and resist any reduction of the paper strength of the force. At the head of his battalion the MP had ample opportunities to display his patriotism, public spirit, and generosity.

The political pressure of the militia was not exercised solely through its own members in Parliament. Local MPs added their own influence to demands from the force. "I am in daily, almost hourly receipt of letters from Colonels, and Captains and corporals and Mayors and Wardens and constables and parsons about this Essex Battalion," complained one MP to the Minister of Militia, "and either you have to give them a sixth company or I have to retire from public life and I don't care a d – – – which alternative finds favour in your eyes."[53]

Officially, even more than other branches of government the militia was supposed to be divorced from politics. As Prime Minister, Sir Mackenzie Bowell listened with apparent astonishment when a deputation charged that political influence had interfered in militia administration.[54] In one of his first speeches after taking office, Dr Frederick Borden, Laurier's minister of militia, announced: "I know no Conservative, I know no Liberal in the militia force."[55] In fact, as his own correspondence reveals, he knew them very well. So did his predecessors. They had helped to make the Militia Department one of the most comprehensive engines of patronage in the government. It had many advantages for the role. In addition to its complete dissemination across the country, the rewards its applicants sought were relatively cheap. The salaries of militia staff officers were low. Promotion in the militia itself might cost the recipient more in new uniforms, subscriptions, and loss of other income than he would receive in pay and allowances. Those Canadians who passionately sought the satisfaction of social standing could find in the Militia Department an avenue to rank, uniforms, and the status of a gentleman. To command the Canadian contingent at Edward VII's coronation, the government chose not a hero of the recent war in South Africa but a millionaire financier who had helped some of the ministers with their investments.[56]

The Militia Department offered a variety of favours. For enthusiasts or gentlemen at the end of their means there were about thirty places on the staff. Humbler aspirants could become caretakers or labourers.

Members of parliament could be rewarded with new drill sheds or repairs to old ones. Militia officers could be gratified with an extra issue
of uniforms for their battalion. Like other branches, the Militia Department did its best to ensure that its spending went only into the
pockets of supporters. "What in Hell does this mean?" demanded a
Conservative MP when he found a Militia Department advertisement
in a hostile newspaper. "It is really no use my fighting your battles here
if you continue giving this paper the means of supplying himself with
powder. Stop it at once."[57] Even in the midst of the North-West campaign of 1885, the rules of patronage were not suspended. A typical
telegram from a Winnipeg politician directed the Minister of Militia to
"... give contract for biscuits to Thomas Chambers. He is a good Conservative ... The man that has it now are [sic]Grits and bad ones at
that."[58]

Government MPS – or defeated government candidates in constituencies held by the opposition – had authority over much local militia
patronage. A Kingston MP was warned by the Minister of Militia that
if he did not hurry up and nominate a new master tailor for the artillery
school, "the Battery people will have to go in kilts."[59] Few towns offered
as much military patronage as Kingston but many towns could hope to
be the site for an annual camp, with its excitement and profitable contracts. "Quit delivering long speeches," demanded one member's backers,
"and get down to business." The MP did as he was told and won a camp
for his town for two successive years, despite the existence of more suitable sites nearby.[60]

In theory, the political influence of MPs, militia politicians, and the
general public should have been balanced by a countervailing departmental interest, operating through the permanent officers and officials
of the department. In practice, such an interest was unusually weak. In
organizing his new department Cartier had followed the current British
War Office model, creating a military branch under the Adjutant
General and a civil branch under a Deputy Minister. The latter had responsibility for almost every aspect of administration, from the supply
of clothing to the management of militia land and buildings. The first
Deputy Minister, George Futvoye, was an elderly lawyer and civil servant with few apparent qualifications for the job. Another of Cartier's
appointments, incidentally, was his private secretary, Benjamin Sulte,
a future historian of French Canada, who spent the rest of his working
life in the department. Cartier's organization meant that the Militia

Department was unique in the federal government in having two permanent heads, neither of them clearly designated the senior. Although the Deputy Minister received a smaller salary than the Adjutant General, his involvement in the crucial problems of patronage as well as his Canadian background tended to bring him closer to the Minister than the head of the military branch.

The Militia Act reserved the appointment of Adjutant General to persons "educated in the military profession" who had achieved field officer rank in the British regular army.[61] The senior military position open to a Canadian officer was the appointment of Deputy Adjutant General at headquarters. From 1868 to 1895 Lieutenant Colonel Walker Powell was the senior officer in the Canadian militia of Canadian birth. This permanent feature of the department had begun his career as a Liberal MP and he owed his initial appointment to the militia staff to John Sandfield Macdonald in 1862. Powell had a gift for making himself amenable to politicians of both parties and by 1868 he was sufficiently popular that Cartier, on introducing the Militia Bill, paid special tribute to his "ability and fidelity." Ministers and Generals were to come and go but Walker Powell, immersed in the details of administration, went on, resigned to the limits both of his career and of the militia as a whole. His point of view is apparent in a letter to a more demanding militia officer: "It is a pity to see such fine material as we have in our active militia so badly cared for, but there is such a difference of opinion among public men as to what the Dominion policy on this point should be as to cause our indefatigable efforts to be productive of less good results than should suffice to repay us for the time and labour devoted to the force."[62]

Junior officers and officials in the Militia Department had even less reason to protest the political management of its affairs: in many cases, they were the beneficiaries of political influence. Each of the nine military districts was commanded by a Deputy Adjutant General and each of the twenty-one Brigade Divisions was entitled to a Brigade Major. While the militia lobby resented the money spent to pay these officers, the opposition objected to the creation of thirty new vacancies for political appointees. National feelings were aroused when Cartier gave six of the senior appointments to British half-pay officers. Command of the predominantly French-speaking sixth military district at Montreal went to A. C. de Lotbinière Harwood, a Quebec Conservative who had no military experience at all.[63]

While department officials in Ottawa had the protection of a rudi-

mentary civil service act, staff officers and officials elsewhere had no such
security. They could be, and on occasion were, dismissed without right
of appeal. It was acknowledged that their salaries were too small to
allow them to save for their retirement and their gratuity, if they reached
the age of superannuation, was limited to two years' pay. If they died
on the way, their widow had to be content with two months' pay. Few
Canadian officers enjoyed private means – indeed, a plea of genteel
poverty was one of the commonest justifications in proposing a man for a
staff appointment. Having secured their appointments by political influence, officers used the same channel to seek further advancement. The
correspondence of a minister like Sir Adolphe Caron is crowded with
requests for extra allowances, better quarters, or a transfer to a more
congenial station. There is also evidence of a sprinkling of special favours
– a fur collar from Winnipeg, a special riding crop from England, the
services of an orderly from the battery at Kingston. It is clear that the
Militia Storekeeper at Quebec contributed substantial sums to Caron's
election fund in 1887 and again in 1891.[64] Of course, outspoken officers
could also be put in their place. When an artillery officer, the reputed
author of satirical articles on the state of the militia, had the temerity to
ask Caron for an extra allowance, his reply was a ponderous rebuke:
"you are sufficiently paid as we are not allowing any extra pay for having
the institutions of Canada run down by officials."[65]

All of this suggests that British critics were right in condemning the
Militia Department as a sort of military Tammany. Such a judgment
might be too harsh. If political considerations seem to have been omnipo-
tent in such fields as the distribution of contracts, in such matters as appointments, promotions, or the resolution of disputes between militia
officers, they were only weighting factors. In urging his nominee for a
vacancy in 1897, H. H. Dewart observed: "... no one who knows anything about the Liberal workers in this county and the City ever needed
to ask where Dr. Nattress was."[66] Nattress, who got the appointment, was
also a militia surgeon of long standing, a veteran of the North-West
campaign of 1885, and a distinguished practitioner. Ten years before, a
place was found for Lieutenant Colonel John Gray, a defeated Conservative candidate whose financial affairs were in disorder. However,
the appointee was also a distinguished militia officer who had commanded one of the most efficient field batteries in the force.[67]

While it may be just for posterity to moderate its judgment on the
extent of political patronage and influence in the Militia Department, it

was harder for contemporaries to measure its extent. They knew that
political considerations affected them. The change of a government or
even of a minister could alter their prospects unless they were sufficiently
popular or well-connected to have friends in all parties. It was this atmosphere which a later GOC of the militia, Major General Hutton, tried
to describe:

The direct result of what is called "political pull" is that officers have in the past
thought little of their professional attainments & how they do their duty, but
much of how they may curry favour with influential politicians! Discipline has in
the same manner been reduced very nearly to vanishing point as Officers have not
dared to enforce orders, or carry out instructions for fear of "running against a
snag" in other words encountering adverse political pressure, which might turn
them out of their appointments ...[68]

The solution for the mistrust and intrigue engendered by political
influences has normally been the introduction of an outsider, immune
alike from the benefits and sanctions of the system. That was part of the
role that a British officer in command of the militia was expected to play.
In providing that the Adjutant General as senior officer in the militia
must also be a British senior officer, Cartier had acknowledged that no
Canadian militia officer, for a long time to come, would have sufficient
experience to advise the government on its military policy. By also giving
him responsibility for the discipline of the force, Cartier had also apparently provided the necessary authority, immune from political influence.
Events soon showed that the apparent was not real.

Cartier's chief adviser in designing the Canadian militia system had
been the Adjutant General of the Canadian provincial militia, Colonel
Patrick MacDougall. It would have been hard to find a better qualified
officer for the task. MacDougall's father had helped to organize the
Nova Scotia militia over forty years before. MacDougall himself had
spent ten years in Canada as a junior officer. In England he had won a
high reputation as a military historian and thinker, and in 1858 he had
been selected as the first commandant of the new Staff College. His appointment as Adjutant General of the Canadian militia at a time when
Canada seemed threatened by American invasion was a tribute to his
military reputation. Colonel Garnet Wolseley, a contemporary of Mac-
Dougall in Canada, later recalled that he "was gifted with the most
charming, the most fascinating manner toward all men – by no means a

poor recommendation for anyone who tries to get on well with politicians."[69]

As Adjutant General MacDougall had worked hard. Scattered rural companies of militia were amalgamated into new county battalions. A large camp at Laprairie brought militia officers from the whole province together for their first serious training under the command of the brilliant Colonel Wolseley. In framing the Militia Act, MacDougall had pressed as hard as he could for Cartier to provide equality of sacrifice between those who served and those who stayed at home. He had insisted that discipline would be impossible in a force which could not compel its members to honour their three-year engagements. Humiliated by his failure to convince Cartier and by the reduction in his salary as a result of the 1868 revolt by the parliamentary colonels, MacDougall had come close to resignation.[70] He was dissuaded perhaps partly because Cartier agreed to restore the original salary levels for the staff by means of non-statutory allowances and to raise the Adjutant General's pay to $4,000 a year.

The resignation was only postponed. Major Mackenzie Bowell of the 49th Battalion and a leading spokesman of the militia lobby was also the editor and publisher of the *Belleville Intelligencer* and a prominent Orangeman. Engaged in a complex dispute with the Deputy Adjutant General of his district, Bowell instinctively turned to his newspaper as a means to attack his superior officer. When MacDougall called him to account for such a gross act of insubordination, Bowell promptly invoked both his journalistic and parliamentary immunity. Despite an opinion from the law officers that Bowell was, in fact, amenable to military sanctions for his conduct, the cabinet was more concerned with his political influence, refusing to allow more than a mild reprimand for him and the staff officers in the controversy. Disgusted by his impotence to maintain discipline or to protect his subordinates, MacDougall finally resigned.[71]

The MacDougall-Bowell conflict was only the first of a series of battles which British officers commanding the militia were to wage with their politically minded subordinates. Like his successors, MacDougall had to accommodate himself to circumstances in which three elements were already working: there were the militia officer-politicians, uncertain allies and dangerous enemies; there were the other politicians (and voters), suspicious of all military men and sceptical of the received doctrines of military policy; finally, there were his ministerial superiors, more aware of the political environment in which the militia had to live than of the requirements of military efficiency.

MacDougall's successor was a very different man. Colonel Patrick Robertson Ross was only forty when he was appointed Adjutant General. He had won youthful advancement as a commander of irregular cavalry during the Kaffir Wars in South Africa and as a young infantry officer in the Crimea. Thereafter, his career had stagnated. In contrast to Mac-Dougall's reforming zeal, Robertson Ross saw himself as the agreeable and co-operative subordinate of his Minister. Such a view of his position exasperated the British military authorities in Canada. General Lindsay held him responsible for the Canadian mismanagement, delay, and political interference in the arrangements for the Red River expedition. "If he had been left to himself," Lindsay later complained, "the force would have been found half-equipped."[72] Lord Dufferin, who arrived in Canada to become Governor General as Robertson Ross was leaving, inherited some of the prevailing British prejudice. In a private letter to the Colonial Secretary, he passed on the Ottawa gossip that the Adjutant General owed his position to Cartier's affection for his pretty young wife.[73] Even the Adjutant General's fidelity to his Minister and his elaborate flattery of the Dominion's militia system in his annual reports could not guarantee him immunity from political attack. The Toronto *Daily Telegraph*, in an attack on the Militia Department clearly inspired by Cartier's enemy, Colonel George T. Denison, complained that "At our large camps instead of practical training in the art of war, instead of useful instruction, we have bombastic and useless shows, got up for the glorification of an inefficient Adjutant General, and in order to create a political effect in favor of his patron and his party."[74]

Robertson Ross had some distinct achievements to his credit. The ingenious idea of creating two permanent artillery batteries as "schools" probably came from him. The report of his visit to the North West in 1872 led to the organization of the North West Mounted Police. If his annual reports were effusive and sometimes poorly written, they also included many of the criticisms and suggestions which his successors were to repeat with such monotonous frequency. However, for British officers who had their own standards for measuring his military competence, Robertson Ross was plainly inadequate. General Lindsay's most urgent recommendation to both the Canadian and British governments in 1870 was that the militia must be placed under an officer "whose rank and experience carry weight."[75] In a covering letter to Cardwell, Lindsay emphasized the need to appoint a British general to command the force: "The military efficiency of the Militia in my opinion depends upon having a thoroughly competent officer at its head. His appointment would not only raise their efficiency, but would be a guarantee that the military and defensive forces of Canada, in their natural and gradual development, would be organized upon the same system as those of the United Kingdom."[76]

In 1870 both British and Canadian governments had ignored Lindsay's advice. Another initiative to change the status of the senior officer in the militia came from Robertson Ross. In his annual report for 1870 he emphasized the added responsibilities the militia had acquired since the British withdrawal and suggested that, in consequence, he should be promoted to major general and his title changed to General Officer Commanding. Colonel Powell would become the Adjutant General and both he and the Deputy Adjutants General in the military districts would be promoted.[77]

The proposal had certainly been approved in advance by Cartier. The militia staff officers had already complained that their existing rank of lieutenant colonel gave them no precedence over other militia officers and the Minister could believe that promotions all around would give satisfaction. Since salaries depended on the appointment, not the rank, no extra cost was involved. The necessary amendments to the Militia Act were prepared and circulated.

At the War Office the changes won little favour. Advised by General Lindsay, both Cardwell and the Duke of Cambridge objected strongly to Robertson Ross's scheme for his own promotion, and their protest was embodied in a confidential despatch to the Governor General, Lord Lisgar.[78] A despatch containing serious strictures on a senior officer's competence is not an easy weapon to use and Lisgar limited himself to showing it to the Prime Minister. He found that Macdonald was opposed to Cartier's planned promotions but he also found that the Minister of Militia was firmly committed to going ahead. The War Office countered with delaying tactics, "losing" the correspondence; by the time they had conceded a Canadian right to at least grant militia rank, Cartier's moment had passed. Defeated in his Montreal East constituency, the blow to his prestige, combined with the rapid onset of Bright's disease, removed him from an active role in politics or administration. Already under the shadow of the Pacific Scandal, he left for England in search of medical treatment. He died there on May 20, 1873. With him died Robertson Ross's hope of becoming even a militia major general. A few months later he resigned his appointment and returned to England, still only a Colonel.[79]

Sir John A. Macdonald continued to believe that his government needed a British military adviser, and for a moment he even believed that he could obtain one at British expense. With the departure of the garrison, Cardwell also proposed to eliminate the Governor General's Military Secretary. Lisgar objected to this reduction of his establishment and Macdonald tried to come to his aid. His arguments deserve to be quoted at length, illustrating the viewpoint of a man who was to play a central role in militia policy-making until 1891.

Macdonald contended that it would be impossible for Canada to appoint a British major general to command the militia. If the General tried to see that the Dominion lived up to her share of the 1865 agreement, there would be friction: "The Canadian Parliament would certainly not vote the money to pay him. He would be looked upon with jealousy by the Militia authorities, would hold an exceedingly anomalous & unpleasant position without command or influence and his sole duties would be a sort of espionage, and might be considered in that light." At the same time he acknowledged the need for such outside inspection – at least when the Liberals were in office. He and Cartier would spare no pains to keep the force efficient:

But here, as in England, we have a peace at any price party who look upon all monies expended for Military purposes as thrown away – the turn of the political wheel may bring that party into power or what is more likely, may cause the formation of a government to whom the support of the Peace Party would be important. In such case, without any obvious breach of the engagement, the expenditure might be diminished on the ground of economy, the number of days drill decreased and the discipline gradually relaxed.

In the light of later events, his final argument is interesting:

When I held the place of Minister of Militia, I found difficulty in maintaining discipline and punishing breaches of it from the political influence brought to bear upon me in favour of offenders of rank and position and on one or two occasions I am afraid that I was forced to give too much weight to the political side of the question. With a competent Military Secretary, the Gov. Genl. would always be able to make his mind up how far he could yield to political pressure without injuring the discipline of the Militia Force.[80]

The joint appeal of Lisgar and Macdonald had no effect and the War

Office ceased to pay for a Military Secretary for the Governor General.*
Lisgar's successor, the Earl of Dufferin, managed to provide himself with
a military adviser by the expedient of appointing an officer, Lieutenant
Colonel Henry Fletcher of the Scots Fusilier Guards, as his private secretary. An added advantage of Fletcher was that his wife, Lady Harriet,
made a suitable companion for Lady Dufferin in her North American
exile. Fletcher, "though not particularly brilliant or quick" in his
master's judgment, proved "very sensible and trustworthy."[81] He was
also almost the ideal embodiment of the Military Secretary Macdonald
had envisaged. He reported extensively on the Canadian militia, visited
the United States Military Academy at West Point, and advised the
Canadians on their own military college. He even printed and circulated
at his own expense a pamphlet on militia reform.[82] However, for all his
energy and interest, Fletcher had no official position. He could be
thanked for his advice but he could do nothing to implement it.

The departure of Robertson Ross in August 1873 meant that the senior
appointment in the militia was vacant. Although Colonel Powell became
acting Adjutant General, as a Canadian he was barred from permanently filling the post. Meanwhile, Canadian politicians had other
preoccupations. Macdonald's government was borne to its disastrous
defeat over the Pacific Scandal. On November 7, 1873, a new government was formed under Alexander Mackenzie, the Liberal leader, and
early in the following year he won a substantial majority of the seats in a
general election.

In opposition the Liberals had played the normal role of criticizing
militia extravagance, but their new Prime Minister had his own opinions
on future Canadian military policy. Some of them must have derived
from his own experience as a major in the 27th Lambton Battalion.
Mackenzie's "Address to the Electors of Lambton," virtually the Liberal
platform for the 1874 campaign, called for the revision of the militia
system and promised that the force would receive "the immediate and
urgent attention of the government with a view to increasing its efficiency."[83] This was vague enough but the first session of the new Parliament was presented with legislation to establish the military college at
Kingston, the most lasting memorial of the Mackenzie ministry.

* Subsequent Governors General did appoint their own Military Secretaries –
  Lord Melgund who accompanied Lord Lansdowne was the most prominent
  – but they held no official position with either the British or Canadian governments.

The Prime Minister also took up the problem of the command of the militia. Lord Dufferin was relieved to find that his prime minister had military inclinations. Seeing the command of the militia as an essential channel for British influence in Canada, the Governor General had already been exploring the field for candidates to fill the post of Adjutant General. The array of talent was unimpressive. His own secretary would have been ideal but it would have cost Fletcher his career in the Brigade of Guards to accept the appointment. Other officers proposed by the Duke of Cambridge all had faults. Colonel Middleton, who wanted the position, was "a little rough in appearance perhaps." Colonel Luard's temper was allegedly not as good as Middleton's. Colonel Jervois, the fortifications expert, was merely "not a bad officer." Colonel Laurie, already serving on half-pay as a militia staff officer in Nova Scotia, was "less preferred" than the others.[84] Dufferin was dismayed at the prospects and he suggested to the Prime Minister that a better list could be compiled if the rank of the appointment were raised to major general. For his own part, he promised to use his influence to get a first-rate man, with the final choice left to the Canadian government.[85] To his delight Mackenzie agreed. Accepting his own side of the bargain, Dufferin next directed his attention to the Duke of Cambridge and to his old friend, the new Conservative Colonial Secretary, Lord Carnarvon.

After a year and a half in Canada, Dufferin had a shrewd perception of the difficulties a British general would encounter. A passage in his letter to the Duke of Cambridge is an admirable summary of the problems which were to arise:

The Officer commanding the Canadian Militia occupies a very difficult and by no means a very pleasant situation. He is the servant of the Dominion and completely subordinate to the Minister of Militia. There is at this moment no very great military spirit in the Country – the Canadian Parliament is always averse to Military Expenditure and cannot believe peace will ever be interrupted. The person responsible therefore for the efficiency of our Army is constantly fighting an uphill game, and it requires a man of great energy, ability and resource, to make the most of the means placed at his disposal. His relations wtih the head of his Department also require tact, temper and judgement, as everything depends upon his winning the confidence of the Minister who controls it, without exciting his jealousy, – and thus obtaining the favourable consideration of his views.[86]

His letter to Carnarvon was more blunt. He did not want a "deserving officer" or one who "has claims." He wanted an officer who realized that

he would be subordinate to a Canadian minister, but tactful and re-
sourceful enough to get his own way. "Above all things, he should not
be a hoity-toity gentleman, with a supercilious contempt for colonials,
and the somewhat homely type of society which of necessity prevails in a
new country."[87]

Mackenzie seems to have had little difficulty in converting his colleagues. The main obstacle would have been expense but this was easily
avoided. The new General Officer would have the same pay and allowances as the previous Adjutant General: $4,000. Powell's title would be
changed to Adjutant General but his pay would be unaltered. The only
extra expense would be $1,000 to provide the General with an aide-de-
camp. Although the pay was small for a British general, the Dominion
was assured that the War Office would continue to credit the officer
selected with his half-pay.

The next task was to find the man. The Duke of Cambridge made
an unavailing attempt to persuade his reforming subordinate, Major
General Garnet Wolseley, to accept voluntary exile in Canada, and then
turned to Major General Edward Selby Smyth.[88] A further six months
were consumed by negotiations over the details. On the strength of a
favourable report from Lord Carnarvon, Dufferin had little difficulty in
persuading Mackenzie that the right man had been found, but it took a
good deal more correspondence to establish that the appointment would
be for five years, that no official residence would be provided, and that
the General could choose his own aide-de-camp. The negotiations were
concluded by a Canadian order-in-council on September 11, 1874.

CHAPTER TWO

Selby Smyth

Justifying the Militia

Major General Edward Selby Smyth took up his new post on October 1, 1874. It was his first contact with Canada. Born a Belfast Irishman, the son of a soldier, he had spent most of his regimental service in India and South Africa, participating in a long series of minor campaigns. In 1861 he had been appointed Inspector General of Militia in Ireland and had spent some of his time organizing flying columns against the Fenians. His last active appointment before coming to Canada had been as General Officer Commanding in Mauritius.

Apart, perhaps, from his service in Ireland, there was little in his background which appeared helpful for his new appointment, but Carnarvon had formed a good impression of him. "He is quite a gentleman, I should say in manner and impressed me favourably," he wrote to Dufferin. "My only doubt is whether he has a great deal of 'go' in him but this is only a personal doubt and nothing that I can hear confirms it. He is said to have been 'a very smart officer' and yet I feel sure that he is kind and conciliatory in disposition."[1] To the Duke of Cambridge, Carnarvon expressed mild regret that his nominee was not ten years younger, but at fifty-four the General was far from being an old man.[2]

The new General proved completely acceptable to his new employers. "Mackenzie is delighted with him, and I understand he has made a most favourable impression upon the head of the Departments with which he is connected," Dufferin reported.[3] A month later he wrote to the Duke that Selby Smyth was "just the kind of man we wanted and wherever he has gone he has won golden opinions from those interested in the reorganization of the Military system."[4] Almost the only criticism was of the type represented by a Toronto *Globe* complaint that the Major General had chosen a British aide-de-camp instead of favouring native talent.[5]

Selby Smyth's arrival almost coincided with the appointment of a new Minister of Militia, the fourth since Confederation. Cartier's immediate successor, Hugh McDonald, had been a Nova Scotia opponent of Confederation whom Macdonald had conciliated with cabinet office. McDonald's role in the department was negligible and when the government was defeated four months later he was appointed to the Nova Scotia bench.

Alexander Mackenzie, facing enormous difficulties in forming the first Liberal government, was persuaded to accept William Ross, a former Conservative from Cape Breton Island, as his Minister of Militia. Within a month, Mackenzie had acknowledged his mistake. "The man's an ass," he complained to his chief Ontario lieutenant, Edward Blake, "and I wonder we never knew it with six months knowledge of him."[6] It took Mackenzie eight more months to force out a minister whom he found to be indolent, indiscreet, and incompetent. In September 1874, after an ultimatum that Ross must either accept the Collectorship of Customs for Halifax or go emptyhanded, Mackenzie was rid of him.

To replace Ross as a Nova Scotia representative in the cabinet, Mackenzie was anxious to get A. G. Jones, the MP for Halifax. Jones refused, protesting that he was not prepared to sacrifice his own business. Instead, he persuaded the Prime Minister to turn to William Berrian Vail, a Digby merchant and the provincial secretary for Nova Scotia. Vail, he claimed, would make a better leader for the Nova Scotia MPs as he was tired of provincial politics, had more time for public office, and had "served an apprenticeship putting up with other people's whims."[7] Vail accepted the invitation and took office on September 30, a day before the General.

It was still necessary to amend the Militia Act to provide for the appointment of a Major General to command the force. Thanks to the excellent impression Selby Smyth had made during his first few months in Canada, the government encountered very little opposition to the change. Even Peter Mitchell, after a customary protest at the "enormous expenditures" which would be involved, professed himself satisfied after a personal and private explanation from Vail.[8]

What criticism there was of the change took the form of complaints that the command of the militia was denied to Canadians. The popular Colonel Powell, who had in effect commanded the force for more than a year, now had to revert to a lower position. There were Canadians in and out of Parliament who maintained that a British general was not necessarily suited to the Canadian command. McKay Wright, a Conservative from the Ottawa Valley, warned that an English officer "would, before he could be of much service, have to unlearn much of what he had learned in his profession in Great Britain."[9] Captain R. J. Wicksteed, in a lengthy pamphlet extolling the militia system, declared that "For the purposes of our country, the judgement of Lord Elcho, the English volunteer, should weigh heavier than that of the Duke of Cambridge, the English Commander-in-chief, but the advice given by one of our own Brigade Majors should far out-weigh in value to us that of these two officers combined."[10]

When Vail and Selby Smyth entered the Militia Department, six years had passed since Cartier's Militia Act had come into effect and four since the bulk of the British troops had left. A number of commentators have left accounts of the militia as they saw it in those formative years. Colonel Fletcher claimed to have found signs of deterioration as early as 1872. Inspecting militia camped at Lévis and Kingston, he could praise their spirit and good conduct. He was surprised to find that the officers were of all ages and observed that they seemed like "sensible, homely men, who would probably do their work well on service." One efficient staff officer, he discovered with evident astonishment, was a saddler by trade. On the other hand, he judged that the troops were "not as smart or as clean, as ought to be after making all allowances," and he concluded that the memory of the well-disciplined British garrison was fading fast.[11] In the pamphlet he published a year later Fletcher commented on the "apparent ignorance" of faults which would "attract the attention of all who were conversant with military affairs."[12] In the absence of a model, efficiency faltered.

The departure of the British was not the only reason for the failings of the militia system. To its officers, the decline in discipline seemed to be due to the need for company commanders to remain sufficiently popular to attract recruits. Lieutenant Colonel Robert H. Davis, a country doctor and the commanding officer of the 37th Haldimand Battalion, described

in fictional terms the life cycle of a typical volunteer company. Having
depicted the enthusiasm with which the Slabtown volunteers were
formed, Davis goes on:

Drill is commenced forthwith, military ardor burns high in the breasts of every
volunteer, and there is an average attendance of forty or fifty men. The captain
is stern and attentive, and the company really makes wonderful progress. The
rifles and the uniforms arrive, the men are paraded and have a shooting match
– and a second company could be organized on the spot. The first year, the
company is a perfect success; the next, a slight weakness is apparent; the third
year, there is a decided falling off; the fourth year, the captain thinks he can
muster about forty, if he gets time enough; the fifth, – well, he don't know, "the
men, you see, were called out to drill last year at a bad time; a good many of them
lost their hay, and some more lost their places, and they didn't like the way they
were treated when in camp at Jericho," etc. The sixth year, the captain and
ten or a dozen men are all that remains of that famous company.[13]

Conditions of service did not help recruiting. Men who joined to
impress their friends with their splendid uniforms were quickly disil-
lusioned. The government insisted that clothing could only be replaced
at five-year intervals and a new recruit was likely to be issued with a
shabby jacket, a threadbare greatcoat, and a pair of trousers which, in
the absence of dry-cleaning, were very much as their previous wearer
had left them. The cap was the round, uncomfortable, and cordially
detested "pill box" or "soap dish." A volunteer provided his own boots,
shirt, and underclothing.

In camp, a militiaman found that the government provided no food
for the first and last days of camp and for many years no pay on Sundays.
At night he shivered under a single worn-out blanket, despite annual
complaints that this was inadequate for chilly spring or autumn evenings.
During the day he practised monotonous elementary drill movements or
marched off to the range to fire his twenty rounds at a distant and
unresponsive target. If he had been in camp before or knew his captain
well, a militiaman might become a sergeant or a corporal, or escape drill
altogether by being assigned to some regimental duty. At the end of the
camp came a grand review and perhaps a sham battle. There would certainly be speeches from officers and politicians. Going to camp was an
experience which a large number of Canadian men underwent at least
once in the late nineteenth century. Not many chose to go twice.

To many militia officers, like Colonel Davis, the troubles of the force stemmed largely from its reliance on voluntary enlistment. They urged the government to invoke the section of the Militia Act creating a Regular Militia and so relieve them from their recruiting difficulties. That these were real was demonstrated in 1872 when the second of the three-year enlistment periods envisaged in the act was due to begin. In MD 2, covering central Ontario, where the local staff officer was almost alone in favouring the voluntary system, men were readily forthcoming. There were 5,900 men in camp at Niagara, with vacancies for only twenty-nine more. That situation was unique. Elsewhere, the warnings of staff and commanding officers were justified by half-strength battalions and vanished companies. The most serious collapse was in the two French-speaking districts of Quebec. Several battalions, including the senior French-Canadian unit in the force, the 4th Chasseurs Canadiens, ceased to exist. Visiting the camp at Lévis, Lord Dufferin noticed that many of the French-Canadian soldiers were too old or too small for service, evidence of the desperate efforts of their captains to fill the ranks.[14]

Manpower was not the only problem of the militia. Making his first tour of inspection in the autumn of 1874, Selby Smyth was shocked to discover the deterioration in the condition of the arms and equipment distributed among the militia units. It was evident to him that the whole system of care and inspection was at fault, particularly in the rural battalions. The overwhelming administrative burden in the militia system fell on the troop, battery, and company commanders. They had to recruit their own men and they were also expected to look after their arms, equipment, and uniforms. To help with the cost each captain was entitled to an allowance of forty dollars a year. A few took the responsibility seriously, building storerooms, hiring men to clean and oil the rifles, and keeping strict accounts. The great majority of rural officers did not. Poor men for the most part, they regarded their allowances as small compensation for their pains in keeping up a company. Selby Smyth discovered that rifles, knapsacks, and clothing were likely to be heaped into a back room of a captain's house or piled in disorder in a nearby shed until they were needed for the following year. Some captains allowed their men to keep their uniforms throughout the year, and looked the other way when a militia greatcoat was worn for rough farm chores. Although large numbers of the Snider rifles had been rendered useless by neglect, Selby Smyth found that in the whole Dominion there were only two government armourers to put them right.

Another problem was that the brigade majors, whose chief duty was to inspect the militia companies and keep an eye on their stores, did not measure up to their work. Not only were they politically vulnerable to pressure from influential, if incompetent, militia officers but their pay was based on the number of companies they could report as efficient. The evident failure of the brigade majors led the new General to wider criticism of the staff as a whole. There were too many of them, particularly since most of them were busy for only a quarter of the year. In some cases he found that they were unqualified, and in most cases they were too firmly rooted in their local communities to exercise any strict or unpopular supervision over their subordinates. Recalling his own younger days as an inspector of militia in Ireland, Selby Smyth was certain that fewer, more energetic, staff officers would put an end to the mistreatment of equipment, the padded muster rolls, and the dubious claims which drained away militia funds.[15]

The Major General had solutions for most of the evils and difficulties he encountered, some of them based on the administrative system of the British militia, others founded on an expansion of the tiny nucleus of permanent troops. Impressed by the success of the two artillery batteries in keeping up the efficiency of their component of the militia, Selby Smyth urged that similar service could be supplied to the infantry by organizing permanent infantry companies at Kingston, Toronto, and Quebec. To improve the administration of the militia he proposed that stores and rifles be taken out of the hands of company commanders and concentrated at battalion headquarters. Recalling the regular army adjutants and instructors who were part of the British militia organization, he suggested that each Canadian battalion should have a full-time lieutenant, sergeant major, and sergeant attached to it. As a compensating economy, the brigade majors would be eliminated.[16]

When these proposals were published in the annual report of the Militia Department, they were sharply condemned. In the Toronto *Globe*, George Brown quickly detected the threat of a standing army, "small it is true at first in its dimensions" but liable to be increased at the first outburst of military excitement.[17] Wicksteed, in his pamphlet, launched a direct attack on the schemes of British advisers like Fletcher and Selby Smyth. He was firm in rejecting any permanent force: "Let us beware, my friends, of the growth of that deadly incubus, a standing army, and nip in the bud any scheme which, in the guise of military schools, Government police, caretakers or otherwise, could eventually saddle the country with a full-blown military machine, a far greater scourge to its supporters than to its enemies."[18]

Selby Smyth's proposals made commendable military sense but they were politically unrealistic. The dangers of offending militia captains by withdrawing their equipment – and their allowances – were self-evident. Among volunteers, however, the General's popularity was at least partially redeemed by his criticisms of the staff. Mackenzie Bowell, perhaps on those grounds alone, described Selby Smyth's report as "the most practical he ever knew to be presented to the Parliament of Canada."[19]

The one problem for which Selby Smyth had no solution was recruiting. It was settled by events. The economic depression, first noticeable in 1874, was in full evidence a year later. The effects were apparent in militia strength. While some men were more reluctant than usual to risk their jobs by asking for leave to go to camp, they were outnumbered by those who were happy to earn even fifty cents a day. The government, faced with falling revenue, cut its spending, particularly on the militia. By 1876, desperate economies pared defence expenditure to its lowest point in Canadian history: $500,452. When the figure was announced in Parliament, MP s cheered the news.[20]

Looking for savings which would do the least harm to the long-term strength of the force, Selby Smyth chose to protect the organizational structure. Some units were disbanded but the great majority continued, with their authorized strength in rank and file cut by as much as a third. With the paper strength of the militia cut from 45,000 to 37,000 men, there was money enough to train just over half the force each year. Again seeking for short-term economies, the Major General managed to persuade the government that the first priority must be given to training the most technical of the arms, the field artillery. Next came the militia units in the cities, partly because they were relatively cheap, partly because of their growing importance in suppressing the disorders which could arise from the economic distress. Despite all the inclinations of a rural-based government, the rural militia battalions came last. When the other priorities had been satisfied, the rural units would be fortunate to drill once in two years.

Arrangements designed as a makeshift for temporary difficulties hardened into a pattern of training which was to last until 1896. After a few years of experiment with training the militia at their battalion or even company headquarters, a routine emerged which was followed for eighteen years. After Parliament had passed the annual militia estimates, usually in the spring, sometimes much later, calculations would be made of how much would be available to train the force. Then the units were selected, at first by local staff officers, in later years by militia headquarters. The field artillery and city battalions were always chosen. The balance was made up from rural corps. These were usually assembled in a camp in their military district for twelve days of drill. In the central provinces the favoured time for camp was late June or early July, but elections and other political accidents sometimes forced postponement of the camps to September with its colder weather and the competing attractions of the harvest season.

This routine had political consequences. Annual camps for the militia became a hardy perennial among political promises. The hostility of the most politically vocal part of the force, the rural militia, to any other form of military spending, hardened because of their own grievance. At the same time, their dominant influence prevented any structural reorganization which might have reduced the organization to a size small enough for annual training within the regular militia appropriation. For all the talk about the languishing state of the force, there was a remarkable stability in the number of sub-units during the years of bitter financial stringency between 1875 and 1896.*

The depression solved the manpower problem, but it created others. Severe economy fostered administrative paralysis in matters large and small. In 1873 the roof of the Montreal drill shed collapsed under the weight of snow; it took fifteen years before it was rebuilt. In 1871 Cartier had authorized medical chests to be issued to militia camps but no arrangements were made to check or replace the contents. Year after year, the "old, dirty tin boxes" went to and fro. In 1878 a medical officer at Kingston reported that he had gone through six of them, trying to make up a complete kit. Such medicine as he found proved to be worthless: "The pills had to be broken between stones to give them any particular virtue having been in stock since the chests were first issued. In urgent and even dangerous cases, I had no immediate means to command to treat actively excepting those furnished by myself."[21] Ten years later the annual Militia Department report included similar reports from nearly every military district.

It was in this environment of austerity that Selby Smyth and his successors were compelled to work. Unlike some of his successors, Selby Smyth was prepared to accommodate himself to his circumstances. As much a prisoner of the doctrines which dictated economy in public expenditure as were Mackenzie and his colleagues, he turned his thoughts

*See Appendix c.

from major and expensive reforms of the militia to the battle for its very
survival. His annual contributions to the departmental report grew
steadily longer and more rhetorical in their justification of a militia organization in the absence of any apparent enemy. The quality of his
prose may be judged from an extract of his report for 1877: "It is our
duty, therefore, whether through the sunshine of peace or the darkness
and gloom of war, still to advance shoulder to shoulder, until we have
prepared for those who come after us a safe camping ground on the
shores of the great future; then and not till then, can we take the rest of
the weary – confident that so far as in us lies we have done our part to
ensure that this land shall remain one and indivisible – till wars and contention cease in all the world."[22]

The events of the 1870s soon furnished a more practical justification
for the militia. As employers dismissed workers and tried to cut wages,
the rudimentary labour organizations, legal only since 1872, tried to fight
back. Canadian official opinion was alarmed at the unusual experience
of industrial conflict and feared the spread of the more violent struggles
then being waged in the United States. It was a theme which the Major
General could cheerfully commandeer. In his 1877 report he grandly
warned: "... we must never lose sight of conscience and honour nor for
a moment permit the chance that Communism should with impunity
make a grand experiment on the smallest portion of that collection of
properties termed the British Empire."[23] In the following year, finally
admitting that the risks of American aggression were no longer very
great, he pointed out that the military problem for both countries was
how to protect the "law-abiding population" from the mob.

The extensive provisions for military aid to the civil power which
Cartier had incorporated into his 1868 act had soon proved to be one of
its most defective features. Taken with little adaptation from the pre-
Confederation Militia Act of the province of Canada, the provisions
ignored the implications of the new federal system. Full responsibility for
calling out the militia, and paying for it when called out, rested with the
municipalities, but these were now subject only to provincial authority.
Responsibility for law and order also lay with the provinces. If summoned by local magistrates, militia officers were obliged by the act to call
out their men, and it was from the local authorities that the officers had
to recover the money to pay and feed their troops. If the municipality
refused to pay, the officer had no alternative but to take the case
personally to court. Refusals to pay were common. In the bitter cir-

cumstances of a riot or strike, mayor, councillors, and magistrates were
frequently at loggerheads. In many parts of Canada there were no
municipalities to sue.

In the midst of the confusion were the militiamen, waiting for their
pay. In 1875 troops called out three years before at the time of Cartier's
election campaign in Montreal East were still waiting for their pay. The
Montreal council refused the bill claiming that Conservative magistrates
had ordered out the militia as a partisan scheme. In 1876 militia were
sent to the Lingan colliery in Cape Breton Island at the request of the
owners. Two years later the impatient militiamen were threatening to
sue their captain for their pay. The opposite situation occurred on Vancouver Island in 1890 when coal company officials, who were also
magistrates, were quite willing to pay for a force of militia to overawe
their strikers.[24]

These and other obscurities in the law did not prevent the militia from
turning out regularly against strikers and rioters; the chance for excitement was too good to be missed. On the other hand it did reveal a certain
immaturity in Canadian self-government. While politicians worried
about the obvious dangers of using volunteers against their neighbours,
neither Liberal nor Conservative governments could bring themselves to
remedy the most obvious flaw in the system. The section of the act was
repeatedly amended: it grew from forty-eight lines in 1868 to a hundred
and nineteen lines in 1904, but it was not until then that a government
found the imagination to remedy the confusion.[25]

The pay difficulty and the possible unreliability of the slightly trained
militiamen could both be overcome by organizing the small units of
regular soldiers that Selby Smyth had advocated soon after his arrival.
At Quebec, Colonel Strange and his battery turned out frequently
against striking dock workers or to separate warring factions of French
and Irish. Lord Dufferin, who had established his summer residence
at the Citadel, found reassurance in the small body of permanent
troops and he took every opportunity to point out their value to his
Prime Minister.[26] Quebec was exceptional. The two largest cities in the
Dominion, Montreal and Toronto, had no such protectors. Instead, they
depended on their own police and militia. In each city certain battalions
were already emerging as smart middle-class social clubs as well as military organizations. The combination was an added guarantee of their
reliability in combatting civil disorder.

The Grand Trunk strike at Belleville illustrated most of the problems of military aid to the civil power. On December 31, 1876, employees of the railway struck against a proposed cut in their wages. Despite his indignation at the strikers' defiance, Mackenzie refused a demand by the railway's general manager that the government intervene. It was not a federal responsibility. Less phlegmatic, the Mayor of Belleville called out the somewhat disorganized local militia. The combination of bitterly cold weather and the New Year festivities meant that only a few soldiers appeared. Finding that the strikers were behaving peacefully, the few refused to attack them. The excited mayor promptly telegraphed to Toronto to demand the services of the Queen's Own Rifles, one of the crack battalions of the militia.

Despite the season and the cold, the men of the Queen's Own were delighted at a chance for action. On January 2 two hundred armed volunteers set off for Belleville in a special train. With a melodramatic flourish an armed guard was posted in the engineer's cab. At Belleville the interlopers were met by a shower of coal and stones, but with bayonets fixed the soldiers quickly forced the strikers from railway property. However, the men had the last word. Within three days the company gave up and the old wages were restored.

In the business community the affair provoked anger and alarm. "The men had simply made up their minds to force the company to comply with their wishes," declared a shocked Toronto *Mail*, and demanded to know how it had been allowed to happen.[27] In Parliament Colonel James Brown, a Liberal MP and commanding officer of one of the Belleville battalions, showed himself no friend of the strikers but he also denied that the local militia had failed.[28] The trouble arose from the mayor's panic. As for the men of the Queen's Own, they had to wait for their pay until their commanding officer could win his suit against the Belleville corporation. They were, however, permitted to keep the only winter clothing they had been issued for the trip – a red woollen muffler.[29]

Religious conflict, another aspect of the 1870s, provided an even greater strain on the discipline of militiamen than battling strikers. The gloom and tension of the period provided the setting for a revival of the traditional conflict between Catholics and Orangemen, with occasional outbreaks of the violence of earlier decades. In 1875, while the bulk of the Montreal militia were escorting the body of Joseph Guibord, the rationalist printer, to burial in consecrated ground, Toronto volunteers were on duty to prevent Orangemen from breaking up Catholic pilgrimages through their city. Although city police bore the brunt of the struggle on October 3, 1875, the troops marched along parallel streets, ready to intervene.[30] In the ensuing years militia were called out to meet the threat of Orange riots in Saint John and Charlottetown, but the real focus of danger was Montreal, the commercial heart of the Dominion and the meeting place of roughly equal French- and English-speaking communities. In both 1876 and 1877 the city's Orangemen had been persuaded to postpone their annual "walk," but when one of their members was killed in a street scuffle on July 12, 1877, there was a hardened determination that in 1878 the Orangemen would march.

It was also an election year and the Prime Minister was under acute pressure from supporters and opponents of the proposed demonstration. Taking his cue from George Brown, who had used the same argument to defend the Catholic pilgrimage marchers in Toronto in 1875, Mackenzie at last declared that the Orangemen should be protected in their civil right to use the streets to walk to church. The Mayor of Montreal, J. L. Beaudry, felt differently and with the overwhelming support of his council ordered that the march be cancelled. His hand was strengthened by a hastily adopted provincial statute banning such processions.

As Beaudry prepared to enforce the law with the aid of his city police and a force of special constables, Montreal Protestants reacted. In their role as magistrates a minority of aldermen signed a requisition calling out militia to protect the Orangemen. Mackenzie, who would have much preferred not to intervene, now claimed that the requisition tied his hands. A force of three thousand militia was hastily assembled, including the men of the permanent batteries from Quebec and Kingston and from the battalions in the Eastern Townships. Lieutenant General Sir Edward Selby Smyth (he had been promoted and knighted in 1877) came down to take command.

Torn between the conflicting purposes of the Mayor and the Protestant magistrates, Sir Edward was in an impossible position. Fortunately, Beaudry took the initiative. On the morning of July 12, as the Orangemen assembled in their hall, the Mayor surrounded it with police and special constables. When the procession emerged, Beaudry arrested the first six Orangemen to appear. The rest fell back in confusion. For the remainder of the day they stayed besieged in their hall. By late afternoon Beaudry allowed cabs to pass through his cordon to take the Orangemen to their homes. By nightfall the last of them had crept away. Meanwhile, several blocks away the troops stood under arms awaiting orders to intervene. In spite of frantic telegrams from the Orangemen to the Prime Minister, orders never came.[31]

The day was Beaudry's triumph. There was also at least a suspicion that the fire had gone out of the Orangemen less on account of the police and special constables than because many of their more ardent spirits were mustered in the ranks of the militia, drawn up under the General's eye. The federal government took what credit it could for saving Montreal from chaos but it also acknowledged that its legal position was uncertain by an unprecedented grant of $10,000 to pay the troops.

The Montreal affair in 1878 was the largest single concentration of Canadian troops in aid to the civil power until the Quebec conscription riots of 1917. It was not the only military excitement in Canada that year. In April, 1878, a German ship, the *Cimbria*, sailed into South West Harbour in Maine. Almost daily reports in the American press warned Canadians that her hold was filled with Russian guns and that she carried hundreds of Russian sailors, ready to fit out and man privateers if Britain went to war with their country.[32] The remote Russo-Turkish war had suddenly come very close to Canada and on a frontier Canadians had scarcely considered – their coasts.

Apart from the British defences at Halifax and some tumble-down fortifications at Saint John, the Atlantic coast was defenceless. At Sydney there were guns but no gunners. Elsewhere there were gunners but no guns. What guns were available were smooth-bores, useless against armour-plated ships. Even Quebec had scarcely a gun which could hurt an armoured warship. Moreover, as the inevitable accompaniment of every Canadian crisis, there were fresh rumours of Fenian plots and preparations.[33] The Liberal government, with so many other preoccupations, reacted reluctantly to the new problem. The cabinet authorized $10,000 to be spent for precautionary measures. Lieutenant Colonel Strange was ordered from Quebec to the Maritimes to put the available defences in order and an urgent request was sent to Britain for a "fleet of fast cruisers" to meet the threat of the *Cimbria*'s privateers. In response to a British suggestion, Lieutenant Colonel D. T. Irwin, French's successor in command of "A" Battery at Kingston, was sent to Victoria to take charge of the defences there.[34]

If Canada's Atlantic coast was dangerously exposed, her Pacific coast was utterly defenceless. This concerned Britain as much as Canada since the Royal Navy's only dockyard on the Pacific was at Esquimalt, near Victoria. Not a gun was mounted for its defence. Although British

Columbia had been constituted as a military district from the moment it entered Confederation, its Deputy Adjutant General, Lieutenant Colonel Charles F. Houghton, a former Conservative MP, seems to have found it impossible to organize militia units. High wages and the mobility of frontier people left few men with the leisure for military pursuits. When Irwin arrived he found that he not only had to construct a battery from the elderly guns grudgingly loaned by the Royal Navy but that he had to recruit and train the gunners as well.[35] Irwin's make-shift battery at Macaulay's Point was to be the first stage in the very long story of trying to arrange adequate defences for Esquimalt.

For the first time since 1870 the Canadian government had been forced to consider defence seriously. The 1878 scare was the genesis for a number of developments in the Canadian defence system, including an infant arms industry. It also was the beginning of an equally significant theme in Dominion military policy, the part Canada could play in an imperial war beyond her shores. In both areas, Sir Edward Selby Smyth played a significant role in guiding his government.

The British reaction to the sudden possibility of war with Russia had reflected on a much wider stage the alarm and confusion experienced in Canada. Early in the crisis a committee had been formed under Admiral Sir Alexander Milne to advise on emergency measures to protect colonial ports, including those on both coasts of Canada. The Milne Committee report on the Atlantic coast recommended that Canada should spend $50,000 to buy modern guns and to maintain permanent artillery detachments at only two ports, Saint John and Sydney.[36] At the height of the war scare the proposals might have seemed modest. In Ottawa, where Mackenzie had earlier boasted that Canada would be "above shirking her duty in providing for the defence of her own coasts,"[37] the mood had cooled when the cost of protection was known. It would be cheaper to let the Russians destroy everything, some ministers observed.[38] Selby Smyth, quick to perceive that the British recommendations were too ambitious for his government, offered a cheaper expedient. In 1870 Canada had fallen heir to about four hundred smooth-bore cannon. The enthusiastic Colonel Strange knew that Sir William Palliser, a British engineer and artillerist, had developed a process for converting smooth-bores into rifled cannon, good enough to cope with armoured warships. Having had his invention rejected by the War Office, Palliser was only too pleased to offer it to Canada. To win Canadian good will he even presented two of his converted guns to the government and

Strange mounted them on the walls of the Citadel at Quebec. Even more encouraging was Palliser's decision to have a third gun converted in Canada by the Montreal Engine Works.[39]

Selby Smyth urged the Palliser plan on the government as an adequate, if less than ideal, solution and the cabinet, "in view of the probable peaceful solution of the threatened Russian war," agreed.[40] Before much more could be done there was a change of government. The new Minister of Militia, L. F. R. Masson, was a Montreal man, well aware of the benefits of having government work done in his city. Conservative election statements had been well adapted to the economic nationalism inherent in manufacturing cannon in Canada and the Palliser scheme went on. Gilbert & Son, owners of the Montreal plant, were given a contract to manufacture ten converted guns and their carriages.

Before any of the guns had been completed the firm went bankrupt. Captain Edward Palliser, Sir William's younger brother, tried to persuade the War Office to take over the work but, perhaps because they were annoyed at the Canadian temerity in taking up a process they had rejected,[41] the British officials refused. Undaunted, the younger Palliser came out to Canada in 1884, surveyed a site at Quebec, and proposed to the government that he would build a factory to convert all the obsolete ordnance in Canada's possession. Once again the Militia Department was interested but it took its time in considering the financial implications of the project. Early in the following year, when the North-West Rebellion broke out, Palliser left to take part in the campaign. When he returned he found that the department had turned its attention elsewhere and the plan to manufacture artillery in Canada lapsed for another thirty years.[42]

Another manufacturing idea to emerge from 1878, again with the joint sponsorship of Selby Smyth and the Conservatives, was more successful. The Dominion had been completely dependent on Britain for all the munitions of war, including ammunition for the militia's Snider rifles. Since 1870 only enough cartridges for the annual target practices and for sale to rifle associations had been purchased from England and in 1878 the General discovered that there were reserves of only 160 rounds per rifle. The need was obvious. When a private firm refused to take on the task of making ammunition, the General proposed that the government should build its own cartridge factory at Quebec, using surplus buildings inherited from the British. The incoming Conservative government gave the suggestion close study. Since the Snider had been

superseded by the Martini Henry rifle in the British Army and supplies
of ammunition might soon become more expensive, a Canadian factory
might be a cheaper alternative to rearming the whole militia with a new
rifle.[43] With evident reluctance the War Office agreed to help arrange
for machinery for the new factory. Captain Oscar Prévost, a lawyer
turned artillery officer, was appointed superintendent and sent to England to learn his work.

It took four years before the factory was in operation. When it was
unpacked in Canada the machinery was found to be defective and in-
complete. The buildings at Quebec had to be renovated. The government failed to arrange for spare parts and these had to be manufactured
by local mechanics. Only by 1884 was the factory in full production and
its ammunition approved by a board of officers. A year later the North-
West campaign gave the new establishment a chance to prove itself by
turning out a million and a half rounds in two months.[44]

Greater self-sufficiency in the materials of war was one outcome of the
1878 scare. Greater interest in Canadian participation in imperial wars
was another. As long as Canadians were preoccupied by threats on their
southern frontier and the coasts, it seemed impossible to Selby Smyth
that the best men of the militia could be allowed to leave the country.
Yet the prospect of an Anglo-Russian war had inspired many militia
officers to volunteer their services.

Sir Patrick MacDougall had arrived at Halifax to take command of
the British garrison, and it was he who raised the issue in formal terms.
In a memorandum to the War Office he proposed to organize a division
of ten thousand Canadians which he would lead to the front.[45] When the
MacDougall proposal was confidentially sent to the Canadian government Selby Smyth was dismayed. Without wishing to oppose a plan
intended to help Britain he pointed out to the Canadian ministers that
uncontrolled recruiting for such a contingent would disorganize the militia. With his obsession about men "of Communistic or, as may be termed,
Fenian proclivities," he predicted that the outbreak of war would bring
an invasion of such folk from the United States. If MacDougall would
only raise his men from the ranks of the unemployed, all would be well,
but even four or five thousand such men would be "as large a quota as it
might be safe to deduct from the fighting element of the Dominion – at
all events until sufficient time elapses to prove how far this effervescing
Communism may develop itself with hostile intent upon the territory of
Canada."[46] The Canadian ministers agreed.

The 1878 crisis passed but MacDougall's interest in obtaining Canadian manpower for the overstretched British Army continued. The work of Sir Alexander Milne's committee had been assumed by a British royal commission under the former Conservative colonial secretary, Lord Carnarvon. The atmosphere seemed appropriate for new schemes of imperial military co-operation. Through the Marquis of Lorne, Dufferin's successsor as Governor General, MacDougall submitted to the Canadians a plan for a "Royal Canadian Reserve." There would be seven battalions of Canadian volunteers, based on the existing militia organization. The officers would be largely Canadian but the corps would be inspected and paid for by Britain. Its members, as well as agreeing to accept active service when needed, would train for a month each year and be paid sixpence a day.[47]

The scheme had attractions. It would not disrupt the militia and in time it might furnish well-trained non-commissioned officers. For many militia officers it seemed far preferable to Selby Smyth's plans for expanding the permanent artillery batteries into a standing army.[48] It would also cost Canada nothing. The General, however, had been working on his own scheme to organize infantry battalions in Canada which would then serve in England and eventually return to become a Canadian regular army. His plans inevitably influenced his reception of the different MacDougall proposal. Selby Smyth could naturally see the advantage to the militia of the "Royal Canadian Reserve" and, provided the reservists were the sons of substantial farmers and artisans and not "tramps and the floating population of the towns," he believed that they would probably meet their obligations. Yet, in a later memorandum to the royal commission, he warned that British control of the reserve would probably run afoul of Canadian nationalism.[49] Sir John A. Macdonald was also asked by the Carnarvon Commission to comment on the MacDougall proposal. The Prime Minister, from whom the British always seem to have expected more imperial enthusiasm than they received, was ready to allow the British to recruit men for the reserve at their own expense but he went on to warn the commission that it would be unrealistic to ask a Canadian Parliament in peacetime to guarantee a contingent in event of war.[50] Discussion of the MacDougall scheme seems to have come to a sharp halt in Whitehall as soon as the British ministers realized that they would be paying the full cost.[51]

In Britain the Russian war scare of 1878 gave birth to a new concern for imperial defence; in Canada it led the government to turn inward.

Sir Edward Selby Smyth seems to have shared this reaction and to have encouraged his government to think in parochial terms. When the Admiralty refused bluntly to detach warships to protect Canadian commerce from the *Cimbria*'s privateers, it was the General who tried to persuade the Canadians to set up their own naval organization. His reaction to MacDougall's plan to lead troops to a British war was to think of Canada's own borders. His reception of the "Reserve" scheme was in sharp contrast to the imperial enthusiasm of the Governor General. Certainly, on the issue of Canadian contributions to imperial military efforts, the General was reflecting the prevailing public opinion in the Dominion. His grasp of political realities contributed to his success in surmounting the complications which had arisen during his term of office. Selby Smyth collaborated successfully with two different Liberal Ministers of Militia and with a Prime Minister who continued to dominate the affairs of the Militia Department. He then managed a successful transition from Liberal to Conservative government in October 1878.

The General was probably assisted by the weakness of William Vail, a man who failed to live up to the testimonials of his Nova Scotia colleagues. "He was never of any use to me," Mackenzie later informed his brother. "In debate he was so awkward that I fairly dreaded his getting to his feet."[52] Mackenzie was a severe critic of his Ministers, but even by gentler standards Vail's contribution to his department seems to have been modest. In 1877 both Vail and his fellow Nova Scotian, A. G. Jones, were victims of the Conservative campaign against Liberals who had violated the Independence of Parliament Act. Both men had violated the statute by being shareholders in newspapers which had profited from government printing contracts. Both were forced to resign their seats. Vail pleaded hard against being compelled to face a by-election, threatened to resign, and begged to be appointed the Canadian Commissioner to the Paris Exhibition. Mackenzie stood firm. The Minister finally faced his Digby electors and his fears were realized by a substantial defeat.[53] Jones, who had originally proposed Vail for the post, had not yet been renominated for the Halifax seat and Mackenzie promptly made him Minister of Militia in Vail's place. The Halifax voters sent him back to Parliament and in the remaining ten stormy months of the Mackenzie government he showed himself to be the best of the three Liberal ministers.

Selby Smyth had been sufficiently popular with his Liberal superiors to be proposed for the KCMG at the same time that seniority raised him to the rank of lieutenant general in the British Army. The following year the General faced a new Conservative ministry and a new Minister.

In opposition the Conservatives had offered no specific militia policy. Individual members had attacked extravagance, the permanent staff, and the new military college, and had proclaimed themselves the best friends of the rural militia, but when the staff had actually been cut the Conservatives were chagrined to discover that it was their own appointees who were sacrificed. The Conservatives had launched few of their barbs at the General Officer Commanding. In 1878 Mackenzie Bowell had been annoyed by a passage in the General's report for the previous year calling on militia MPs to use their influence more constructively for the benefit of the force,[54] but this was hardly the basis for fundamental antagonism. Indeed, Selby Smyth probably hoped that the Conservatives would be the means of achieving overdue reforms and in his first report to the new government he went so far as to condemn the political influence which kept useless and inefficient militia units in existence.[55]

As Minister of Militia in his second government Macdonald chose a forty-five-year-old Montreal lawyer, Lieutenant Colonel L. F. R. Masson. The choice seemed appropriate as Masson had been a brigade major on the staff until 1868. He had then served in Parliament for eleven years and seniority as well as ability dictated his selection as one of Montreal's French-speaking representatives in the cabinet. Mackenzie Bowell, the leader of the parliamentary colonels, became Minister of Customs. With Masson sick during much of the 1879 session it was Bowell who presented the new government's militia estimates. He could report that the old abuse of paying the brigade majors by the number of efficient companies had been abolished. Henceforth they would receive a regular salary of $1,200 a year. Sadly, in view of his past campaigns, Bowell could only report the elimination of one staff position.[56]

During his brief period as Minister, Masson's chief preoccupation was the refusal of French Canadians to play their proportionate role in the militia. A group of French Canadians in Montreal proposed to reorganize the defunct 4th Chasseurs Canadiens, dressing them in a version of the Zouave uniform to commemorate the young French Canadians who had volunteered for the Papal Zouaves in 1868. The promoters could argue that while the rest of the militia, with their faithful imitation of British uniforms and military customs, followed one stream of Canadian tradition, it was legitimate that a French-speaking corps was en-

titled to reflect a purely French-Canadian military exploit. Masson, who
had played a part in organizing the original Zouaves, urged the project
on the government. There could be no objection to reviving the battalion
since French Canada already had much less than her fair proportion
of the militia. The only objection was to the uniform. Lord Lorne, as
governor general, insisted that no foreign pattern of uniform could be
allowed in the Canadian militia. In England the Duke of Cambridge
denounced the Zouave uniform as fancy dress. Others more diplo-
matically suggested that the costume might produce confusion in a war
with a French or American enemy. Masson countered by agreeing to
change the uniform colour from grey to red. The argument came to an
end in January 1880 when ill health forced Masson to give up his portfolio. The would-be organizers who had spent more than five years on
their task finally gave up.

There is no evidence that the General became involved in the affair.
The dispute was largely conducted between Masson and Lorne through
a rather cynical prime minister. If Masson's health had survived he
might have overcome British intransigence and succeeded in adapting
the militia to an alternative tradition of potentially greater appeal to
French Canada. Instead, he failed, and he had no successors with the
will to make comparable changes.[57]

Masson's resignation forced Macdonald to make some emergency
alterations in his cabinet. The former Minister reluctantly agreed to
accept the nominal post of President of the Council while Sir Alexander
Campbell agreed to move to the Militia Department.

There had to be other changes as well. Sir Edward Selby Smyth's
appointment was due to end in 1879, the year in which he also reached
the official age of retirement. In Britain the prospective change of command led to reconsideration of the whole structure of military authority
in North America. Would it not simplify matters if there were only one
British general in Canada instead of two? It hardly made sense that the
Lieutenant General Commanding at Halifax should have the same rank
and precedence as officers who had commanded the entire garrison of
Canada. Since 1870 he had been responsible only for a small fortress
and a garrison of less than two thousand troops while the other general,
junior in rank, held a command stretching from the Atlantic to the
Pacific. Moreover, the chain of authority between the two officers was
by no means clearly established to British satisfaction. In 1870, to the
indignation of Sir Hastings Doyle, Colonel Robertson Ross had bluntly

refused to consider him as his superior officer in matters relating to the militia.[58] Similar conflicts had flared intermittently in the ensuing decade.

When the Canadian government applied for a short extension of Selby Smyth's term, the Colonial Secretary, Sir Michael Hicks Beach, used the opportunity to suggest that the two appointments might in the future be combined. The Canadian government refused even to consider it. There were two objections to amalgamating the two commands, both of them from the Canadian standpoint insuperable. The first was that the general at Halifax, thanks to his traditional precedence, still acted as administrator of the government in the absence of the Governor General. It would simply not do for the officer commanding the militia, the employee of the Dominion government, to assume such eminence. The other objection, closely related to the first, was the Canadian government's insistence on the undivided loyalty of its subordinate: "An Officer having no command but that of the Militia and owing his primary obligations as regards duty and administration to the Government of Canada would be more likely to adopt loyally its views and policy in Militia matters than the Commander of the Imperial Troops for the time being."[59]

For all its reluctance in assuming responsibility for its own military policy, after a decade the Canadian government had become jealous of its authority. Canadian politicians were coming to realize that there was no automatic identity of interests with British defence policy. The commander of the militia might be a British officer but he was the servant of the Canadian government alone.

On May 31, 1880, Selby Smyth officially vacated his appointment. A man of substantial private means, he was able to retire to his estate in Surrey and he was never again actively employed.[60] There had been disappointments for him in Canada. Several of the reforms he had urged materialized only under his successor. Under his command the militia had deteriorated in equipment and training. He had not been popular with all his subordinates: Colonel George T. Denison was, as usual, among the slighted.[61] However, in the minds of many Canadians he had been a success. A private fortune, a cheerful, easy manner, and a shrewd sense of the limits of his authority had been Selby Smyth's major assets in Canada. They were not to be shared in equal measure by his successors.

CHAPTER THREE

Luard

Failure of a Disciplinarian

Canadian refusal to consider the amalgamation of the command of their militia with the command of the British troops at Halifax meant that a new General Officer Commanding would have to be appointed. Lord Lorne, alarmed by Masson's evident nationalism, had been fearful that the appointment might be given to a Canadian at the expense not only of efficiency but of sound British influence. In fact, in a "most satisfactory conversation," Sir John A. Macdonald had already assured the Duke of Cambridge that the position would be reserved for a British officer.[1] The new Minister, Sir Alexander Campbell, was also less likely than Masson to succumb to nationalist influences.

The first problem was to find a suitable general and second was to have him accepted without offending decorum on either side of the Atlantic. An added complication was that the process of consultation in 1874 had not been recorded. Lieutenant Colonel Charles Panet, Futvoye's successor as Deputy Minister, was sent to interview Alexander Mackenzie. The former Prime Minister had to explain how the Duke of Cambridge had provided a short list from which the Canadians had been able to make their selection.[2]

In England it proved more difficult to find suitable candidates than in 1874. The command of the Canadian militia struck most officers as remote, unexciting, and rather expensive. The most eminent of those considered, Lieutenant General Arthur Hardinge, the Queen's secretary, found that Her Majesty could only spare him for really active service.[8] The Duke of Cambridge's choice narrowed to Colonel Richard Amherst Luard, one of the officers he had considered six years before as a possible Adjutant General for the Canadian militia.

Another candidate had profited from the interval to make his own interest in the position known. He was Major General James W. Domville, an elderly retired artillery officer, father of a particularly pertinacious Conservative MP and the president of the rapidly failing Maritime Bank of Canada.[4] The risk that the Canadians might perhaps appoint such an applicant to the post appears to have hastened the War Office officials. Ten days after Domville's candidacy was notified to London, the War Office learned that Colonel Luard had been accepted.[5]

In his advice to the Duke on the qualities needed in a good successor for Selby Smyth, the Governor General had suggested that he should have tact, bravery, experience with volunteers, and private means. "An officer who could afford hospitality would have great influence among the militia officers in other than merely military respects."[6] It was wise guidance. Luard qualified in two respects. He had proved his courage during campaigns in India, and at the siege of Canton he had been the first to scale the walls of the Chinese city. Luard had also served as an inspecting officer of volunteers and had spent some years in Halifax during the early 1870s. At fifty-two he was far from being an old man. At the same time, his career had not been outstanding. He had lacked both tact and wealth and the reputation for bad temper which the Duke had mentioned six years before was soon to be justified. His lack of means became apparent to his new employers when he pestered them for advances to meet his travel expenses. These requests, coinciding with reports from other sources about the new General's limitations, came close to persuading the Prime Minister to reconsider the appointment.[7] Warned that he must take the post as it stood or look elsewhere for employment, Luard set sail without his advance. On August 5, 1880, soon after reaching Canada, he was gazetted to the command of the Canadian militia.[8]

Luard settled his family in a house near the vice-regal residence of Rideau Hall and set out on an extensive inspection of his new command. Most of the year's camps had been held in the spring but the new General managed to find a few rural battalions undergoing training. His first impressions were not very favourable.[9] Two-thirds of the men in the ranks were raw recruits, receiving barely six full days of training every other year. At St Helen's Island opposite Montreal, Luard found that valuable stores were left completely unguarded at night. At Quebec he saw that the walls of the fortress had in places tumbled into the ditches. After a little over a month he was back in Ottawa bursting with determination to put matters right. After reporting his findings to both the Duke of Cambridge and his Minister, Luard went on to insist that there must be new infantry schools in conjunction with the two permanent artillery batteries at Kingston and Quebec, and a new school at Montreal with both French and English elements. For the Maritimes, he decided, companies detached from the British garrison at Halifax could set the local militia an appropriate and more economical example.[10]

Although he himself might choose to be a reformer, Luard did not find that mood reflected in the government. If Conservative candidates had promised militia reform, once in office their government altered few Liberal policies. Any reform proposal was defeated by the ministerial view that "the present state of the finances did not render it opportune."[11] Almost the only favour the rural militia received immediately from the new government was that more of them were gathered into district camps rather than training in the parochial surroundings of their local headquarters.

There were militia officers who could echo Luard's desire for reform. A. S. Woodburn, launching the *Canadian Military Review* in 1877, bitterly condemned such politically inspired extravagances as paying allowances to company officers who utterly neglected the rifles in their charge: "We want the real requirements of the force attended to, so as to enable it to become efficient. We want the militia question dissociated from party politics so that disinterested counsels may prevail in the management of the force. If public apathy is removed and these essentials are granted us, the patriotic spirit which has so far struggled on, despite all discouragements, in the maintenances of the force, will soon work out the rest of the problems."[12]

Woodburn's magazine died miserably after one issue. Dr Fred Strange, a Conservative MP and an officer in the Queen's Own Rifles, had little better fortune when he presented his own ideas on militia reform to Parliament. Referring to the "languishing state" of the force and using his own statistics, Strange proceeded to show that if the paper strength of the militia were cut from 37,000 to 20,000, the savings would not only allow the whole militia to be trained annually at a higher rate of pay but would even return $45,000 in savings.[13] The speech was thoughtful and moderate but it was delivered to an audience of rural colonels. Any reduction in strength would almost inevitably be made at the expense of the rural battalions and it was an added provocation that it should be proposed by an officer of one of the "smart" city regiments. Lieutenant Colonel Arthur Williams, commanding officer of the 46th Durham Battalion and also a Conservative, typified the rural reaction with the comment that "... the rural corps, as a rule, did not understand the art of dressing themselves with that neatness that so marked the city corps, but he felt satisfied that when endurance and pluck were required that those from the country would be found to be quite equal in efficiency to those corps that the hon. gentleman seemed to praise so highly."[14]

Strange's ideas were adopted by Luard and they won more support from the Minister of Militia than from militia officers. At the end of October 1880 Campbell presented his cabinet colleagues with a draft order-in-council recommending that the militia be cut to twenty thousand. He even admitted that he would have preferred to cut the volunteers to ten thousand, so as to be able to afford two small battalions of regulars, "a practical and useful force better able than anything the country now has to cope with domestic or Indian troubles ..." By the more conservative reduction he still hoped to train the full force for sixteen days a year and to provide more permanent troops. In addition to the two batteries there would be small infantry companies at Kingston and Quebec, a half-company of engineers to repair the fortifications, and enough horses to train the cavalry.[15]

Although the *Globe* probably reflected public opinion when it referred to regular troops as "a permanent force of idlers," leading Canadian politicians had moved a considerable way towards accepting the necessity of a standing force. During his last harried summer in office, Alexander Mackenzie had found time to assure Lord Dufferin that he was considering the formation of two or three small battalions of infantry to train junior officers and non-commissioned officers for the militia. It would be, he suggested, a second stage in the programme he had begun by opening the military college.[16] The arrival of Lord Lorne brought another advocate of a standing army to Canada, although the Governor General seems to have been concerned chiefly with providing himself and Princess Louise with the military guards and escorts appropriate to their dignity.[17] Macdonald had also been persuaded by the disorders of the 1870s and the rumours of Indian trouble in the North West that at least a nucleus of a permanent force was needed.[18] The problem was political. It would not be a popular measure with Canadians in general or the militia in particular. To cut the militia by seventeen thousand men would mean that at least two thousand militia officers, often the most influential figures in their small communities, would be deprived of rank, status, and allowances, all to create a standing army. Almost inevitably Sir Alexander Campbell's order-in-council was quietly dropped.

Luard had more immediate success with another proposal which had been urged by his predecessor six years before. In spite of his belief that staff officers in the militia should hold their appointments for only five years and then be transferred to another district, Selby Smyth had never been able to move them. Now there was action. Barely two months after his arrival Luard learned that the government had approved the retirement of three of the oldest staff officers and the rotation of all the others. Henceforth, the cabinet ruled, no appointment would last for more than five years nor would it be held by any officer over sixty-three years of age.[19]

The order was necessary, overdue, and bitterly resented by most of those affected by it. Most officers had been in the same place since they were appointed, sometimes for all their lives. A few had combined business with their military duties. Lieutenant Colonel Osborne Smith, ordered back from Winnipeg to his native Montreal, preferred to resign rather than forsake his land speculations. Unfortunately for him, the Winnipeg land boom promptly collapsed leaving him to plead for a pension. Colonel John Wimburn Laurie, the British half-pay officer who combined the command of the Nova Scotia militia with the development of a prosperous farming estate at Oakfield, was ordered to British Columbia. He spent one year at Victoria and then resigned to return to farming. Other staff officers deserved more sympathy. Obliged to buy uniforms, keep a horse, and maintain a social position, few who lacked private means or a business income could escape debt on salaries of $1,700 or $1,200 a year. The three officers forced into retirement had to be content with small gratuities; within a few years, one of them was granted a minor clerical job to keep him from want.[20] A brigade major who was transferred from Kingston to Montreal, Lieutenant Colonel P. W. Worsley, found that he could neither sell nor rent his house. In desperation he left his family behind – and was soon even more hopelessly in debt from the expense of keeping two establishments.[21] Inevitably, staff officers exerted all the political influence they could muster to prevent their transfers, but to little effect. Only two officers managed to save themselves: the two French-speaking Deputy Adjutants General were not compelled to change places. The rest either moved or resigned.

Luard's shake-up of his staff was accompanied by other changes in the higher ranks of the militia. In Great Britain the abolition of the purchase of commissions led to a series of secondary revolutions in the pay and career structure of army officers. While the Major General continued for the time being to draw his British half-pay and his Canadian salary, other British officers in Canada were now informed that they could no longer draw half-pay or even their pensions while they filled an active militia post. Protests on their behalf and for a Dominion "in its military infancy" were forwarded by the Governor General, but to no effect.[22] Colonel Strange, having calculated that his pension would only be $100 less than his Canadian pay, resigned as Inspector of Artillery and turned to ranching in Alberta. Other officers with poorer pension prospects felt compelled to stay. In the long run the effect of changes in the pay and conditions of service of British officers would mean that able men could be ordered to take up appointments, including those in the colonies, which they had earlier been able to refuse. In the short run it meant that such appointments were far less attractive for able young officers without private means.[23]

There was also a change at the head of the Militia Department. After more months of ill-health, Louis Masson finally insisted on withdrawing from the government altogether. Macdonald was ready to promote a young Quebec City lawyer, Adolphe Caron, to the cabinet, but there were political obstacles to overcome. Among Quebec ministers there was a delicate balance in representation between spokesmen for Montreal and Quebec and Masson's departure meant that the vacancy was for Montreal. After much negotiation a Quebec City minister was persuaded to accept a vacant judgeship. Caron could thus be brought into the government in company with a Montreal area MP, J. A. Mousseau.[24] Sir Alexander Campbell became Postmaster General, an office from which his patronage responsibilities for Ontario could be even more effectively exercised. On November 8, 1880, Caron became Minister of Militia. He was to hold the post for more than eleven years.

The manoeuvrings behind Caron's appointment were a fitting prelude to a career which was to be devoted to the manipulations and negotiations of patronage politics. At thirty-seven he was the youngest member of the cabinet, but in some respects he was already an anachronism.

Although he had spent seven years in Parliament as MP for Quebec County, his real claim to office was as a representative of the purest old *bleu* tradition: Catholic, conservative, authoritarian. His father, René Caron, had ended forty-two years of faithful service to successive generations of conservatism as Lieutenant Governor of Quebec. His wife was a daughter of François Baby, a descendant of one of the historic ruling families of the province. Caron himself was also one of the *assimilés* – "a Frenchman speaking English better than the English," said the *Shareholder,* with evident approval.[25] He belonged to an English-speaking law firm in Quebec and his circle was the group of predominantly English-speaking merchants and lawyers who controlled the affairs of the city. His own character was impetuous, generous, and vain. In politics, he was determined to make his way as a loyal follower of the Prime Minister.*

Unlike some of the previous Ministers, Caron had had no previous connection with the militia, although his identification with Quebec City and its growing military patronage gave him a direct interest in the administration of his new department. One early decision, for example, was to replace the surgeon of the artillery school at the Citadel with a close personal friend, Dr Colin Sewell.[26] In Quebec matters Caron could rely on his Deputy Minister, Lieutenant Colonel Charles Panet, the former commanding officer of the 9th Voltigeurs de Québec. In 1874 Mackenzie had appointed Panet to the Senate, but when George Futvoye retired a year later Panet arranged to succeed him as Deputy Minister. Despite his Liberal connections, Panet seems to have retained the confidence of his Conservative ministers. Sharing language, background, and social contacts with Caron, Panet was inevitably a more congenial and influential adviser than a British major general.

It could hardly have been otherwise when the general was Luard. The Minister and the General had conflicting goals; both were in a hurry to achieve them. Luard was determined to eradicate inefficiency and indiscipline and to establish his own standards of order in the force. Caron's purpose, with the blessing of Macdonald, was to popularize his department and to alleviate the discontents which might make enemies of militiamen in the next general election. Caron's arrival meant that

---

* There is perhaps a temptation to judge Caron more severely as a notorious *patroneux* simply because his personal papers have survived in such profusion. He simply played the game by the known rules and without blushing.

Luard's opportunity for drastic and unpopular reform was over. When the cabinet granted the Militia Department an extra hundred thousand dollars for 1881, Caron used it to give the rural battalions twelve days in camp instead of six. Even opposition MPs had to approve.[27]

Within months of Caron's appointment, Lord Lorne had realized that the wrong general had been sent to Canada. A quiet and confidential suggestion that Luard be shifted to some other position, perhaps the command at Halifax, was rejected by the War Office and the lines for the open conflict which broke out in the summer of 1881 were drawn.

Both Luard and Caron set out that summer to visit the camps. Luard respected the basic good qualities of his men. They were "sober, willing and intelligent" and only lacked proper instructors and training.[28] Unfortunately, as he went from camp to camp, this sympathy was concealed behind abrasive criticism. Militiamen, accustomed to Selby Smyth's benign advice and praise for what were, to the volunteers, genuine sacrifices of time and money, reacted angrily. At London a colonel who had been rebuked in front of his men rode off the field and sent in his resignation, an incident which drew widespread publicity. It was Caron's task, following behind, to pacify the indignant officers and to moderate their grievances. The Governor General, well aware of the friction, promised to warn Luard about his "unnecessary nagging criticism."[29]

It was easy for politicians to see Luard as the caricature of a choleric, hide-bound, military reactionary. The truth was more complicated. The general certainly believed in the traditional merits of close-order drill and he insisted that troops should learn to fire by volley rather than individually. However, it was his more progressive ideas which provoked the greatest indignation among his subordinates. In his inspections Luard paid attention to neatness and cleanliness but his scorn was reserved for the elaborate parodies of British full dress which some militia officers had adopted. In his annual reports Luard inveighed against pipeclay. Instead of gaudy and expensive uniforms, like the hussar pattern adopted by many militia cavalry regiments, he wanted cheapness and simplicity. He was unimpressed when a Montreal battalion paraded before him in the imported finery of Highland dress. He conducted a persistent campaign to replace the militia's ancient, worn-out, buff crossbelts with a modern form of equipment so that a soldier on service would have a more comfortable way to carry his food, water, and ammunition.[30] In most respects, Luard's reforms would have meant a more sensible, workmanlike militia.

The General's model of what could be achieved by the militia was the Queen's Own Rifles, the Toronto battalion which had turned out for the Belleville strike in 1877. In his first annual report in which Luard found little else to praise, the Queen's Own were congratulated "not only for their excellent appearance, equipment and drill, but also for the number of what may perhaps be termed 'extra subjects' they have taken up."[31] Men of the battalion were found practising signalling, ambulance work, and even digging trenches. Luard was probably told that the Queen's Own also boasted successful football and lacrosse teams, organized regular dances and excursions, and even produced well-drilled detachments for local theatrical productions.[32]

The Queen's Own was only one of the best of a number of fashionable city battalions. Like the 5th Royal Scots of Montreal, the 63rd Halifax Rifles, and several other corps, it emerged during the 1870s not merely as a military organization but as a combination of social club, sports club, and fraternal lodge. Enthusiastic corps boasted pipe bands, shooting clubs, gymnasts, and even an occasional choir. Throughout the year there were mess dinners, company dinners, church parades, and sham battles. Above all, there were outings. On public holidays special trains delivered militia battalions in the splendour of scarlet tunics, colours, and bands to the smaller cities of the Dominion. In the late seventies Montreal and Toronto competed for the grandest military review. In 1879 the famous preacher, Henry Ward Beecher, persuaded five hundred men of his New York National Guard regiment to join the Canadians in Montreal for what was certainly the most spectacular military assembly in Canada for many years.[33]

Such activities cost money. While rural battalions existed on government pay and allowances, sometimes supplemented by a grant from the county council, the city units depended on their officers. The Toronto *Globe* reported that one local battalion spent $4,000 a year for its maintenance. Revenue came from the proceeds of band concerts and benefits. In one regiment the officers paid an entrance fee of $20.00 and annual subscriptions ranging from $48.00 for majors to $24.00 for newly joined subalterns. There were also company funds to which the officers contributed and for which even the rank and file handed over their drill pay.[34] Popular regiments built up substantial assets in mess furniture, silver, band instruments, and uniforms. Inevitably, some units also got into serious financial difficulties.

The enthusiasm of the city militia battalions was an obvious military

asset for Canada, but there were also some significant problems. Because
the battalions were as much private clubs as military corps there was a
threat of domination by a family or political clique. "You can always
rely on the Grenadiers being a *good Conservative Regiment*," its colonel
assured Macdonald in 1890.[35] Ten of the first twenty-one officers of the
Governor General's Bodyguard of Toronto were Denisons and many
of the others were related to the family by marriage. Some small units
were quite literally the property of their commanding officers. Lieutenant Colonel Thomas Scoble, a Toronto militia enthusiast, raised his
own company of engineers, hired an instructor, and bought most of the
equipment from his own pocket. A few years later, infuriated by criticism
from an inspecting officer, he resigned his commission and disbanded
the corps. The cost of being a militia officer meant that the higher ranks
were often reserved for wealthy men. "If a gentleman has not the means
to supply himself with a proper outfit, and his aspirations are military-
inclined," declared the *Canadian Militia Gazette*, "let him take up a
private's post." The suggestion that officers should be placed on a level
with their men by giving them their uniforms would be "degrading in
the extreme."[36]

Only an exceptional enthusiasm for military pursuits and family associations with the English aristocracy enabled William Otter, a poorly
paid clerk for the Canada Land Company, to rise to the command of the
Queen's Own Rifles and to turn it into a corps efficient enough to catch
Luard's attention. Otter was exceptional, too, because he gave priority
to military efficiency. Despite their smart uniforms and drill, many city
corps were of limited military value. Because they were able to train only
in the evenings and on occasional public holidays, the city volunteers
never went to camp. Few of them fired their rifles except at sham battles.
In the practical work of soldiering, the rural militia probably received
better training.

The awkward similarities between a regiment and a private club
meant that periodic quarrels among the officers, often related to charges
of financial mismanagement or the admission of new officers, could produce awkward scandals. What would have been dissatisfied murmurings
or a rowdy general meeting in a club became conspiracy and insubordination in a military organization. Regimental disputes frequently broke
into the open when aggrieved contenders sought support through the
newspapers or through their political contacts. The 10th Royals in Toronto came close to dissolution when three captains charged that their

colonel had mishandled the regimental funds. After several investigations, much publicity, and general bad feeling, virtually all the officers were forced to resign and the battalion was reconstituted under the command of the Toronto chief of police.[37] Money was also at the root of the troubles of the 53rd Sherbrooke Battalion in 1881. With the unit in chronic financial difficulties, some of the older officers decided that their juniors should waive their right to promotion so that more affluent, if unqualified, gentlemen might be brought in over their heads. They also planned to force the colonel, who had held command for twelve years, to resign. A series of angry resolutions and bitter exchanges led to the involvement of the militia authorities and the removal of several of the officers of the battalion.[38]

In both disputes the aggrieved on both sides could at least unite in blaming Luard for unfair or arbitrary interventions. Regimental disputes were not peculiar to the Canadian militia. Veteran British officers would have had experience in dealing with them in their own army, but what regularly defeated them was the refusal of Canadians to behave like British regular officers. As MacDougall had found in his clash with Bowell, militia officers had no hesitation in using the weapons of publicity and political influence when their military interests were affected. Military discipline depends, in great part, on an accepted differentiation in the roles and expectations of the soldier and the civilian. Such a sense of difference was instinctively alien to Canadians in and out of the militia. The fact that such a doctrine had to emanate from an officer as unsympathetic as General Luard did not make it more palatable.

Of course, even for politicians, the doctrine sometimes proved convenient. During the summer of 1881, for example, Caron had authorized the local Conservative MP to establish a canteen at the militia camp at Picton, Ontario. The camp happened to be on the property of Lieutenant Colonel Walter Ross, a former Liberal MP. Ross also happened to be acting as camp commander and thus believed himself to be in an official position to forestall this small act of patronage. A detachment of militia ejected the canteen operator and threw his canteen over the fence. For this rather violent exercise of authority, in defiance of the Minister's orders, Ross was reprimanded in General Orders.[39] The incident drew wide comment and was raised in Parliament. There was the blatant use of patronage. In temperance circles there was the allegation that Conservatives were promoting the sale of liquor to innocent boys. Above all, it seemed odd that it was a Liberal officer who was singled out for public rebuke, a punishment inflicted only once before. The Minister insisted that the full responsibility for the disciplinary measure rested with General Luard.[40]

There was no doubt that Caron did use his authority for partisan ends and that other Conservatives were prepared to insist that he do so. When Major George Patullo, a prominent Liberal organizer, contrived a scheme to get command of the 22nd Oxford Rifles, Caron cheerfully informed the Prime Minister that, in response to local Conservative protests, the Liberal's promotion had been postponed "jusqu'aux Calendes grecques".[41] At Belleville a Conservative colonel got permission to recruit two extra companies on the assurance that "it would kill, largely, Col. Brown in the next Election."[42] Perhaps more justifiably, Caron agreed that the dates for militia camps in 1882 would not be allowed to conflict with the spring general election. "[N]obody will be troubled by any camps at present," he informed the Prime Minister.[43]

As Caron devoted himself to preparing for the first electoral test of his ministerial career, his relations with the General approached an impasse. Luard's second annual report was little more than a list of earlier and unheeded recommendations. The General, himself, would gladly have resigned but he could not afford the luxury. If he gave up active employment before July 1882 he would revert to the rank of colonel and be obliged to retire. "Only by going away," he confided to his friend, Colonel Otter, "can I pass the time safely."[44] The government gladly granted Luard leave for three months and Caron launched a campaign to have him replaced by Major General Strange, the former commander of the artillery school at Quebec. The British did nothing to help the Canadians out of their difficulty with Luard. The Duke of Cambridge refused to recommend a retired officer like Strange, and the Prime Minister with considerable reluctance consented to the General's return.[45] Between them the Prime Minister and the Governor General attempted to work out means of preventing future quarrels. Macdonald was prepared to admit that Caron had "misunderstood his position and duties" but went on to suggest that if Luard, "under Your Excellency's advice, will content himself with drawing his salary and winking at the irregularities occurring among irregular troops, all will be well."[46]

The General had hardly been back in Canada for a month when he was again in conflict with the Minister. On September 7 he went out to watch the annual competitions of the Dominion Rifle Association at the Rockcliffe Ranges near Ottawa. One match involved teams from

militia battalions firing in full uniform and equipment. As the team from
the 8th Royal Rifles of Quebec City was being paraded for inspection
after their practice, Luard noticed that the officer in charge, Major Erskine Scott, had obtained a towel from a spectator to complete one of
his men's kit. Although in civilian clothes, the General pushed forward,
identified himself, charged Scott with cheating, and ordered him to be
placed under arrest.

Far from being congratulated for his intervention, Luard found that
he had upset a hornet's nest. Major Scott was a prominent citizen of
Quebec. His fellow major in the 8th, Charles Pentland, was Caron's law
partner. Colonel J. W. Laurie, the retired staff officer who had been presiding over the match, claimed that he had seen no cheating. The Dominion Rifle Association protested that Luard had no authority over
their competitions. Luard, who publicly compared Scott to a dishonest
jockey, refused to admit that he had exceeded his authority. He had
discovered an officer in uniform cheating and his indignation was not
abated when he discovered that Scott and his influential friends were in
direct correspondence with the Minister. Caron was politically embarrassed by Luard's action and his Quebec associates allowed him no peace.
Armed with their briefs he persuaded the cabinet that Luard, not Scott,
was at fault. With the support of the government he compelled Luard
to release Scott from arrest and, a few months later, to allow him to succeed to the command of the battalion.[47]

The Scott affair ended whatever small hope there might have been for
reconciliation between the two men. Seizing an opportunity to demonstrate the discipline which, as he tactlessly told a reporter he had been
sent out by the British government to enforce, he had been driven into
an humiliating retreat.[48] Although Caron later claimed that he had been
forced to threaten resignation to win his point in the cabinet, he does not
really seem to have found great difficulty in mobilizing support for what
had seemed, prima facie, an indefensible case.[49]

The first parliamentary session after the Conservative victory in 1882
gave Caron a chance to present the first real revision of the Militia Act
since 1868. His major innovation was that at last there would be provision for more schools and a formal recognition that there was a permanent component of the force. Caron had also planned changes to
ensure that there were no more Luards. His draft bill provided that the
command of the militia would henceforth be open to any officer who
held a British commission, a qualification shared by Major General

Strange and dozens of other officers in Canada. Lord Lorne immediately protested, urgently reciting arguments for limiting the appointment to British generals on the active list. The range of suitable men would be larger; fresh appointments every five years kept the commander in touch with current military developments; above all, by not being political, a British general could deliver a Canadian government from temptation: "When party and political influence in the area of patronage should cease, as in the case of the selection of the Officers of the armed force of a country, it is of value to provide a plan by which the Government may be put under the least temptation to act for any but military reasons."[50]

Macdonald and Caron yielded to the Governor General and the proposed amendment was removed. However, relations within the department continued to deteriorate. As in other government departments in Ottawa, final decisions on even trivial matters could only be made by the Minister in person. Caron refused to make himself available to the General. "During the Session of Parliament," he tartly noted, "my first obligation is to attend to the House and to the Members of Parliament who represent the various constituencies, and who have the first call on my time."[51] Yet when the General submitted a claim for routine travel expenses, for which there had been no prior ministerial authorization, Caron minuted, "in matters of this kind in future I must insist upon all expenditure of money being first submitted to me."[52] In the summer of 1883, when the Adjutant General went on leave, Luard replaced him by the only other military officer at headquarters, Lieutenant Colonel Irwin, the Inspector of Artillery. To Caron, who had promised the vacancy to Powell's civilian clerk, Luard's act was "simply a piece of impertinence on the part of the General which should not be tolerated."[53]

Caron had some excuse for his parliamentary preoccupation in 1883. The revised Militia Bill was his first experience of piloting legislation through the House of Commons and it included a few tricky passages. Many of the changes merely reflected the experience of fifteen years. Several new offences were defined, references to the non-existent Regular Militia were removed, and a provision for the appointment of a Quartermaster General was added. The real innovation, the new permanent corps, appeared in Section 21. It allowed the government to raise a troop of cavalry, three companies of infantry, and three batteries of artillery for permanent service. This was the "standing army" that politicians and editorial writers had warned against. The fiction that "A" and "B" Batteries were merely embodied militia was at last dropped.

Caron had prepared for the innovation with some skill. He printed a memorandum from the popular Colonel Powell to explain why the new schools were not only necessary but economical. He chose a post-election session when opposition morale would be low. Since the whole new force was to be limited to only 750 men, critics could hardly claim that it would be a fearsome threat to constitutional liberty. Predictably, the opposition condemned the change as an extravagance, but the only dangerous opposition would have come from the Conservatives in the militia lobby. Caron helped to neutralize their objections by providing elsewhere in his bill that henceforth militia officers would be paid according to rank and not at the old flat rate. On May 25, 1883, the new bill became law.[54]

The next task was to create the new schools. The third battery, intended for Victoria, was deferred for the time being, although an officer was sent to the west coast to become its first commanding officer and perhaps to assure British Columbians that more was on its way. The cavalry troop was organized at Quebec under the command of Lieutenant Colonel J. F. Turnbull, a local militia officer and a close personal friend of the Minister. The three infantry schools were to be located in former British barracks at Fredericton, Saint-Jean (near Montreal), and Toronto. Two of the three infantry commanders, Lieutenant Colonels George Maunsell and Gustave d'Odet d'Orsonnens, had been on the militia staff. Luard's small remaining influence helped to secure the command of the Toronto school for his friend, Lieutenant Colonel William Otter of the Queen's Own Rifles.[55]

In other respects Luard's advice was ignored. Caron had explained to his friend, Dr Sewell, that the schools would "give me a chance of providing for some good young fellows who have a taste for military life."[56] The General was completely bypassed by Caron in sorting through the flood of applications for the new commissions. While most of the eventual appointments had some military justification, Luard complained that one proposed captain had already acquired a reputation for drunkenness. Lord Lorne, who agreed with the General, was assured by Macdonald that since all the other nominations were apparently very good and the exception was supported by all his French-Canadian colleagues, it was necessary to give way for one doubtful case.[57]

Luard even failed to impose his wishes on the new commandants of the schools. All four of them were sent to England in the summer of

1883 to be attached to British regiments, while the General remained in Ottawa struggling to get decisions from Caron about repairs to barracks, the enlistment of soldiers, and the patterns of uniform. "I have sent to Maunsell the Minister's telegram saying there is ample time," Luard wrote to Otter, "but he always does think there is ample time – and then hurries on at the end."[58] Luard was particularly anxious that his four colonels should start a fashion in the militia of simple, inexpensive uniforms. Caron refused to back him up. As a result Turnbull was able to adopt the elaborate hussar uniform that Luard detested while the other officers were allowed to buy the expensive uniform of British staff officers.[59]

Delays in repairing the barracks, selecting the officers, and recruiting other ranks meant that it was April 1, 1884, before the infantry schools were open and October before the cavalry school was ready.[60] By then, Luard's career in Canada was over.

In the fall of 1883 the General set out as usual to inspect camps. He had seen most of the same corps in 1881 and he now found evidence of improvement. On September 20 he reached the camp at Cobourg. With the competing demands of harvest work, it was always difficult to muster enough militiamen in the autumn, and most of the battalions were under-strength. The weakest was the 46th, commanded by Colonel Arthur Williams, the Conservative MP, with only 151 of its authorized 252 men. Luard was in a bad temper at Cobourg. Unmounted staff officers were ordered from the field. An adjutant in difficulty with his horse was told to get down and walk. Officers were scolded in front of their men for faults of dress and drill. In the ensuing review, Williams' battalion managed to get out of position and to draw more of the General's wrath.

At the luncheon after the inspection the atmosphere was tense. Colonel Casimir Gzowski, the venerable patron of the Dominion Rifle Association, was present as a guest. Among other comments, the aged engineer complained that MPs were indifferent to the national importance of shooting. Colonel Williams, a little heated, accused Gzowski of insulting Parliament. Luard, also out of control, intervened to silence the MP and to contribute some of his own views on the subject of parliamentary institutions.

There was an immediate outcry at the General's conduct. Newspapers of both political colours rushed to denounce him. Williams, "glad to be the humble instrument in a cause which certainly requires in the public interest the highest consideration," consulted Caron on how best to proceed.[61] Lord Lorne, now at the end of his term in Canada, appealed to the British authorities to find Luard another post before he was dismissed.[62] Caron, in Quebec to meet the incoming Governor General, suggested to Macdonald that the moment was opportune to get rid of the troublesome general.[63]

Lorne's successor was the Marquis of Lansdowne, a much cooler politician. Having persuaded his ministers that newspaper articles hardly provided grounds for instant dismissal, he set himself to persuading Luard to resign, the Duke of Cambridge to offer him another appointment, and Colonel Williams to withdraw his complaint. In all three purposes he was successful. On March 5, 1884, Luard left Ottawa for the last time to take command of a brigade at Aldershot.[64] On his departure Williams withdrew the complaints he had laid with the Secretary of State about Luard's alleged breach of parliamentary privilege. When the subject was at last debated in the House of Commons there was little to discuss.[65]

Luard's failure was a setback for British influence in Canada. The MP s who had demanded that the command of the militia be opened to Canadians had been given fresh arguments. At the same time, the torrent of denunciation soon brought a counter-reaction. Lord Alexander Russell, the British commander at Halifax, reported to the Duke of Cambridge after a visit to central Canada: "Many people have spoken to me in favour of Luard since he left, saying that he had done more for the Militia of Canada than any previous Adj. Gen. [sic] and that the reason he did not get on with the Minister of Militia is that he shewed up the deficiencies and shortcomings of the system."[66] There were also Canadian defenders. In the parliamentary debate which had been expected to destroy him there were as many who defended the General as denounced him, and they included both Liberals and Conservatives.[67]

Luard's problem in Canada arose not from policy differences with the government but from a conflict of authority with the Minister. Each dispute had arisen from a political challenge to the General's authority over discipline.[68] Even Macdonald recognized that Caron's position was often administratively indefensible, however reasonable it might be from a political standpoint. The problem was that Luard's impetuousness, poor judgment, and lack of self-control regularly made his position indefensible as well. Once the dispute had become personalized, one of the two men had to go. The problem itself remained.

CHAPTER FOUR

Middleton

Complacent Placeman

With Luard's departure the involved procedure for choosing a successor had to be undertaken. Once again some Canadian politicians had their own candidate for the post. Major General J. W. Laurie, the former staff officer who had preferred his Nova Scotia farm to the lonely command in British Columbia, was determined to command the militia. As a former British officer who had been promoted to major general on his retirement, he believed that he was qualified. Even more important, as an affluent and influential Nova Scotia Conservative, he had enlisted the support of Sir Charles Tupper, minister of railways and canals, Nova Scotia's chief spokesman in the cabinet, and perhaps Macdonald's closest political ally.[1] With Tupper enlisted for the campaign, Laurie might be excused for assuring Halifax friends that the position was as good as his.[2]

Another man was an equally ardent candidate for the post. Colonel Frederick Dobson Middleton was then completing his tenth year as Commandant and Secretary of the Royal Military College at Sandhurst. In forty years of service he had fought in New Zealand, India, and Burma. He had twice been recommended for the Victoria Cross. Now, as he approached his sixtieth year, he faced retirement. The appointment in Canada was the sole alternative. In 1868, while serving with his regiment at Montreal, he had married Eugénie Marie Doucet, the daughter of a French-Canadian lawyer, and their joint desire to return to Canada perhaps explains why Middleton had been listed ahead of Luard in the Duke of Cambridge's list of possible Adjutants General for the Canadian militia in 1874. As well as making his wishes known at the Horse Guards, Middleton sought to improve his standing in the Dominion by entertaining the four Canadian colonels in England in 1883. They returned as emissaries for his cause. He also sent for a copy of Caron's new Militia Act and returned it with appropriate compliments.[3] Long before Luard had left, Caron was satisfied that Middleton would be his successor. When he was certain that a contest for the position would develop, the Minister himself warned the Colonel to have his testimonials ready.[4]

The new appointment created problems of politics and protocol. In April Caron made his own position clear to Macdonald. Supported by a note from Colonel Powell, he argued against the possible selection of Laurie. The militia, he declared, did not want a commander who had spent "twenty years engaged in farming and manufacturing pursuits" and who could not possibly have kept up with his profession. As for Middleton, as well as having the highest testimonials, he would only hold the position for five years, a fair guarantee that the commander of the force would remain up to date: "My own conviction is that Major General Laurie would be if appointed more of a permanent occupant of the position as I can imagine that the influence he has brought to bear in his favour today might be strongly used to keep him in office after a period of five years."[5]

Having declared himself, Caron was prepared to wait. Tupper had been appointed Canadian High Commissioner in London, and at the end of the 1884 session of Parliament he would leave to take up the post. By postponing an appointment until his departure, Caron avoided the risk of a battle with Laurie's supporters.[6]

The problem of decorum was potentially more complex. Lord Lansdowne wanted to retain for the Duke of Cambridge the prerogative of first presenting the names of officers for formal consideration by the Canadian government. He was anxious to avoid the possibility that Canadian ministers would submit the names, leaving the Commander-in-Chief with the invidious task of explaining why an officer like Laurie or Strange was unsuitable. The fact that Middleton was the only serious British applicant as well as being Caron's personal choice meant that Lansdowne had his way. In reporting his negotiations to the Duke, the Governor General felt satisfied that he had established a procedure which would preserve a British initiative in making appointments in the future.[7]

Middleton reached Canada on July 13, 1884. Canadians learned that their new general was very short, very red-faced, and quite friendly. Middleton was pleased with his welcome although he confessed to the Duke of Cambridge that he did not know how long it would last: "I cannot help thinking that Your Royal Highness has read these people a lesson by employing General Luard and not listening to their barking and yelping at him and that to a certain extent I shall benefit from it."[8]

Middleton was careful to share such unflattering thoughts only with the Duke and the Governor General. He accepted Lansdowne's advice to take stock of the Canadian militia and its recent history before attempting to establish his own authority. To Caron he appeared obliging and constructive. After a series of quick visits to militia establishments in eastern Canada, the new General compiled the most flattering annual report for the department since the time of Robertson Ross. The new schools had "performed wonders," the military college was specially praised: "there are very few institutions of a similar character equal to it in Europe and none that are better."[9] Middleton was clearly determined to make himself acceptable to his new employers.

In 1884 events in Egypt and the Sudan reawakened Canadian interest in the possibility of being involved in Britain's imperial wars. The military occupation of Egypt in 1882 had obliged the British to withdraw one of their battalions from Halifax but the Canadian government had displayed no enthusiasm for replacing it with its own troops and very little for a variety of schemes to recruit Canadians for the hard-pressed British Army. A Canadian permanent force officer, Major Joseph Hébert, went to Egypt in 1882 to serve with a British battery, but he died of fever soon after his arrival.[10]

Two years later the organization of a relief expedition to save Gordon at Khartoum produced an emotional atmosphere in Britain which quickly spread to more imperially minded Canadians. The Dominion became at least indirectly involved when the British government, through the Governor General's office, hired a force of Canadian boatmen to help the expedition up the Nile.[11] A swarm of militia officers volunteered their services to command the boatmen and a few were accepted. General Laurie, denied the command of the contingent, turned to drafting a scheme to raise a brigade of Canadians to serve the Empire under his command.[12]

None of these activities were of official interest to the Militia Department. The Prime Minister consistently maintained that the British were entitled to recruit men in Canada if they wished but that it was not the concern of his government. Nor was the Sudan. As for militia colonels, with their volunteering, Macdonald dismissed them as merely "anxious for excitement and notoriety."[13] The Conservative Toronto *Mail* commented, perhaps a little unfairly: "The idea in London appears to be that the Dominion is a vast annual camp and that we shall feel offended if we are not permitted to take a hand in this campaign. This extraordinary misconception has doubtless arisen from exaggerated cable reports of the war feeling in this country."[14]

The man who had to take responsibility for volunteers, voyageurs, and General Laurie was Lord Lansdowne's military secretary, Lord Melgund, himself a keen amateur soldier. Melgund was delighted by the enthusiasm of the militia officers. He even encouraged General Laurie's scheme in the face of advice from less euphoric officers like Colonel Otter, and tried to obtain Canadian sanction for the recruiting.[15]

On the other hand, General Middleton played almost no part in these imperial arrangements. Nor did he fill a much larger role in an obviously more relevant task. For years, particularly since 1878, correspondence on matters of imperial defence had been accumulating in the Militia Department. In 1882 the Liberal leader, Edward Blake, had pressed Caron for copies of all correspondence with Britain on defence matters since 1870. Before replying, Caron referred the material to Major G. R. Walker, a British officer employed as an instructor at the Royal Military College at Kingston. Walker advised against publishing any of the documents, pointing out that the evidence of Canada's defencelessness would be of value to an invader.[16]

That had to satisfy Blake, but by 1884 Caron had become convinced that a more thorough approach to the problems of dealing with such correspondence would have to be developed. In many cases the British had been waiting for years for replies to even routine circulars. The Minister set up a "Commission on the Defences," with Lord Melgund as Chairman and General Middleton and Colonel Panet as members. The secretary was Colin Campbell, once a Royal Navy assistant paymaster and now a junior clerk in the department. The committee met only once, decided that its work would be limited to coast defence, and left its affairs in the hands of Lord Melgund and Campbell.[17] Melgund soon acquired other preoccupations and Campbell struggled on alone throughout 1885, collecting and sorting documents. The commission's only report was entirely prepared by Campbell and consisted of no more than a catalogue of years of unanswered correspondence and disregarded reports. The documents themselves were bound in nine large volumes and deposited in the Minister's office.

In this undertaking Middleton took little evident interest. When Campbell referred reports to him the General claimed that he had no time to read them although, as the rather querulous old clerk complained, he did have time to go skating.[18] When a new Russian war scare developed from the Pendjeh affair in early 1885, bringing a new flood of volunteering from excited militia officers, Middleton proposed vaguely to both Caron and Melgund that he might put himself at the head of a force of five thousand Canadians to be trained for possible service, but no definite steps were taken even to draft a plan.[19] Any such musings were interrupted in March by news of serious trouble in the North West.

A Canadian garrison had remained at Winnipeg from 1870 until it was finally disbanded in the summer of 1877. The "Manitoba Force" was a lonely and forgotten detachment, the Canadian counterpart of the scattered American army garrisons below the border. After 1874 the North West Mounted Police was dispersed across the North-West Territories of the Dominion and the troops at Winnipeg had little to do. For most of them, the sole attraction in joining was the large land grant at the end of their service, a prize which frequently found its way into the hands of Winnipeg land speculators.[20] As long as the Manitoba Force existed, there was little encouragement for the volunteer militia in Manitoba. A few tiny companies had come into existence for a threatened Fenian raid in 1871, but they disappeared so rapidly afterwards that the local staff officer had to hire a private detective to track down some of the rifles and equipment.[21] As in British Columbia, the high wages and mobility of a frontier population offered thin material for a militia organization, and by severely restricting the numbers trained each year, the Militia Department offered no compensating encouragement. As a result, the Canadian government's authority from Winnipeg to the Rocky Mountains was reinforced by little more than the few hundred Mounted Police.

Military district number 10 covered Manitoba and the entire North-West Territories but in 1885 it had no organized units outside Winnipeg. In 1879, when the annihilation of the buffalo brought starvation to Canadian Indians and when a large number of Sioux crossed from the United States, an emergency session of the cabinet authorized $11,000 to raise and equip six companies of militia in the territories. After a few months, when further reports indicated that the apparent threat had subsided, the government tried to rescind the decision, only to learn that five of the six companies had already been organized. However, as no further money was forthcoming to train or supervise the scattered little units, they had ceased to exist long before 1885 and their rifles were placed in storage.[22]

In the 1880s the military threat in the west seemed to have shifted to Manitoba, where the collapse of the land boom and farm prices produced unexpected hardship and a militant Farmers' Union. At militia headquarters such rumblings were conveniently associated with Fenianism and Caron reacted by proposing that a fourth infantry school should be established at Winnipeg. When the farm union uttered threats of secession, a new militia battalion, the 90th Rifles, was hurriedly authorized for Winnipeg and an armed guard was placed over the small store of arms and ammunition in the city. The military officer in charge of these preparations was Lieutenant Colonel Charles F. Houghton, transferred in 1881 from his post in British Columbia. When the Prime Minister asked his son, Hugh John, a Winnipeg lawyer and a veteran of the Red River Force, for an opinion of an officer who might occupy a key position, the reply was hardly encouraging. While Houghton might be a good fighting soldier, "day in and day out he drinks more than is good for him." The younger Macdonald also concluded: "he has not much head and still less judgement."[23]

In the event, preparations in Manitoba were not needed against farmers or Fenians but against the Métis and their Indian allies. In 1884 Louis Riel, the leader of the Métis government at Fort Garry in 1870, returned to his people at their new settlement, Batoche, on the North Saskatchewan. Soon rumours and reports of a fresh Métis uprising, this time supported by the Indians, were reaching Ottawa. They could not have come at a worse time for the government. The Canadian Pacific Railway, Macdonald's dream of linking east and west, was virtually bankrupt. The Dominion's credit, pledged to the CPR, was exhausted. In the way of desperate men, the cabinet hoped that the Métis troubles would pass. Party newspapers called reports of rebellion "a monstrous exaggeration."[24] On March 25, 1884, the Montreal *Gazette* compared the troubles to "a petty riot" in any well-settled part of old Canada.[25]

The next day a small police force, accompanied by volunteers, clashed with a party of Métis at Duck Lake, north of Batoche. When the government men struggled free they left ten of their dead behind. News of the battle spread. The police abandoned Fort Carleton and with hundreds of terrified white settlers fortified themselves in the town of Prince Albert. Further west news of the battle reached Big Bear's band of Crees. On April 2 his braves murdered nine white men at Frog Lake. Other whites, including three women, were taken prisoner. The Indians then surrounded the police post at Fort Pitt. On April 15 the policemen escaped from their fort and reached Battleford where more police and five hundred civilians had crowded into the small stockade. Terror spread across the prairies as Indians pillaged Hudson's Bay Company stores and seized cattle and horses. Nourished by rumours of massacre, reinforced by recent memories of the merciless Indian wars of the American plains, white settlers from the Rockies to as far east as Winnipeg were panic-stricken.

In Ottawa a government which had ignored the danger signals for months now reacted sharply. Three days before the Duck Lake disaster, Edgar Dewdney, the lieutenant governor of the North-West Territories, asked for a "military man."[26] Mindful of the deficiencies of Colonel Houghton, Macdonald ordered Middleton to start immediately for the west. The General reached Winnipeg on March 27 to find the city convulsed by rumours and alarms. Houghton had already left for the territories with a company of the 90th Rifles and Middleton followed with the rest of the battalion, making camp at Qu'Appelle, the nearest point on the CPR to Batoche.[27]

Middleton's departure meant that there was no one left in Ottawa with the remotest experience of organizing a campaign. The stream of messages coming along the telegraph wires left no doubt that the trouble was serious. General Custer's disaster was a recent enough reminder of the hazards of Indian wars and politicians and public alike wildly exaggerated the military skill of the Indians and Métis and the ruthlessness of their leaders. The military problems Canada now faced seemed enormous. "It is such a vast country that it is impossible to see where the trouble may end," a Conservative editor wrote to Tupper. "Of course it will be put down, but the cost in life and treasure will be very great."[28]

In the circumstances Macdonald and the government had to rely on Middleton as a sick man relies on a doctor. The Prime Minister did send one long and self-deprecatory letter of advice to the General, urging the advantages of mounted troops and the desirability of guarding the railway and the border, but it was his only contribution to campaign strategy.[29] Although the Minister of Militia later acquired a taste for appearing at miltia field days, he too was prepared to leave the tactical decisions to Middleton. Deluged by anguished appeals from those prairie communities which could find access to a telegraph line to send troops, rifles, and cannon to their immediate rescue, Caron resolutely referred the demands to Middleton. In Ottawa his task was to provide the troops and supplies his General needed.[30]

At Qu'Appelle, Middleton was much more sanguine than the politicians in Ottawa about the military problem. From Winnipeg he had wired: "Matter getting serious. Better send all Regulars and good City Regiments,"[31] but he was soon busy discounting the fears of excited settlers. As for the force of Mounted Police, voluntarily locked up in Prince Albert and Battleford, he regarded their appeals for prompt relief with conspicuous contempt.[32] The General's plan was to strike with his full force at Batoche, encircle the little town so that Riel and his followers would be trapped, and crush the rebellion at its heart. If he could move quickly, he could safely leave his communications unprotected and ignore the urgent pleas of unprotected prairie communities. The problem was how to move quickly. The governing factors in Middleton's planning were administrative.

Chief of his difficulties was transportation. As his militiamen drilled and in many cases fired their rifles for the first time in their lives, Middleton tried to improvise a transport organization. S. L. Bedson, a retired British officer and the warden of Stony Mountain Penitentiary, was appointed transport officer. Another former officer, Major W. R. Bell, manager of the Qu'Appelle Valley Farming Company, hired teams and drivers for an exorbitant ten dollars a day. "I am trying to keep down expense here as much as possible," Middleton wired the Minister, "but fear it will all cost money."[33] All the circumstances pointed to the need for mounted troops but Middleton soon learned that the grass to feed the horses would not appear on the prairie until May. Until then, every pound of forage would have to be transported. "These scoundrels have just selected the time when the roads will be almost impassable, the rivers the same, and all the teams are required almost immediately for seeding," he reported to Caron.[34] The key to the solution of his transportation difficulties was the shallow, rambling South Saskatchewan River, but until the spring run-off from the Rockies, there was too little water in the river to float a steamer. Until then, Middleton had to rely on waggon trains to carry all that his force needed. It was an expensive way to carry supplies. In twenty days on the trail a team would eat half its own load of hay. To delay, however, meant leaving the rebellion to ferment for another month. Middleton decided to march.[35]

Back in Ottawa Caron's first task was to hurry forward reinforcements to Middleton. Although there were more than a hundred miles of gaps in the uncompleted CPR line north of Lake Superior, no other route for sending the troops was considered. The CPR construction superintendent was ordered to make arrangements to convey the men along the broken line. Within a month almost all the 3,300 militia from the east had made their arduous passage under his management. While construction hands gathered sleighs and flatcars to carry the soldiers and their equipment along the unfinished railway, Caron called out his forces. On March 28, only a day after Middleton's call for men had been received, 780 troops had been called out. Commanders of detachments soon learned of the Minister's sense of urgency: "... wish you to travel night and day. I want to show what Canadian Militia can do."[36] Officers on the spot found that instantaneous mobilization had its problems. At Toronto Colonel Otter had to appeal for two days grace while townspeople hurriedly collected winter clothing and underwear for his men.[37] At Kingston the Mayor found that the wives and children of the men of the permanent battery had been left without money and a special relief fund had to be organized for their benefit.[38]

Under pressure from the Governor General, MPs, and militia officers, Caron called out still more militia. The two Toronto battalions, the Queen's Own and the 10th Royals, had been the first to be called. The two French-speaking city battalions, the 9th Voltigeurs from Quebec and the 65th Carabiniers from Montreal, both commanded by Conservative MPs, were next to be called. To satisfy rural Ontario two composite battalions were organized, one under Luard's foe, Colonel Arthur Williams, MP, the other under Lieutenant Colonel W. E. O'Brien, MP. Later, the 7th Fusiliers from London, the Montreal Garrison Artillery, Colonel Denison's Governor General's Bodyguard, and a composite battalion from Halifax were among the units sent to the North West. The prospect of fighting stimulated military enthusiasm and Caron was besieged in his office by a host of applicants for military employment. One of them, sent off in command of a company of Ottawa sharpshooters, has left a picture of Caron, "a remarkably handsome man, a regular Adonis," working feverishly in his office while the corridors outside almost bulged with expectant and eager militia officers.[39]

Everything had to be improvised. Regulations were hurriedly drafted to provide pensions for the wounded and for dependents of the dead. Special field allowances were authorized for the officers. Apart from allowing militia units to have their own surgeons, there was no medical organization for the militia. Caron gave the task of organizing hospitals and ambulances to Dr C. M. Douglas, a former British army surgeon who had won the Victoria Cross eighteen years before. After a few days Douglas concluded that the task was hopeless. The Minister was urged to approach the United States army medical department for help "on the grounds of common humanity."[40] Instead, Caron turned to yet another Conservative MP, Dr Darby Bergin, commanding officer of the 59th Stormont Battalion. Within a week the First Field Hospital under Dr Thomas Roddick of McGill University had been organized and was on its way to Winnipeg. It was closely followed by Senator Michael Sullivan, another Conservative doctor whom Caron had appointed Purveyor General.

The journey of the troops along the CPR line was a feat of both organization and endurance. Working desperately against the time when the spring break-up might make movement impossible, the railwaymen organized teams and sleighs to ferry soldiers and their equipment across the thirteen different gaps in the line. Meanwhile, men who a few days before had been clerks or craftsmen tried to adapt themselves to an alternation of marching and freezing on open flatcars in temperatures that often went below zero. By the time the 9th Battalion passed over the line the railwaymen had nailed boards around the flatcars and tacked on canvas for a roof, but Georges Beauregard and his comrades scarcely appreciated their relative comfort: "Nous étions une cinquantaine par boîte, entassés les uns sur les autres, ruisselants de la pluie qui nous tombait sur le dos par torrents. Pour la première fois nous avons pu connaître ce qui était que la misère. Pas moyen de nous rechauffer nous avions à peine le courage de chanter pour nous remettre le coeur."[41]

The destination of the troops was Winnipeg, where a base was hastily improvised. Lieutenant Colonel W. H. Jackson, a militia staff officer from London, arrived there to find himself the only officer in the city. A few days later a telegram arrived from Caron appointing him to take charge of all administrative arrangements for the campaign.[42] Winnipeg was also the headquarters for the Trade Commissioner of the Hudson's Bay Company, Joseph Wrigley. The firm, with its network of trading posts, its reserves of food, and its waggons and river steamers, was to play as important a part as the CPR in helping the government to overcome Riel. It had a ready-made logistical organization which the military authorities could only have matched after months of delay and expense. Although the company, like others, "adhered to the time-honoured prac-

tice of getting all they possibly could out of the government,"[43] its
positive contribution to the campaign has often been ignored. No other
firm or combination of firms in the North West could have supplied the
unexpected and sudden demands of a force of several thousand men so
quickly or efficiently.

Although the Minister rarely intervened in Middleton's tactical arrangements, he did insist that subordinate staff officers like Jackson
respect the political pressures of Winnipeg Conservatives. The General
himself was forced to accept the services of a number of unwanted officers. At Calgary Major General Strange closed his ranch, moved his
family to the safety of the town, and decided to go to war with the
Indians he so cordially detested. Middleton was obliged to put him in
command of a column to pursue Big Bear, though his own opinion was
that Strange "was what you call in this country a 'crank' and with a
little religion in it which is dangerous."[44] Major General Laurie was
even more unwelcome, but he was also accepted, after elaborate arrangements were made to ensure that he would not out-rank Middleton. To
his own disgust Laurie was assigned to the command of the base at Swift
Current, a post from which his fussiness managed to cause Middleton
repeated annoyance.[45] Middleton would also gladly have rid himself of
Colonel Houghton but hints, followed by a virtual appeal to Caron,
brought no relief. Instead, Houghton continued to provide a focus for
the growing number of malcontent officers in the General's column.[46]
On April 11, in response to a request from Caron and to piteous appeals
from Battleford for relief, Middleton formed yet a third column under
Lieutenant Colonel Otter. On April 13 Otter and five hundred men left
Swift Current. It took five days to get the troops and their long waggon
train across the South Saskatchewan, but by April 24 Otter was in Battleford having marched his men an average of thirty miles a day.[47]

The main column left Fort Qu'Appelle on April 6. The weather and
conditions for marching were at first appalling. On the first day, soaked
by snow and sleet, the men travelled only twelve miles. That night the
temperature fell and by morning it was twenty-three degrees below
zero. It was a suitable start for a march which led the militiamen
through blizzards and forced them to wade through sloughs up to their
waists. On April 17 the column reached Clarke's Crossing on the South
Saskatchewan. The slow marching had enabled several contingents from
eastern Canada to catch up with Middleton. Although he regretted the
absence of the men with Otter, he felt sufficiently strong to split his

force on either side of the river. It was an essential part of his strategy to trap Riel at Batoche. Middleton believed that communication between the two wings would be possible by use of a steamer. Unfortunately, the steamer did not arrive. Laden with reinforcements, supplies, a field hospital, and a Gatling gun, the steamer *Northcote* only left Swift Current on April 22. By then, the first run-off had gone down the river and the level of the shallow stream was falling. The captain had claimed that it would take him only four days to reach Middleton; it took fourteen.

It was also on April 22 that Middleton's force, now divided by the river, left Clarke's Crossing for Batoche. Two days later at Fish Creek Middleton's wing ran into the first Métis resistance. The little column was saved from a disastrous ambush by half-breed impatience and its own scouts. The untried militia just managed to hold their ground but the engagement cost ten killed and forty wounded out of a total of only three hundred and fifty men engaged.

The battle also cost Middleton his high self-confidence. The troops camped on the battlefield and the two wings were reunited. While Middleton waited impatiently for the steamer to arrive with reinforcements and medical assistance for his wounded, he reported confidentially to Caron that without his presence the battle would have been a disaster:

You will probably have heard that I exposed myself needlessly. That is not the case. I was perfectly aware that it would have been dangerous not only to my troops but also to the whole N.W. territory if I was knocked over and I can assure you that I did not want to be knocked out, but I saw that one of two things had to be done: either I must retire the men which would have ended in a rout, or I must do my duty to the Government and run certain risks. I did so and am glad to say was successful, ably and energetically aided by my 2 aides who deserve well of Canada.[48]

The Governor General, who had reports direct from Lord Melgund accompanying the expedition, was also aware that Fish Creek had nearly been a catastrophe. His own view was that Middleton should have been kept in Ottawa and that Melgund, younger and more imaginative, should have had the command in the North West.[49]

While Middleton's men waited with growing impatience at Fish Creek, the two other columns were busy. Without consulting Middleton, Colonel Otter decided that an attack on the nearby Cree camp at Cut

Knife Hill would discourage the Indians from their continuing attacks on property around Battleford and from joining Riel. With the approval of Governor Dewdney,[50] he and a large detachment of his force set out from Battleford. At dawn on May 2 he reached the Indian encampment but surprise was lost. When the troops failed to press their attack the Crees recovered their spirits and proceeded to infiltrate around Otter's flanks. Both of the cannon the militia had brought from Battleford collapsed under their rotten carriages and Otter soon decided to withdraw. It was the restraining hand of Poundmaker that saved the retreating militiamen from further punishment. The foray cost eight soldiers killed and fourteen wounded and Middleton, when he heard of it, was understandably displeased.[51]

Further west, General Strange painfully improvised a force at Calgary. Wild West legends to the contrary, he found the local cowboys to be almost completely unarmed. Reinforced by militia battalions from Winnipeg and Montreal, Strange left Calgary on April 20. He reached Edmonton ten days later, having dragged his train of waggons across swollen rivers and through swamps of prairie gumbo. It took him two weeks to fortify the town and to construct makeshift barges to carry his men and supplies down the North Saskatchewan. On May 14 the pursuit of Big Bear began in earnest.[52]

By then, the serious military phase of the rebellion was over. On May 7 Middleton at last felt able to resume his advance. Two days later in heavy bush outside Batoche he again encountered the Métis. There was a confused engagement with a well-concealed enemy and Middleton was torn between the choice of withdrawing to his previous campsite or remaining. At length he made up his mind to continue the battle but Lord Melgund was sent back to Qu'Appelle to order up all the available reinforcements and to report on the situation to Ottawa. For two days the militiamen marched and skirmished outside their hastily fortified camp and fretted at their lack of success. On May 13 the morning was spent in an elaborate feinting movement, abandoned when the main body of troops did not hear the signal to attack. A furious Middleton marched his men back to camp. Early in the afternoon, in circumstances never satisfactorily explained, the men in the battalions guarding the front began to advance. As the volunteers surged forward, their comrades in the camp swarmed out to follow them. The Métis, almost out of ammunition and unprepared for the assault, fled. There was scattered resistance in the village of Batoche itself but by nightfall the Métis rebellion had collapsed.[53] Two days later, Louis Riel, who had scorned to escape, surrendered to three of Middleton's scouts.

The campaign was not yet over. On May 28 Strange's column finally came into contact with the main body of Big Bear's Crees at Frenchman's Butte. The Indians easily held off the militia until fire from Strange's single cannon caused most of them to panic. However, since the militia had also fallen back the Crees were able to return, collect their property, and resume a more orderly retreat. As a result, the Canadian troops had to spend most of June in a futile pursuit of Big Bear through the swamps and bush of northern Saskatchewan.

In fact, after Batoche all was anti-climax. The militia became fed up with the blundering pursuit of the Indians or with guarding mounds of hay or canned beef along the line of the CPR. "It would be an outrage for men to be detailed from their professional or other profitable business avocations for a longer period than the exigencies of the public service demand," declared one eastern editorial writer,[54] and the government was hardly less anxious to liquidate an expensive operation. On June 22, when the last white prisoner had been recovered, the troops began to come home. Middleton had planned to end the campaign with a triumphal review in Winnipeg but the plan was deluged under torrents of rain. Instead, the mayor ordered the city's taverns to remain open all night and the troops, who had been denied liquor throughout the campaign, were thus allowed a more congenial celebration. By July 20 the last of the eastern militia were on their way home, leaving only the permanent troops and some local militia to guard the dying embers of revolt.

The sudden collapse of Métis resistance had come as an enormous relief to Macdonald and his colleagues. The campaign had been a remarkable feat of improvisation. An army of 5,456 men had been organized, more than half of them brought from eastern Canada over the uncompleted CPR in bitter winter conditions. A transport service of 1,771 men and over four thousand animals had been created. Above all, the campaign had been completed in only three months. The costs were real. The force had lost twenty-six men killed and over a hundred wounded. The bill for the military share of the campaign was more than three million dollars. Yet, until Batoche fell, the government had anticipated far worse. Middleton, on whom responsibility for success or failure had rested, was voted $20,000 by Parliament. The British presented both Caron and his General with a KCMG and the War Office went on to confirm Sir Fred in his British rank of Major General. After pressure from Lord Lansdowne and the Colonial Office, the War Office also paid for the cost of a medal for the troops and civilians who had taken part in the campaign.[55]

For so successful an affair the 1885 campaign generated a disturbing amount of ill-feeling and dissension among its senior participants. The real heroes of the campaign had been the men in the ranks, enduring cold and hunger, performing impressive feats of marching, and developing the discipline to overcome their lack of training and equipment. They had to be satisfied with a medal and a small land grant. The senior officers wanted glory. If, like Colonel Denison, they had been left behind to guard supplies, they were indignant at being denied a chance for action. If they had seen fighting, they condemned the all-too-apparent blunders of others.

Perhaps some of the atmosphere of recrimination was inevitable. Former British officers like Strange, Laurie, and Houghton bitterly resented the fact that the command had not fallen to them, and even before the campaign was over they were using their political channels to campaign against Middleton.[56] Many Canadian officers did the same and Caron had encouraged many of the militia politicians in the field force to communicate their views directly to him. Middleton had not won the affection of his Canadian subordinates. There was no question that he had done well in the campaign. He had displayed considerable physical courage and, for a man of his years, surprising physical stamina. At the same time, his disdain for the military accomplishments of his militia officers was an ill-kept secret. They were, he assured Caron, "fine fellows," but "they knew nothing, of course, except marching past and a few drill manoeuvres ..." whereas their half-trained men needed the best possible leadership.[57] When the official report of the campaign was published, those who had been looking forward to special mention of themselves and their exploits found that the General had been sparing of both praise and blame for those under him. Disgruntled subordinates claimed that "Old Fred" was simply keeping all the credit for himself. "It is thought by many who had opportunities of judging," wrote a Conservative MP who had served with Middleton, "that the General would have gained more honour & a more lasting reputation, had he displayed more willingness to accord a share of honours to others who merited."[58]

Typical of the tangled disputes was the debate about who had ordered the final charge at Batoche. In his report Middleton claimed the credit but many of those present insisted that it was due to Canadian initiative, chiefly that of Colonel Arthur Williams, the Conservative MP whose men had been among the first to attack. Since Williams had died shortly before the end of the campaign, some of the more excitable militia officers claimed that he was a martyr to the General's tyranny.[59] It was an absurd claim in itself but it reflected the impatience of men who now felt that they had little further need of British tutelage. Colonel Panet, the deputy minister, sent to Colonel Otter for details of his little battle at Cut Knife Hill so that he could present it in its "true light." It illustrated, he suggested, "the fact that Canadians can fight their own battles without foreign help."[60]

The acerbity of the officers' feelings might have been dulled if all the ambitious and aggrieved could have been suitably decorated for their services. However, having given Caron and Middleton their knighthoods, the British authorities judged the campaign by the standard of their own small wars and agreed to offer only three minor decorations. There was no way that this meagre recognition could have been distributed to give satisfaction. Middleton himself proposed seven officers for the CMG, and Caron too pressed for a longer list of honours. The cabinet preferred to let the matter drop, limiting their pressure to obtaining a bar to the campaign medal for those who had actually been under fire.[61] The dissatisfaction of the officers remained and, since custom decreed that a commander was responsible for obtaining recognition for his subordinates, Middleton remained the target for their bitterness.

The discontent of ambitious militia officers seemed a minor discord in the aftermath of victory. Both Caron and Middleton seemed to have fortified their positions, and the militia organization for all its faults had passed the test of actual service. The General now sought to convert the Mounted Police into a military garrison for the disaffected territories. Anticipating such a change the government offered the command of the police to Lord Melgund. Although he refused the post rather than expose his wife to the rigours of living in Regina, Melgund supported Middleton in urging the appointment of a future General Officer Commanding of the militia, Major Edward Hutton. By then, the government had thought better of the plan to turn the police into soldiers and the commissionership was given to a Canadian.[62] The Militia Department was allowed to organize a company of permanent force mounted infantry at Winnipeg as a school for the local militia and a force in case of further trouble. For the latter role it was no longer needed. The completion of the CPR ended the era of frontier insecurity and Middleton, who had planned to lead a flying column to the North West in the spring of 1886, was able instead to bring home the outlying garrisons of permanent force troops.

Far from gaining lasting political advantage from military success in 1885, however, the Conservatives had engineered their own long-term destruction. In May Riel's surrender had brought the campaign to a satisfying climax; six months later his trial and execution brought French and English Canada to their most bitter confrontation in generations. In ten years the execution of Riel was to help make the Liberal party, by then purged of its radicalism, the voice of French Canada. It was to throw the Conservatives back to the base of Protestant, pro-imperial Ontario.

This transformation affected the militia. In the long term it hastened the identification of its most active spirits with the Conservative party. Correspondingly, it weakened the standing of the force in Quebec. Both of the French-Canadian MPs who had led their battalions to the North West supported the pressure to save Riel. The experiences and service of their men became a minor theme in the verbal battle between English and French Canadians and increasingly between Caron and his own province.[63]

The Minister was, indeed, in a special position. Alone among his French-Canadian cabinet colleagues he had condemned Riel without moral or political reservation. His loyalty to Macdonald, his education, and his clerical and English ties made such a reaction inevitable. His mental and physical involvement in the suppression of the Métis rising had set him apart from the profound emotional response in Quebec to what was seen as an act of English revenge.[64] Convinced like Macdonald that the excitement would die for want of fuel, and indignant and contemptuous of Conservative MPs who endorsed Riel's cause, Caron set himself to recover his party's political position by a more systematic exercise of every weapon of political patronage. To Caron the "glaring injustices" which affected elections were government printing contracts given to hostile newspapers.[65]

Although the Prime Minister's son assured Caron that he could have a safe seat in Manitoba, the Minister was determined to save his own riding of Quebec County and as much of the surrounding region as he could. Being Minister of Militia was an asset to be exploited. The presence of the cavalry and artillery schools, the cartridge factory, and a large militia store meant that about a sixth of the annual departmental

budget was spent in Quebec and Lévis.[66] Caron took personal control of
how it was spent. His own dealer, Joe Bigaouette, supplied the horses for
the schools and a constituent, Mrs Mary Brophy, supplied the oats. It
would be a "Kilkenny cat concern" if she ever lost the contract, he once
confessed. "My life would be a long agony."[67] As Minister he could
arrange for three companies of his county battalion to spend the winter
of 1885–6 in the Citadel at Quebec. It was a pleasant alternative to a
winter of unemployment or ill-paid work in the woods, and it was expected to pay political dividends.[68]

Patronage also meant services for Quebec and for personal friends of
the Minister. Caron resented the pressure from cabinet colleagues to fill
unnecessary staff appointments or to create new places for their clients.
"You see Caron 'has broken out in a new place' and goes in for economy," Macdonald noted jocularly when the Minister refused to appoint
a full-time quartermaster for the tiny cavalry school.[69] Caron was more
accommodating with his friends. The middle-aged brother of a Montreal
friend was appointed as a subaltern in the new mounted infantry school
at Winnipeg. Unfortunately, the twin garrison menaces of boredom and
drink soon proved too much for him as they did for some other Caron
appointees. On the other hand, at least one of the young men who won
their commissions through political influence with Caron, Harry E.
Burstall, rose to military distinction commanding the artillery and then
a division of the Canadian Corps in the First World War.[70]

In his determination to increase the patronage potential of his department, Caron had to struggle with his cabinet colleagues. One of his
triumphs was to win direct control over the repair and maintenance of
barracks, fortifications, and drill sheds from his chief Quebec rival, the
influential Sir Hector Langevin, minister of public works. Caron justified
the transfer as an opportunity to employ the graduates of the Royal Military College, but five years afterwards the department's engineering staff
consisted of only two architects, neither of them RMC graduates. The real
change was that Caron, not Langevin, had the final say in the distribution of drill sheds.[71]

Another area in which departmental policy and political advantage
coincided was in buying an increased proportion of the militia's clothing
in Canada. Caron resumed a policy which the Liberals, for the sake of
cost and quality, had abandoned. The chief obstacle to the change was
the problem of manufacturing the special scarlet cloth which the Canadians, in imitation of the British, had adopted for their militia uniforms.

In 1886 W. E. Sanford, the largest woollen manufacturer in the Dominion, accepted the challenge to manufacture the cloth in return for an unprecedented three-year contract. By 1890 the department could report that everything worn by the militia was made in Canada.[72]

This practical application of the Conservatives' National Policy brought protests from the opposition and from many in the force itself. The cost of manufacturing the clothing in Canada was high and the quality, at least initially, was low. Sanford was paid a third more for tunics than it cost to have them delivered from England. Evidence submitted to the Public Accounts Committee in 1889 suggested that some of the cloth bore a strong resemblance to shoddy, while the dyes changed colour dramatically when exposed to the light of the sun.[73] Some years later an ambitious graduate student, W. L. Mackenzie King, was to prove that militia clothing was manufactured in dreadful conditions of sweated labour.[74]

Criticism of the system would have been at least less partisan had all the contractors, secure in their three-year contracts, not been prominent Conservatives. W. E. Sanford was appointed to the Senate in 1887 and Bennett Rosamond, the Almonte wool manufacturer, took over the Lanark North riding in a by-election in 1891. The clothiers tended to be frank about their relationship with the government. In 1887, negotiating his unusual contract, Sanford was careful to remind Caron that he was also busy trying to raise money for the newspaper the Conservatives planned to establish in Toronto.[75] Hollis Shorey, the Montreal clothier who manufactured the militia's trousers, was even more direct. In a letter to Macdonald he explained: "some time during the last general elections a gentleman called on us at the request of the Minister of Militia for a subscription toward the elections, and promised that if we gave it, no more tenders would be asked for three years but that we would have the work at the then prices." Shorey went on to explain that tenders were now, unexpectedly, being invited: "I have not put my name down for a subscription to the 'Empire' and my sons and myself have come to the conclusion not to do so until I hear from you in reply to this letter. We have always subscribed & worked for the Conservative party and shall continue to do so, but our general subscriptions to the last general elections were heavier than usual, and if we are not to get this contract we cannot afford to subscribe liberally in this case.[76] Shorey's business with the Militia Department in the following year made him its third largest contractor.

Caron's political preoccupations and even his influence on behalf of unsuitable candidates for permanent commissions did not bring him into conflict with Middleton. The General's opinion of his Minister was far from flattering: "he is before all things a politician, is not an able man and is as vain as Frenchmen usually are," he confided to the Duke of Cambridge. "He is however a great favourite of the Premier, Sir John Macdonald, who finds him useful, I am told, in carrying out shady political jobs."[77] This was a private view. In his official and social contacts with Caron, harmony reigned. In a series of annual reports Middleton made unexceptionable recommendations for better shooting, more training, and less elaborate uniforms. He even provided an unsolicited testimonial for the decrepit Snider rifles, pointing out in 1887 that they had just been adopted by the British for their police in Burma. It was a tranquil, complacent interlude for the department and the force.

What helped to control Middleton's feelings about his superiors was his anxiety about his income and career. "I would not hesitate to leave this country of vain, drunken, lying & corrupt men," he wrote to Lord Melgund in 1886, "but I cannot afford to 'chuck up.' "[78] By 1885 the regulations which prevented British officers from drawing their half-pay or pension while in colonial government service had been extended to the General Officer Commanding the Canadian militia. With superb bureaucratic timing the news reached Middleton at his moment of military triumph in 1885. Both Laurie and Strange were also informed that they would lose their pensions for the period they had spent on active service during the North-West campaign. Both Caron and Macdonald went to work on behalf of their officers. "A half pay officer may become an idler, a farmer or a billiard marker and still draw his pay," Macdonald commented to the Governor General, "but if employed in the line of his profession by a Colonial Govt. he forfeits it."[79] In Strange's case the British authorities eventually relented, but for Middleton there would be no concession.

The General, having lost almost half his official income, next faced compulsory retirement. In November 1887 he would reach the age limit for active service. The British had at last begun to take a direct interest in the quality of the officers they seconded for colonial service and had even intended to make this a theme of discussion at the 1887 Colonial Conference. When the gathering concluded, the Canadians were officially informed of Middleton's pending retirement and that the War Office was willing to nominate a successor.[80]

Sir Charles Tupper, back in the cabinet as Minister of Finance, looked forward to the vacancy with some satisfaction. Since 1869 he had periodically found jobs in the Canadian government for his son-in-law, Colonel D. R. Cameron of the Royal Artillery. Cameron was now approaching retirement after an undistinguished career, and Sir Charles planned that he should enjoy a final term in command of the Canadian militia. Caron again fought back against the Tupper influence as he had in 1884. Since Cameron as a retired officer would have no better claim for the post than Middleton, he was forced to be satisfied with a temporary prize, the secretaryship of the Fisheries Commission.[81] Then Caron turned on the British. With the support of the Governor General, the Minister forced the War Office to concede that the militia command was at Canada's disposal. To arguments that the force needed a commander in touch with modern developments, Caron answered that Middleton was still needed to manage changes already underway. Although Middleton was placed on the British retired list (with the rank of lieutenant general), he found that his term in Canada had been extended until 1892. "I fondly hope and trust," he wrote to Caron, "that you will never regret your action in this matter."[82]

The new developments for which Middleton was allegedly needed were the formation of a new infantry school at London and of the artillery battery so long promised for Victoria. Because high local wages made it virtually impossible to recruit men in British Columbia for the forty cents a day of a permanent force soldier and would have made desertion an irresistible temptation for troops drafted from the east, Caron had made a series of half-hearted attempts to recruit reservists from the Royal Navy and Marines. Their experience would make such men good soldiers while their pensions would deter them from desertion. Meanwhile, in spite of the reports of a small procession of British and Canadian inspecting officers, the defences of the Pacific Coast remained much as Irwin had built them in 1878. In 1886, during a visit to England, Caron was finally persuaded by the War Office that something would have to be done to fulfil an earlier Canadian promise to provide a garrison.[83] After a last attempt to recruit British reservists, the Minister ordered that an artillery battery be organized by drafts from the two existing artillery schools and sent west on the CPR. One possible reason for the decision was that Caron himself was due to visit British Columbia in November 1887. On his arrival at Victoria he was able to point to the newly arrived troops as evidence of Ottawa's concern for local safety. After a few days of accelerated negotiation he was able to announce to a political meeting the site of the new barracks.[84]

This belated gesture was more designed to impress local voters and fulfil the letter of agreements with Britain than to provide an efficient defence. The hundred Canadian gunners were left with Irwin's obsolete guns and eroding earthworks. Two years after their arrival the troops were still without barracks and thirty of the men had deserted. Their dispirited commander was pleading to be transferred to eastern Canada.[85] As late as 1891 the local MP believed that he would get the votes of the remaining gunners if Caron would only agree to spend a few thousand dollars on surveys and roadwork to give the impression that the long-awaited barracks were on their way.[86]

The British government, increasingly concerned about Esquimalt's defencelessness in a Pacific under the growing shadow of Russian naval power, was also being pressed by its own Parliament to show results. Prior to the 1887 Colonial Conference, Lansdowne had pressed Caron for a satisfactory solution but the only result was the disconsolate and ineffective "c" Battery. Lansdowne's successor, the Earl of Stanley, came fresh from his experience as the British Secretary of State for War, but he had little better success in imposing a sense of urgency on the Canadians. On May 2, 1889, in the latest of a series of proposals, the British offered to provide a garrison of marines and the armament for the forts and to supervise the construction of defences if Canada would meet the cost of the troops and works. "C" Battery was to be removed.[87] The Governor General found that his ministers refused to reopen the matter. By building earthworks in 1878 and providing a few gunners a decade later, Canada had fulfilled her responsibility. Britain was welcome to do more but entirely at her own expense.[88]

In pressing his government for a decision on Esquimalt, Lansdowne had found that there was still no machinery for considering those defence questions which lay outside the routine of departmental administration. In Britain the new Colonial Defence Committee had urged all the colonial governments to set up comparable bodies. Caron, whose vision of what was required was still circumscribed by the abortive 1885 Commission on the Defences, finally agreed to set up a new consultative body. In a very long Privy Council report, reciting all the efforts and achievements of Canada in defence since Confederation, he proposed a new defence committee. The members would be Middleton as chairman, Colonel Powell, the adjutant general, Colonel J. R. Oliver, the commandant of the Royal Military College, and Lieutenant Colonel Irwin, the inspector of artillery. In a departure from the pattern proposed by the Colonial Defence Committee the senior British officer in North America was not included. It was argued that he was too remote at Halifax to deal with the total problem of Dominion defence.[89]

For secretary, the key appointment in such committees, Caron was urged to obtain an experienced officer from England. He rejected the suggestion and also passed over Colin Campbell, the devoted but uninspired secretary of the earlier commission. Instead, he asked for the services of Lieutenant John Irvine Lang, a graduate of the Canadian military college who was then serving at Halifax as an officer of the Royal Engineers. It was a politically popular appointment. It also cost Canada nothing.

The committee apparently met only once, early in 1888.[90] For Caron it had served its purpose as a public relations exercise, as a device to sooth Lansdowne, and as a means to dispose of unanswerable Colonial Office circulars on defence. As secretary, Lang spent most of the year surveying fortifications at Esquimalt and showed no inclination to divert a promising career towards Ottawa. Of the other members, Powell and Irwin were administrators, taking their cue on matters of policy from the Minister. During the summer of 1888 Colonel Oliver found himself removed from the command of the Royal Military College when Sir Charles Tupper demanded his place for his son-in-law, General Cameron.[91] The key figure might have been Middleton, but he displayed little interest in the committee. A visit to British Columbia had convinced him that Canada's real interest lay in defending Vancouver, the terminus of the CPR.[92] Lansdowne himself concluded that if the dockyard were to be properly defended it would require a substantial force of Royal Marines.[93]

In any case General Middleton was now in semi-retirement. He was not going to challenge his political superiors when they had made their views on the Esquimalt question quite clear. On past experience he might be excused for believing that so compliant and helpful an attitude would be a guarantee of the tranquil completion of his extended term. He was even negotiating to become president of a Canadian insurance company after his retirement.[94] Then, unexpectedly, his career was in ruins.

Charles Bremner was a half-breed fur trader who had been arrested at Battleford during the rebellion. When he was released he found that his furs, confiscated at the police fort, had been stolen. With the help of a few friendly Liberal MPS, Bremner persevered in his investigation and discovered that the trail led to Middleton and his staff. In 1887 the matter had been raised by David Mills, a leading Liberal, but Middleton had silenced him with a flat denial. However, by 1890 some damning evidence had accumulated. There was proof that Middleton had taken furs to an Ottawa furrier after his return from the campaign. There was a note, apparently from Middleton, ordering the police storekeeper to make up some bundles of furs. The Liberals, bitterly divided by so many of the issues of the Riel tragedy, could unite in condemning theft. Under attack during the 1890 session of Parliament, Middleton demanded an investigation. When he appeared before a Select Committee of the House of Commons he proved to be an equivocating and unsympathetic witness. "I thought I was the ruling power up there," he told MPS, and "that I could do pretty much as I liked as long as it was within reason." The MPS did not agree. The confiscations, they said, were "unwarrantable and illegal"; Middleton's conduct was "highly improper."[95]

When the Select Committee report was published, Middleton was engulfed in a torrent of newspaper abuse. In a pre-election year his conduct was a stick to beat the government. The Toronto *Globe* reflected the tone of many leader writers: "Sir Frederick Middleton has degraded his high position, disgraced the uniform of a British officer and hurt our ideal of the English gentleman. And for years the Government has shielded this titled officer from punishment. He seems still to rest securely beneath the protection of the Militia Department."[96] In Parliament, Edward Blake, the former Liberal leader, devoted more than two hours to pouring out a mixture of learning and invective on the General's conduct, concluding that Middleton should not only pay for his share of the Bremner furs but that he should reimburse the trader for his entire claim of $7,000.[97]

It was apparent that the real attack was on the government. If Middleton had ever had the furs, it was also evident that they had in turn been stolen from him. Other strongly based allegations of looting by Canadian militiamen in the North West had not been investigated although Caron himself had had to go to considerable trouble to recover a church bell stolen by some Ontario volunteers.[98] However, by denouncing only the General, Blake gave the Conservative government an easy escape. By disowning Middleton the Prime Minister soon robbed the Liberals of their monopoly on virtue. When Middleton, bewildered and hurt by the turn of events, submitted his resignation, Macdonald insisted that Caron reword his letter of acceptance to remove any suggestion of sympathetic feelings: it would be "severely remarked upon in Parliament."[99]

Middleton was stunned by his misfortune. His friends rallied to give him a farewell dinner in Toronto, concluded by a flattering address from Goldwin Smith, the leading controversialist of the day; but he was dismayed to find how few friends there were. As a final, desperate attempt to answer the charges against him, Middleton published his *Parting Address to the People of Canada*. In it he tried to rebut the verdict of the Select Committee. He went on to meet another charge, insisting that he had worked hard to secure honours for his officers and listing the names and awards he had proposed. The publication was a gross political error. The *Militia Gazette*, a magazine for militia officers which had hitherto been sympathetic, switched off its support. As shrewder politicians had realized five years before, those included in Middleton's list were furious that they had not been recommended for higher honours while a much larger number was indignant that they had not been included at all. "Poor Middleton," Caron charitably observed, "made an awful muck of it."[100]

Although British official opinion rapidly concluded that Middleton had been the victim of a political conspiracy, it was the end of his military career. In 1896 he was appointed Keeper of the Crown Jewels in the Tower of London, as plain a rebuke as possible for those who had harried him from the Dominion as a thief. Sir Richard Cartwright, one of the leading Liberals, later acknowledged that Middleton had been very unjustly treated.[101] Yet the blame lay less perhaps with the opposition than with the eagerness of the government to sacrifice a faithful subordinate who had become, at least temporarily, a political liability.

In 1882 Macdonald had recommended that Luard should "draw his salary and deserve it by doing as little as possible." It was advice that Middleton had followed but his removal, when it came, was far more humiliating than his predecessor's. It would be hard to find more contrasting styles of command but both men had failed to win the affection or support of their subordinates or the protection of their superiors. It was becoming apparent that the command of the Canadian militia was, for a British officer, not merely remote, dreary, and ill-paid; it might be impossible as well.

CHAPTER FIVE

Herbert

Military Politician

Middleton's ignominious departure meant that the command of the Canadian militia was again prematurely vacant. In militia circles there was talk of appointing a Canadian. "The position is the legitimate prize of those who have given time and money in helping to maintain the volunteer militia," claimed the Dundas *True Banner*, suggesting that either Colonel Otter or Colonel George Denison, the cavalry expert, would do as well as Middleton.[1] William Mulock, the Toronto lawyer who had become the chief Liberal critic of the Militia Department, indicated that he would present a motion to Parliament to have the command opened to a militia officer.[2] Neither Caron nor Macdonald had the slightest intention of allowing such a change. "It would never do for some half dozen good reasons," Caron told his friend, Lieutenant Colonel George Kirkpatrick.[3] One reason was the lack of politically influential contenders. At the Royal Military College Cameron was turning out to be an unsatisfactory and demanding commandant.[4] After a brief term as the Conservative MP for Shelburne, General Laurie had gone back to England, eventually serving in the British Parliament as well. General Strange made an indirect bid for the post but his eccentric character and his long list of grievances against the government allowed him little consideration.[5]

The only real difficulty was created by the British themselves. In spite of precedents carefully established to guarantee that the Canadian government was consulted, the Duke of Cambridge simply announced that the appointment would go to Colonel Ivor John Caradoc Herbert of the Grenadier Guards.[6] Certainly the new General was better qualified than his predecessors. Herbert was an enthusiastic, educated, and experienced soldier, a veteran of campaigns in Egypt and the Sudan. At forty he had just completed a term as British Military Attaché in St Petersburg, some evidence that he was destined for a distinguished career. For Canada he had the special qualifications of being well-off, fluent in French, and a Roman Catholic.

Such attributes did not immediately mollify the Canadians. Not having been consulted, they took no official notice of the Duke's announcement. In London, where this reaction was interpreted as evidence that Macdonald planned a political appointment, both Lord Lorne and the Duke of Connaught were pressed into service to lend their influence to Herbert's appointment.[7] In Ottawa the Governor General, Lord Stanley, could intervene more effectively. He arranged that other names of applicants be forwarded, talked the Canadians out of an initial preference for the former commandant of the military college at Kingston, Major General E. O. Hewett, by claiming that engineers were "apt to be 'faddy,' " and paved the way for Herbert.[8]

By giving the appointment to Herbert the British had demonstrated their growing determination to impose a higher standard of defence on their self-governing colonies. For Canadians the era of gestures like the 1888 Defence Committee or the sad little artillery battery at Victoria was nearing its end. Lord Stanley, who knew something of Herbert as a former brother officer in the Brigade of Guards, made it plain to Macdonald that the new General would be a contrast to Middleton:

I think he would be a man who would insist on things being smart, and who would not hesitate to speak out his mind in the public interest of the service, to those to whom he was answerable officially. He would be led but not driven. I believe he has private means beyond the average, and he would certainly find re-employment at home, so that he would probably throw up his appointment if his assent, either tacit or expressed, were asked either to neglect of discipline, or to diversion of the money voted by Parliament from the service for which it was given.[9]

Herbert reached Canada in late November to find that campaigning for the 1891 election had already begun. Leaving the task of writing the

1890 report to Colonel Powell, he took advantage of the national preoccupation with politics to have a good look at his new command. His
inspection, extending from Winnipeg to Halifax, gave him "a terrible
insight into the working of the system that exists here."[10] What he found
was the stagnation of twenty years. The military stores had become mu-
seums, "filled with an accumulation of worn-out and worthless equipment, obsolete military stores and condemned utensils ..."[11] Sixteen commanding officers who had held their posts in 1870 were still in command
in 1890. Most of the other senior militia officers held certificates from the
British military schools of twenty years before. Out-dated knowledge was
as significant as obsolete equipment because even officers who were aware
of the shortcomings of the force looked back to an antiquated model.

At the same time, Herbert could find stirrings of reform which he cultivated with greater skill and luck than his predecessors. The complicated
amalgam of nationalism and imperialism which developed in Canada
in the 1890s encouraged sympathy for militia reform. In 1889 Mulock
opened a persistent attack on the corruption and mismanagement of the
Militia Department under Caron, which was to persist in various forms
well into the following decade. Militia officers had been able to sustain
their own periodical, the *Canadian Militia Gazette*, since 1885, and they
used it increasingly to fight for their own interests. Under Caron's guidance the government responded as best it could. Toronto's reward for its
solid loyalty in the 1891 elections was a third militia regiment, the 48th
Highlanders.[12]

Great changes in the Canadian political scene after the 1891 elections
were even more significant in creating a new attitude to the militia. It
was to be the last Conservative victory for twenty years and Macdonald
won it at the cost of his own life. On June 6, 1891, he died. Herbert, who
confessed that he had already "quite fallen under his charm of manner,"
also recognized that Macdonald had been a formidable obstacle to military reform:

His views were very peculiar. Whilst upholding in the strongest manner politically
the idea of the integrity of Canada, as a portion of the British Empire, he would
do nothing practically for the defence either of the Dominion or of the Empire.
He looked upon money, voted for militia purposes, only as a means of gaining
political ends, but he was honest enough to keep that use of it within strict limits,
and consequently cut down the militia estimates to the lowest possible figure. He
knew that at any time he could obtain an increased vote but he also knew that any

money so voted would not yield any corresponding efficiency, but merely add to the party claims which would have to be satisfied from that source.[13]

The other barrier was Caron. Confronted by a mixture of insoluble patronage problems and the inexplicable failure of the nationalist agitation to abate, Caron had abandoned Quebec County for the more remote lower St Lawrence constituency of Rimouski. The dominant interest in his new riding was the Intercolonial Railway and Caron found himself embroiled in the patronage problems of tracklayers and stationmasters. By transferring the site of the militia camp for the district two hundred miles down river to Rimouski for two successive years, Caron had done all that he could as Minister of Militia to reward his new electors.[14] Under the increasingly severe opposition attacks on his management of the Militia Department, Caron's main prop had been Macdonald. For seven months after his patron's death he remained in his old office, but the "session of scandals" which saw the downfall of Sir Hector Langevin did not leave Caron unscathed. There were even rumours in Conservative ranks that he had helped to plot his rival's downfall.[15] When Langevin finally went, Caron reluctantly became Postmaster General.[16] The portfolio he had held for eleven years went to Lieutenant Colonel Mackenzie Bowell, now seventy-one and a mellower figure than the bitter opponent of staff officers of two decades earlier.

Although Herbert cautiously postponed writing his first annual report until Caron had been moved, he was not idle in his first year in Canada. Within two months of his arrival staff officers were directed to persuade their city battalions to spend their holidays and weekends in tactical training rather than on military excursions and ceremonial reviews. In preparation for the camps in 1891 he prepared a precise syllabus for the two weeks of training. "The basis of instruction should be the principle of not attempting too much, but of aiming at a high standard in what is attempted."[17] He himself visited most of the camps, concentrating on the French-speaking militia at Laprairie and Rimouski.

It was hard to know where to begin. While Herbert found the militia artillery relatively efficient, a state he attributed to the permanent schools established in 1871, the infantry and the cavalry were much less satisfactory. "The ideas on training which have been handed down traditionally in Canada," he wrote, "are those of a bygone age, antecedent even to the introduction of the breechloader, and though the more recent changes in certain forms of drill have been adopted, the tactical requirements on which these changes are based have been ignored."[18] Not even this kind of training was general: hundreds of officers in the militia lacked even the most elementary certificate of qualification. As for the staff officers, their appointment had been "in some degree, regarded in the light of pecuniary rewards for past services, rather than as offices involving duties for which energy, activity and technical knowledge are essential attributes."[19] The annual inspections had degenerated into ceremonial march-pasts, a procedure which Herbert attempted to reform by publishing a uniform assessment system for his staff officers.

What most shocked the new General in the course of his own inspections was the state of the permanent corps. From an establishment of 966 men, 497 had either refused to re-enlist, purchased their release or deserted in the course of a year. In 1891 there were 128 convictions by court martial. In an organization intended to provide the rest of the militia with qualified instructors, Herbert found that five men out of six were either recruits or employed in routine duties.[20] It was not hard to find an explanation for the unpopularity of service in the force: low pay, poor food, bad living conditions, and the absence of a pension. At Kingston the artillery barracks had harboured a series of typhoid and diphtheria epidemics. At Winnipeg the mounted infantry school lived in huts first erected for the Manitoba Force, "totally unfit for occupation" during a prairie winter.[21]

The worst abuses often stemmed from inexperienced and sometimes dissipated and negligent officers. At Winnipeg the mounted infantry school had been notorious for years as the site of a succession of scandals. Herbert concluded that "... no measure short of complete and radical reorganization could have been of any avail ..."[22] The commandant saved himself by dying shortly after Herbert's inspection, another officer, son of a prominent Conservative, was removed after a desperate political struggle, and the remaining officers were dispersed to other schools.

The General descended with equal ferocity on errant staff officers. At Halifax the Deputy Adjutant General, Lieutenant Colonel P. W. Worsley, was a former British officer who had reached his appointment after years of penury as a brigade major. Although he owed his initial position to the Liberals, Middleton, who regarded him as a "hard-working and painstaking officer," had secured his advancement.[23] In Nova Scotia Worsley rapidly made himself unpopular with senior militia officers, enforcing forgotten regulations, making conscientious inspections, and at last discovering a little too late that the District Paymaster had been falsifying the pay lists. It was his misfortune that he had already certified the lists as correct before he discovered the fraud. When Herbert reached Halifax and discovered that Worsley was chronically in debt, he assumed that the staff officer was as guilty as the paymaster. Worsley was at first suspended and then removed from his position. Lacking political allies of weight, the unfortunate Worsley found himself penniless, unemployed, and even imprisoned for debt.[24]

If Herbert appeared harsh and perhaps unjust in the case of Colonel Worsley, he readily acknowledged that the failings of the officers were largely due to their circumstances. He saw Worsley as only one of many aging former British officers on the staff, "disappointed men, whose brother officers have risen in their profession at home, while they have not even a pension to look forward to ..."[25] Permanent officers might be appointed for political reasons, but once in the service they had no real prospects of promotion, no security in their old age, and rates of pay which in all but the lowest ranks compared unfavourably with those in the British Army.[26] It was also true that, apart from the Royal Military College whose graduates could rarely obtain permanent commissions without a further endowment of political influence, there were no means for officers to obtain a professional training or to bring their knowledge up to date. It was the absence of a sound military knowledge among their officers which explained why so many of the Canadian permanent force schools were so far below the standards set for the artillery by Strange, French, and Irwin.[27]

Before he could accomplish anything for the force as a whole, Herbert set out to establish his own authority in the department. His first attempt was repelled. Disturbed by the Minister's willingness to act as a court of appeal for officers aggrieved by his own decisions, Herbert approached the Governor General. Lord Stanley, as a former officer, was entirely sympathetic and conveyed his own displeasure to Sir John A. Macdonald. When the Prime Minister refused to consider any limitation on his colleague's authority, Stanley had to beat a retreat.[28] The General soon found it easier to develop his influence in less direct ways. The confused political situation in 1891 was an opportunity to recover some of the authority in the department which he believed his predecessors had sacrificed. Inspecting the camps during the autumn of 1891, Herbert found that excitement over the unveiling of gross corruption in Ottawa created the right atmosphere for ending the humbler abuses of padded pay lists and unearned allowances.[29]

By careful diplomacy the General remained on good terms with Caron until the end, but he welcomed the new minister with relief and expectation. In a weak cabinet Bowell's age and seniority rather than his abilities made him one of the most important ministers. He had also retained the military interests of his younger days. Having postponed presenting the annual report for 1891 until Bowell's arrival, Herbert was delighted to find that the new Minister accepted it almost without amendment. When it was published Herbert confessed to the Duke of Cambridge that, at least for the moment, he was "being more discussed than perhaps any one else in the Dominion."[30] The report was in fact an indictment of Caron's eleven years in office. For the first time the serious state of the permanent corps was revealed. For the first time, too, there was a clear explanation of how badly the rural militia had fared in the departmental budget and how they had been hurt by politically inspired increases in the city corps. The rural volunteers got 44 per cent of the drill pay while the city battalions, only a third as numerous, got 34 per cent. In the host of recommendations, Herbert included a call for a commission of militia officers to work with him to revise the Militia Act and to create a real military system for Canada.

Bowell had barely digested Herbert's report when he received an equally forceful memorandum from the Governor General. Almost every problem in militia administration, from the cloth in the trousers to the desperate need for new rifles, was analysed. A key point, repeatedly stressed, was the need for a clearer division of authority between the Minister and the General.[31]

With hardly an aspect of internal military reform untouched, Stanley and Herbert next began to educate their Minister in the complex history of the Esquimalt defences. While the British, who had been holding marines and armament in readiness since 1889, waited with growing impatience, the terms of the latest British offer were explained and examined. The key feature of the proposal was that Canada would pay a modest sum for a garrison of seventy-five marines and half the cost of the fortifications. Britain would do the rest – from her point of view an offer of extravagant generosity since coast defence was considered a colonial responsibility.[32] The Canadians were not so sure. They resented the brusque British refusal to train men from "c" Battery to handle the modern equipment proposed for the fortifications. Herbert also suspected that his ministers resented the loss of patronage if control of construction contracts was left in British hands.[33] Bowell could also have considered advice from General Laurie[34] that the naval base at Esquimalt was in fact indefensible.* Herbert allowed him no such doubts. It took the General the rest of 1892 and a trip to the west coast with his Minister and "two of the most appalling females I ever encountered," but Bowell was finally persuaded to accept the British terms.[35]

Suddenly, it all had to be done again. Bowell, in Herbert's opinion "thoroughly English and as honest a man as could be found among Canadian politicians,"[36] found himself promoted to the more prominent portfolio of trade and commerce. The new Minister of Militia was James Colebrooke Patterson, a far different figure. In his political role he might have been the western Ontario equivalent of Caron, a political manager and fixer. Patterson was a Windsor lawyer who had risen in politics by the conventional ladder of local and provincial office. His claim to a cabinet portfolio was that he was now the president of the Ontario Conservative Union. At fifty-three he was one of the youngest members of a government of old men. Patterson had another quality which Herbert initially found hard to evaluate; he was lazy. He arrived at his office late in the morning, read little that was submitted to him, and was ill-prepared for parliamentary sessions.[37]

The welcome first fruits of this disability were that the new Minister refused to traverse ground which Bowell had taken ten months to cover. Within a few weeks the Governor General reported a Canadian offer on Esquimalt which came close to the British proposal. The Dominion would buy the sites for the fortifications and pay $150,000 to build them, together with $50,000 for other buildings (offset by $35,000 for what had already been erected). The Canadians would meet the cost of seventy-five marines and maintain a hundred gunners in reserve in eastern Canada. The local militia would be increased to a strength of four hundred. The offer differed from the British proposals mainly by imposing a strict limit on the Canadian liability, but fearful that any bargaining would lead to more years of delay the Colonial Office managed to persuade the other British departments concerned to accept.[38] In the spring of 1893, when Herbert returned to England for an operation, he was able to make the detailed arrangements for the transfer of the fortifications to British control. On August 18, 1893, the advance party of marines reached Esquimalt and the remnant of "c" Battery left for its new station at Quebec.

---

* It was a conclusion the British themselves reached a decade later.

To Herbert the conclusion of negotiations which had been wandering since 1885 was his most substantial single achievement in Canada. For Canadians the settlement should have given less satisfaction. It did represent a considerable financial advantage for the Dominion, but it was also an acknowledgment that she so far lacked the maturity to deal with her own military problems. Serious defence matters were still the concern of Britain, with no more help from Canadians than could be won by hard bargaining. However, maturity might be slow in coming when the country's chief military adviser was also the agent of British policy, specially briefed by the secretary of the Colonial Defence Committee.[39]

Herbert's intention was to place control of the peacetime as well as the wartime defence of Esquimalt and Halifax directly in the hands of the British General Officer Commanding in Canada.[40] The militia in Nova Scotia and British Columbia were to be directly affiliated to the British garrison and placed under the command of British officers. While it made military sense for militia gunners from Halifax to train on up-to-date British equipment rather than to go to Quebec to fire antiquated Canadian guns, there were wider issues involved. Herbert seized the opportunity to open a new military school at Halifax, entirely staffed by the local British garrison. Late in 1894, when Sir John Thompson was buried at Halifax, Herbert arranged that the local militia would be placed under British command for the ceremony.[41]

Solving outstanding problems of imperial defence was a more congenial task for Herbert than grappling with the reform of the militia itself.[42] During Bowell's year in office his military education had not been restricted to Esquimalt. The General had also insisted on showing him military stores filled with rotting and antiquated leather equipment, rusted rifles, and worthless cannon.[43] He was at the Minister's elbow when Bowell inspected the summer camps, seeing for himself the twenty-year decline in training and efficiency. Then, having spent a year in gaining a strong rapport with his civilian superior, Herbert found that he was replaced. Bowell was not gone; in the cabinet he served as a distant but influential ally, but a new man had to be trained.

The year had seen some changes. The boundaries of military districts had been altered to make quicker mobilization possible. The government had at last agreed to replace the decrepit Snider rifles. When Herbert returned to England in the spring of 1893 one of his errands was to find the best way to spend the small sum available for the new rifles. Back in Ottawa Caron was warning MPs that if they wanted to follow in the wake of nations experimenting with new weapons, they would not like the price. General Herbert decided that there might be real economy for Canada if she followed a little behind the lead. The British were then in the throes of replacing their Martini-Henry and one possible alternative had been the Martini-Metford, combining the Martini's single-shot action with a heavy, small-bore barrel. The War Office had ordered nine thousand of them before deciding that they were not good enough. To Herbert, considering the rough treatment they could expect in Canada, the heaviness and simplicity of the Martini-Metford were virtues. He was also influenced by War Office willingness to dispose of them at bargain prices. The Canadian ministers agreed and a thousand rifles were immediately purchased with arrangements made to buy the rest.[44]

Another of Herbert's errands was to fill the appointment of Quartermaster General, authorized ten years before but only filled with Bowell's approval. The officer he chose, Major Percy Lake, was to have a long and influential association with the Canadian militia. Born in 1855, Lake entered the British Army the year purchase was abolished. Lacking means or influence, his ability had taken him through the Staff College with distinction and had brought him a series of staff appointments in Egypt and at the War Office. Like Herbert, he was evidence of the new British determination to send only their better officers to appointments in the self-governing colonies. Lake may also have accepted the position because his father, a retired army officer, had already gone to settle near Grenfell, Saskatchewan.[45] Such ties* did not offset the political difficulties of giving such an eagerly sought position to an outsider. Lake, who had originally been promised a salary of $3,200, found that it was cut to $2,600 and careful steps were taken to ensure that he would be junior to the Adjutant General, Colonel Powell.[46] To help allay indignation among other Canadian staff officers, the appointment of Assistant Adjutant General was created and given to Lieutenant Colonel the Honourable Matthew Aylmer, a brigade major for the previous nineteen years. To meet political complaints of a burgeoning staff, most of the other brigade major appointments were abolished.[47]

Another change directly due to Herbert was the annual publication of fixed establishments for militia units. For years the number of privates had tended to shrink while the proportion of officers and non-commissioned officers and of bandsmen, officers' servants, and grooms had risen

* His brother, Richard, later served as Lieutenant Governor of the province.

sharply. In his 1893 report Herbert pointed out that one man in seven in
the force was an officer, that one in 2.7 men in the ranks was a non-commissioned officer. The Governor General's Bodyguard, the pride of the
Denison family, "cannot be called a military organization," he noted in
an inspection report, "since there are practically no privates in the
ranks."[48] Publishing such figures would at least stop the trend, he argued.
In the same order he forbade the provisional appointment of unqualified
officers, except in the lowest commissioned rank. Experience had confirmed the suspicion that once an officer had been given his rank, he was
much less likely to take the trouble to get the necessary certificates.[49]

Many of Herbert's reforms were unpopular. Commanding officers,
believing that their contribution kept the militia alive, resented criticism.
The General, they felt, made too little allowance for their difficulties in
getting recruits, raising money, and sustaining interest. When Herbert
criticized the city militia for their lack of practical training, he took no
account of the resistance of employers to letting their men go off to camp.
Certainly the federal government gave a poor example. When four companies of Ottawa militia were called out to overawe strikers, the civil
servants in the ranks were docked their pay. Many senior civil servants
had to choose between forgoing advancement or resigning their militia
commissions.[50]

Some of Herbert's critics complained that he was too accustomed to the
wealthy officers of the British volunteer movement.[51] It was a real financial sacrifice for a young Canadian to take the time to qualify at one of
the permanent schools. It took three months to obtain a second-class
certificate while a first-class certificate, the necessary qualification for a
commanding officer or an adjutant, took nine months. On the other
hand, there were many who enjoyed the militia as a club or a hobby, justifying the opinion of fellow citizens that they were part of a decorative
extravagance. One enthusiastic volunteer officer who welcomed Herbert's reforming zeal offered this view of the force: "It seems to me that
the militia has two strong enemies within itself. One is mostly to be found
in rural corps. It joins apparently in order to astonish its country friends
now and then with its gorgeous apparel or in order to go upon a cheap
ten days picnic biennially. The other is mostly in city corps. It is a supercilious thing, wrapped in its own importance. It goes about thinking
'You can't find much fault with us. We are the stuff We are.' "[52]

Herbert's critics increased. Aging, entrenched staff officers, accustomed to leisurely correspondence with militia headquarters, had their

letters returned with memorable rebukes in the General's own handwriting. "It is but too evident ... that this officer looks upon his appointment as a mere sinecure," Herbert noted on one staff officer's letter. "At present he is neither looked up to by the Militia with which he is in touch, nor does he command any confidence from his superiors."[53] Minutes like that made enemies. So did Herbert's efforts to improve the permanent corps.

The withdrawal of "c" Battery in 1893 had been part of a wider scheme to reform the permanent schools begun the year before. If the schools were to be models of organization and discipline for the militia as a whole, they had to be reorganized. Instead of a number of tiny, inefficient, and autonomous units scattered across the Dominion, there would be a regimental organization for each arm. Herbert believed that the uniform system established for the artillery schools in 1883 was one secret of their relative effectiveness. He began by turning the cavalry and mounted infantry schools into "A" and "B" Troops of a Regiment of Canadian Dragoons. The four infantry schools became companies of a Regiment of Canadian Infantry. When "c" Battery came back to Quebec the old cavalry school was forced to find new quarters at Toronto and Herbert reorganized the artillery. A full-sized battery of field artillery was established at Kingston. The nucleus of another field battery and two companies of garrison artillery were stationed at Quebec.[54] With the help of the Governor General, Herbert succeeded in getting each of his new regiments the designation "Royal" and the privilege of wearing the imperial cypher.[55] Of more practical value, Herbert also persuaded the government to send some of the officers and non-commissioned officers to England to qualify at British military schools, the first of a steady trickle.[56]

While Herbert could defend these reforms as in the best interest of the force as a whole, they really marked a major divergence from the trend of Canadian military development since 1868. The basic element in Canadian defence had been the Active Militia. The permanent corps had been created to help train the volunteers, not to supplant them. That was very clear to militia officers and it underlay the antagonism to the permanent officers which spilled over in Parliament and in the pages of the *Canadian Militia Gazette*. Herbert's perspective was different: it was to reproduce in Canada the British military system. The permanent corps would be the nucleus of a regular army. The rural battalions would resemble the British county militia regiments while the militia cavalry, "recruited from the best class of rural population," would be a Canadian counterpart to the British yeomanry. When Herbert looked at the city corps he betrayed some of the disdain which British officers often felt for their own Volunteers. "Experience has shown me," he wrote to Patterson in 1894, "that a large number of the Militia corps raised in towns and cities are military organizations only in name, and that they practically constitute social or political clubs, or lodges of various societies."[57] Development on British lines was the underlying theme of Herbert's reforms.[58]

Certainly Canadian militia officers refused to be supplanted as the chief defenders of Canada by the "political heelers and social pets who have been pitchforked as officers into the permanently embodied corps."[59] For their part, permanent corps officers did very little to mollify militia hostility. While the old "A" and "B" Batteries had helped to develop a feeling of fellowship among gunners, militia, and permanent force, the newer infantry and cavalry schools seemed to develop the antagonism. Militia officers who attended the schools resented the requirement that they purchase a complete set of uniforms. Some of the schools placed great emphasis on instructing their students in the intricacies of mess etiquette. For unsophisticated rural cadets this could be a humiliating ordeal. As for the permanent officers, they bitterly resented the fact that they were not accorded automatic seniority over militia officers of the same rank.

Herbert did nothing to heal the differences between his officers when he encouraged the permanent officers to establish their own organization, the VRI Club, and to publish their own magazine. While the magazine could obviously serve as a medium for sporting and social news among the scattered permanent schools, it did little to improve relations within the force by recording such vignettes as the picture of Colonel Gush who informed the author "... he was a member of Parliament as well as a colonel, and many other bits of information and in less than eight [sic] had introduced me to his corporal who he said, was an excellent man in any shape and form, that he was 'quite proud of him,' and that he was to be his 'Orderly Room Clerk' during the Camp because he was an 'Editor' when at home and therefore 'knows all about Orderly work of a military character.' "[60]

In Captain Sam Hughes, editor of the Victoria *Warder* and Conservative MP for Victoria North from 1892, the militia officers had an uncompromising champion. Born in 1853, Hughes had won youthful acclaim as an athlete of no mean standing. In 1885 when he bought the *Warder* he also discovered a talent for speculation in land and railways which helped to underpin his political fortunes. Hughes's wit, charm, and boundless energy impressed most who met him. He also possessed a politician's supreme gift – an almost superhuman memory. His views were an extreme version of those espoused by the Conservatives in their 1891 campaign. Hughes was a violent imperialist and an equally violent nationalist. He was to become a Grand Master of the Orange Lodge. Indeed, most of Hughes's qualities ran to extremes, including his capacity to pursue causes which entangled his own ego far past any conventional limit.[61]

As early as 1887 Hughes had made clear his view of the permanent corps. Provoked by a suggestion from Middleton that permanent officers should rank above militia officers, Hughes claimed "...the annals of the North West do not indicate that the raw militia were a whit behind the regular." With characteristic bluntness he concluded: "Our advice is get rid of the red tape and train the boys to spot a bull's eye at 500 yards."[62] By the time he entered Parliament Hughes had almost come to advocate doing away with the permanent corps altogether. "The history of nations proves that fresh 'volunteers' always win," he claimed in a letter to Sir John Thompson.[63]

Hughes's influence usually lay less in the quality of his ideas than in the relentlessness with which he pressed them. The pressure which he and other militia officers could mobilize was particularly effective against an indolent and electorally conscious minister like Patterson. When General Herbert returned to Ottawa after his long absence in England in 1893 he found that the atmosphere in the Militia Department had changed. In imitation of Caron's tactics with Luard of ten years earlier, Patterson now refused to see the General, even slipping out of his office when Herbert came to call.[64]

The General's position had been weakened during his absence by the departure of his friend and ally, Lord Stanley. The new Governor General, Lord Aberdeen, was a relatively advanced liberal, overshadowed by an aggressive wife, and almost completely uninterested in the military affairs of the Dominion. Herbert found nothing in common with the Aberdeens and it was with evident reluctance that he turned to the Governor General for some resolution of his now hopeless relationship with Patterson. The outcome was a conference between the two men, with Aberdeen, Bowell, and Sir John Thompson all present to ensure an amicable settlement.[65] From the encounter Herbert seems to have emerged with enhanced influence. Thanks to Bowell's support for the General, Patterson had to realize that his rather feeble effort to force a resignation had miscarried. For his part, Herbert was diplomatic enough to restore his personal relations with the Minister, and at the price of more frequent consultation he had soon restored his predominance.

While the General resumed his work of disciplining and reforming his command, Patterson and his fellow ministers were struggling with another of the recurrent bouts of economic depression which marked the period. As tax revenues fell, economies were ordered. Since arrangements had already been made to rearm the militia with the Martini-Metford, the only quick saving was to cancel the annual drill for the rural militia. "We cannot have both camps and rifles," Patterson told the House of Commons, "and the militia would rather get the rifles and go without the camps for one season."[66] Herbert agreed with the decision.

The next problem was to draft the drastically revised orders for the annual training. The Minister's statement came only a week before the drill season of 1894–5 was due to begin. The task of preparing the orders fell to Colonel Powell. When he was finished, neither Herbert nor Patterson were available to approve them. The General was sick and the Minister otherwise occupied. Rather than risk a week's delay the Adjutant General sent the orders to the printer on his own authority. When he found out, Herbert was furious. It is apparent that relations between the two men had already become strained and the incident was not merely a breach of Herbert's rigid code of discipline, it was a last straw. Colonel Powell was ordered to be suspended and his office door was locked.[67]

To generations of militia officers Powell was the father of the force. Herbert's action was not only extreme as a disciplinary measure; it was also a gross political blunder. As soon as he could Patterson restored the old Colonel to his post, but not before the news became public. With Parliament in session a supply motion gave MPs from both parties a chance to express their feelings in a wide-ranging attack on the General and his notions of discipline. The chief speaker was Sam Hughes and it was his second attack on Herbert in the course of the session. Earlier he had denounced a speech Herbert had made in Montreal, praising the French-Canadian and Catholic traditions of the *Zouaves Pontificaux*.[68] Now he spoke of fellow militia officers who were the alleged victims of the General's bullying and tyranny. One unhappy colonel had even been driven into a Michigan sanitorium to escape persecution.[69] An equally influential critic was Lieutenant Colonel David Tisdale, who had served with Powell years before. Herbert, he claimed, had forgotten that militiamen had other concerns beyond soldiering: "His criticisms are always harsh, his exactions are severe, his demands for minutiae in the force are exacting. I desire to say further that a man who properly understands the force and wishes to make a success of his command will always meet the officers and men in a spirit of conciliation, of instruction and of encouragement, and of one of appreciation throughout."[70]

For once a Minister of Militia defended his General. Briefed by Herbert, Patterson gave the department's side of the cases presented by Hughes, indicating that the afflicted officers had brought on their own troubles by negligence or scheming. "The work of the militia is not a camping-out like a Knights of Pythias excursion," Patterson stoutly declared, "and we want the distinction to be understood."[71] This did not restore the General's popularity. In August 1894 he assembled the four companies of the Royal Regiment of Canadian Infantry from their separate stations and trained them under his own command at Lévis. To militiamen who had been deprived of their own camps, this was simply a provocation.

As Herbert's stock with the militia fell, he also jeopardized his reputation with the cabinet. One of his goals in reorganizing the permanent force had been to make its units interchangeable with those of the British Army. In early October 1894, reading that the British would be sending reinforcements to their Hong Kong garrison, Herbert easily persuaded his Minister that Canada should offer her own regiment of infantry for the task. Without consulting his colleagues, Patterson promptly cabled the offer to London. An angry and embarrassed cabinet had first to endorse the extraordinary offer and then to pray – successfully – that it would not be accepted.[72]

The Hong Kong affair really finished Herbert's usefulness in Canada. His position was obscured, however, by a series of ministerial changes. In December Aberdeen reluctantly invited Bowell to replace the deceased Sir John Thompson as prime minister. Two months later Herbert returned to England on family business.[73] In a further ten months he would have completed the required five years in Canada, but Patterson and Aberdeen recommended that his return to Britain would be a suitable occasion to end the appointment. In a rather revealing eulogy of his

General, Patterson observed: "In a democratic country such as Canada, it is hard to dissociate the Militia Force from the active politics of the hour. General Herbert is a soldier, not a politician, but his qualities as a soldier and an organizer have been acknowledged even by those who belong wholly to the latter class."[74]

The hint was not taken and Herbert officially remained General Officer Commanding. On March 25, 1895, Patterson left the department to become a Minister without Portfolio. His successor was Arthur Dickey, a young Amherst lawyer and the son of a Father of Confederation. He was also an abler man. With an election year approaching, the economic position of the country unimproved, and the Conservative party in utter disarray, Dickey saw his duty clearly. The order for the Martini-Metfords had already been postponed; it was now cancelled. The strength of the permanent corps was cut by an arbitrary 20 per cent. Five months of pressure from the militia lobby culminated in a long parliamentary debate in which MP s from both parties united in blaming Herbert's emphasis on the permanent force as the major cause of the militia's shortcomings.[75]

In his first few months in office the new Minister had repudiated the main theme of Herbert's militia policy and had postponed indefinitely the prospect of rearming the force. Indeed, Dickey seems to have cancelled the general out of his calculations, telling Parliament that he did not believe that Herbert would ever return to Canada.[76] In the circumstances, Herbert seems to have chosen to remain in Britain and to send his resignation by post.

For his services in Canada, Herbert had to be content with a belated CMG, a decoration he plainly regarded as inadequate.[77] The departure from the War Office of his great patron, the Duke of Cambridge, ended the bright promise of his career. He had hoped to succeed Kitchener in Egypt; instead he had to retire on half-pay to await a captain's vacancy in his regiment. He briefly commanded a battalion of the Grenadier Guards, and in 1897 he was given command of the Jubilee contingents from the colonies. Herbert went on to fill a few unsatisfying staff appointments in London and South Africa until he returned to half-pay in 1900. In 1906 he was elected as Liberal MP for South Monmouthshire and he remained in Parliament until 1917 when Lloyd George had him raised to the peerage as Lord Treowen.

It was perhaps paradoxical that an officer whose career had been blighted by politicians should finally join their ranks. In fact, Herbert's achievements in Canada had been due in large part to a considerable skill in timing and in making crucial allies. He had exploited a period of political division and ministerial weakness to create an unprecedented position of authority for the General Officer Commanding. His difficulties had come less from the politicians than from his own militia subordinates. By becoming powerful at a time when he had no ministerial superior powerful enough to counteract his influence, he had also deprived himself of effective ministerial protection. He had made his position a target for all the grievances of militia officers when many of their complaints might legitimately have been directed at his political masters. Herbert's successor would inherit much ill-will and little of his power.

CHAPTER SIX

Gascoigne

Obedient Adviser

The arrangements for a successor to Herbert had little in common with the complex negotiations which had preceded the earlier appointments. Precedents, painfully elaborated since Selby Smyth's appointment in 1874, were ignored. The War Office simply chose Major General William Julius Gascoigne and offered him to Canada. The only delay in accepting his services was due to the absence of Lord Aberdeen on a holiday and to the incapacity of Bowell's cabinet to reach a decision on anything in its state of near-collapse in the summer of 1895.[1]

In a superficial way Gascoigne resembled Herbert. He had also served in the Guards and in Egypt. The differences were more profound. Twelve years older than Herbert had been when he accepted the appointment, Gascoigne lacked the younger man's energy. He also lacked Herbert's ample private means. On the other hand he had some prior experience of Canada: in 1870 he had served as General Lindsay's aide-de-camp. Gascoigne was essentially an ageing, rather limited, and highly conventional soldier. Throughout his time in Canada he seems to have been guided by two principles: respect for authority and the importance of being accepted by Canadians. Within months of his arrival Gascoigne had concluded that his only role was to serve his government as a loyal adviser; of real power and influence he had none:

At present, beyond the moral feeling of dislike to run counter to the opinion of the English Major General: (a feeling which exists only as long as that Officer is not unpopular) that Officer has literally no power whatever: no power of promotion: no power of appointment: no power to prevent the most flagrant injustices: no power literally to do the smallest thing himself: and it is quite impossible without some semblance of power, for any man to be held responsible for the well-being or otherwise of a Force only nominally under him.[2]

Gascoigne officially took up his appointment on September 19, 1895. He was soon initiated into its difficulties. Deciding to forgo his right to appoint a British officer as his aide-de-camp, he picked a young Canadian officer, Lieutenant Alexander MacLean. It was an innocent political error. Not only were other officers and their families affronted at being overlooked but MacLean's family turned out to be Liberal.[3]

A further initiation came when Gascoigne was sent to report on the state of the Royal Military College at Kingston. Since Major General Cameron's appointment as commandant in 1888, the college had been subjected to growing criticism. Although the attacks had come from the opposition, they had been justified by falling enrolment and a quiet warning from the War Office that the quality of the graduates who accepted the few British commissions offered each year had noticeably declined. Cameron's annual reports glowed with optimism about the progress of the institution, dwelling with special pride on the expanding chest measurements of the cadets under his charge and on their accumulations of marks. His explanation of the falling enrolment was reasonable enough: parents were reluctant to launch their sons on an expensive four-year course which offered no formal qualification and small likelihood of a military career at its end. Yet it was also apparent that many of the civilian instructors were old, out of date, and dependent on political influence for their positions. Cameron himself was largely out of touch with the college.[4]

In 1895, to stem opposition criticism, Arthur Dickey revived the college Board of Visitors and ordered it to report. One of the members, the prominent engineer, Sandford Fleming, promptly submitted a minority report, denouncing the college for offering many of the same subjects as a civilian university and demanding that it become solely a military training school. The majority of the board, chiefly militia staff officers, was more cautious. Criticizing some aspects of the institution as a little out of date, the majority recommended that the commandant should be a British Army lieutenant colonel with a maximum tenure of seven years. Then, in a second and confidential report, they made it clear that the college was in fact in a deplorable state and that its reform depended on a sweeping change of staff, beginning with General Cameron: "This officer, it is clear, does not take that interest in his work and does not exercise that supervision over those under him which he should do. To this more than anything else appears to be due that lack of confidence in the college which appears to have spread throughout the country."[5]

Although Dickey published the board's formal report and Fleming's minority opinion, he filed the confidential comment. As one of his first tasks Gascoigne was sent to Kingston to make his own inspection of the college. Despite a strong reluctance to criticize senior officers in the performance of their duties, the General returned to Ottawa satisfied that Cameron was an unsuitable commandant.[6] His report gave Dickey no comfort. Cameron's father-in-law, Sir Charles Tupper, was rapidly emerging as the only man who might pull the Conservatives together and save them from a disastrous defeat in 1896. It was hardly the appropriate moment to uproot one of Tupper's favourite protégés. Gascoigne's report was filed with the others.

Within two weeks of reporting on Cameron, Gascoigne had found a far more serious preoccupation. On December 17 President Cleveland announced to the United States Congress that he proposed to use force, if necessary, to impose a solution to a boundary dispute between Venezuela and British Guiana. In retrospect, the ensuing crisis seems largely unreal, a pre-election gambit, a brief excitement superseded – for the British at least – by the more real dangers of the Jameson Raid and the Kaiser's telegram to President Kruger. In Canada too the Venezuela crisis passed quickly. Canadians were familiar with the tactics of American presidential candidates. The Conservatives were so busy deposing their prime minister that they largely neglected the chance to exploit the momentary excitement of the electorate.

It was in military policy that the effects of the crisis proved to be enduring. For over a quarter of a century war with the United States had been both unconsidered and at the same time the subconscious rationale of the Canadian military system. This meant that militiamen were emotionally prepared for the conflict. At the same time, in every tangible aspect, their organization was totally unready.

Sir George Etienne Cartier: "To create a
military system for the very unmilitary
Canadians was a task worthy of
his stature." PAC

Colonel Walker Powell, Adjutant General, 1875–95: "immersed in the details of
administration ... resigned to the limits both of his career and of the militia as a
whole." PAC

Major General Edward Selby Smyth
and his party during their tour of Western Canada in 1875.
There were complaints
that he did not take a Canadian. PAC

Sir Adolphe Caron, Minister of Militia,
1880–91: "In politics, he was determined
to make his way as a loyal follower of
the Prime Minister." PAC

Major General Sir Frederick Middleton
"... very short, very red-faced, and
quite friendly." PAC

For the rural militia, a few days in camp every other year helped to keep the organization alive. It did little more. The horse lines in a militia camp.
Otter Collection

"We are the Stuff, We are!" Non-commissioned officers of the Governor General's Bodyguard. *Otter Collection*

Some city battalions, like these men of the Queen's Own Rifles, trained conscientiously, if unrealistically, during weekend sham battles.
Otter Collection

Major General E. T. H. Hutton:
"a man cast in the pro-consular mould ..." PAC

As a prerequisite for giving Canada a proper sense of her military responsibilities, Major General Gascoigne (left) had to be replaced. His successor could count on the new Governor General, the Earl of Minto, as a powerful ally. PAC

"A new epoch in military history ..."
General Hutton and the first militia staff course. Fourth from the left: Lt. Col.
Sam Hughes, Col. Hubert Foster, Lt. Col. W. D. Gordon, Lt. Col. Gerald Kitson,
Major General Hutton, Lt. Col. W. D. Otter, Lt. Col. James Mason, and
Lt. Col. F. L. Lessard. *Otter Collection*

A central camp for his "skeleton army": Lord Dundonald visits the site of his
proposed camp at Kazuabazua. *Otter Collection*

"... he had never missed a militia camp in thirty-three years."
Sir Frederick Borden, accompanied by Colonel William Otter, inspects the
militia camp at Niagara. *Otter Collection*

For Gascoigne the crisis had nightmare qualities. His only trained staff officer, Colonel Percy Lake, was sent off to England at the beginning of 1896 with the authority to buy two million dollars' worth of new guns and rifles. Meanwhile, the Deputy Minister obligingly mailed off copies of the more recent departmental reports to bring the records of the United States War Department up to date.[7] On January 1, 1896, the other senior staff officer, Colonel Walker Powell, was finally superannuated, but his assistant, Lieutenant Colonel Aylmer, could not be promoted in his place because he was reportedly a Liberal.[8] Four days later the Minister of Militia himself resigned as part of a cabinet plot to force out Sir Mackenzie Bowell. After an interval of eleven days he was replaced by a veteran Conservative, Alphonse Desjardins. The new Minister promptly stipulated that he would spend only a few days a week on departmental affairs. As president of the Banque Jacques Cartier his real business lay in Montreal.[9]

Gascoigne did the best he could. His general staff consisted of one officer, Captain Arthur Lee, a British officer who was Professor of Strategy and Fortifications at the Royal Military College and the future Lord Lee of Fareham. Lee hastily put together a plan to deploy the available troops to meet an American invasion and then drafted the first mobilization instructions the militia had ever seen.[10] Colonel E. P. Leach, vc, commanding the Royal Engineers at Halifax, was summoned, and together with Lee worked out designs for earthwork fortifications to defend Montreal. To provide commanders for the divisions and brigades to be organized on mobilization, local staff officers were warned that the best of their commanding officers would probably be taken. In April Gascoigne was authorized to form a Reserve of Officers as a means of retaining the extra officers he would need in case of mobilization. The new reserve also provided an excuse to limit the tenure of commanding officers to five years.[11] It was the first such formal limitation the force had ever known.

While Gascoigne worked and worried, militia affairs became for once a significant preoccupation in Parliament. Since it was opposition strategy to keep Parliament talking until its five-year life had expired, defence and militia administration were conveniently topical. With the fading of the Venezuela crisis there were two discernible reactions. One was that the militia had been neglected, that its efficiency had been sapped by partisan favours, and that the Conservatives must be punished for their misconduct. The other, apparently contrary, claim was that the government's action in ordering the two million dollars' worth of arms had been panicky, needless, and unconstitutional, a contention which grew more credible as memories of the December crisis faded.[12]

While the debate on the arms purchases brought the long session to an end, members had also interested themselves in other, less significant, militia problems, particularly in the bitter internal quarrels which had split the Queen's Own Rifles of Toronto and the 5th Royal Scots of Montreal. The two battalions were among the most efficient and popular units in the militia and the quarrels between the commanding officers and their subordinates had made a fascinating public spectacle.

The circumstances in each case were different. Lieutenant Colonel Robert Baldwin Hamilton of the Queen's Own was a poorly paid provincial civil servant who had held his command for seven years. The regimental fund was badly in debt and the three wealthy officers who guaranteed the overdraft announced that they would withdraw their signatures until Hamilton resigned. Colonel Otter, the local staff officer and a man with considerable personal knowledge of the Queen's Own, investigated. He soon concluded that Hamilton had become an unacceptable commanding officer for the regiment. Gascoigne agreed and the colonel was invited to resign.[13]

In the Royal Scots Lieutenant Colonel J. A. L. Strathy, a wealthy Montreal financier, had taken command with a determination to make his regiment a well-disciplined military organization. His second-in-command, Major E. B. Ibbotson, a leading dental surgeon, resented the abrupt transformation of the corps from the comfortable club he had joined, as did many other officers. After a series of abrasive encounters with their commanding officers, so many of them sent in their resignations at once that the battalion was close to disintegration. However, at the price of several visits to Montreal, Gascoigne believed that he had patched up a truce.[14]

Regimental disputes were common enough in the militia but these two held the attention of the two largest cities in the Dominion. In the politically charged atmosphere of 1896 there could only be one explanation for the contrasting treatment of the two colonels. Strathy, the rich and influential Conservative, had been saved; Hamilton, the poorly paid Liberal, had been sacrificed. It was fuel enough to fire debate in both the Senate and the House of Commons.[15] When Parliament dissolved, Sir Charles Tupper replaced Bowell as Prime Minister. In his hastily rebuilt cabinet, his choice for Minister of Militia and Defence was Lieutenant

Colonel David Tisdale, a sixty-year-old lawyer from Ontario's Norfolk county. With less than two months remaining before the general election, Tisdale decided that a stop-gap minister should not make a decision in the Hamilton case. The matter was left, with a mounting accumulation of other decisions, to await the outcome of the contest.[16]

In six months Gascoigne had served three ministers. The post of adjutant general was still vacant although Sam Hughes and other Conservative colonels had spent months lobbying for the position for themselves or their nominees.[17] The future command of the Royal Military College remained unsettled. Lake's purchase of forty thousand Lee-Enfield rifles and four batteries of modern field guns had been endorsed by the cabinet but the dissolution of Parliament meant that there was no more money to pay for them.[18] Within the permanent corps the enthusiasm which Herbert had created seemed to have ebbed away. The VRI Club was kept alive only by a decision to admit senior officers from the militia and by a substantial donation from the General.[19]

Change was in store. The election on June 23 was a convincing Liberal victory. Three days later a desperate Gascoigne wrote to congratulate Wilfrid Laurier and to confess that if there had been no change he would have resigned: "I do respectfully implore you Sir to send me a Minister who will take a real broad interest in the Militia and, above all, one who is likely to stay ... I will faithfully serve any one you send to me, but if a Minister comes who will give the Militia a feeling of rest and security that right will be done irrespective of politics, I believe that you would secure to your side a number of very powerful men who have hitherto been opponents."[20]

Gascoigne was a little precipitate. Sir Charles Tupper clung to office for almost two more weeks and Laurier was only able to announce his new cabinet on July 13. In choosing his ministers he suffered, as a biographer has commented, from "an embarrassment of riches," but that description does not seem to apply directly to his Minister of Militia.[21] The post might have gone to William Mulock, the Liberals' most persistent spokesman on militia affairs since 1887. Instead, Laurier chose to satisfy Nova Scotia's claim to a second cabinet place by choosing Dr Frederick W. Borden, a big, genial, rural physician who had represented King's County almost continuously since 1874. The Militia Department seemed appropriate for a man who had spent twenty-eight years as surgeon to the 68th Battalion and who boasted that he had never missed a militia camp in thirty-three years.[22] "He is a man of means and ability," reported the *Military Gazette*, "with more than the average amount of good practical common sense so necessary in a department where there are so many theorists."[23]

Borden was forty-nine when he became Minister; he was to remain in the department for fifteen more years and to oversee the transformation which prepared Canada for her military role in the First World War. Like many other country doctors of his era he was also a businessman, running an agency of the Bank of Nova Scotia and managing a series of speculations which had built him a modest fortune. He was also a politician, perfectly familiar with the working of influence in his riding and in the militia. Political interference in militia administration had been a minor theme in the 1896 election and it was to become a major chord in the series of battles which swirled around Borden during his first eight years in office. It is therefore important to see how he and his fellow Liberals regarded the problem.

The Liberals had devoted considerable parliamentary time to denouncing the Conservatives for their abuses of power in the Militia Department but they took office seeking revenge, not purification. "As you well know," wrote one of the few Liberal militia officers to the new Minister, "the Dept. has become under your predecessors the bureau for a self-constituted clique and coterie of 'trooly loil' Tory patriots who at all military headquarters were wont to jeer and sneer at, snub and 'set on' every poor officer like myself who dared to call himself a Liberal in politics."[24] A Halifax commanding officer, sure that the militia "will now be properly looked after," demanded the prompt removal of a difficult Conservative subordinate.[25] A Quebec MP offered detailed instructions on the future careers of the permanent force officers in his riding. Only three would be entitled to future promotion. They alone, he claimed, had either remained neutral or supported him.[26] Even the Prime Minister intervened to obtain a special allowance for the son-in-law of a personal friend.[27] There was no limit to the pettiness of the demands. The proprietor of the Peterborough *Examiner* proposed that two disabled veterans of the North-West campaign should lose their tiny pensions for publicly opposing him in the recent campaign.[28]

The new Minister had no inherent resentment against such pressures. They were part of the rules of a political system in which he had been involved for over twenty years. Indeed, as an outsider to power he may have shared the exaggerated belief of oppositions in the influence of purely partisan considerations on policy. In the boundlessness of their

demands on Borden, the Liberals were somewhat the victims of their
own propaganda about the venality of the Militia Department. At the
same time, the Conservatives quickly took up the former Liberal position
of condemning political interference, with the added motive that they
were now protecting their own interests. There could hardly be a change
in the department which did not affect a Conservative appointee, contractor, or decision.

The Conservative campaign occasionally passed over the boundaries
of hypocrisy. Borden found that in their last weeks in office the previous
government had not merely renewed the three-year contracts of their
clothier friends, they had even reached ahead to sign a contract due to
begin in a year's time. Only a few years later Colonel Tisdale, who must
have had some share in this decision, could claim: "... I never knew or
heard of the slightest attempt to introduce politics in any manner whatever into the administration of the Militia Department during the long
years of the Conservative regime."[29]

Borden had no illusions about the Conservative attacks. Accepting the
political conventions of his time he also knew that Liberal partisans
would be justly aggrieved if Conservatives continued to benefit from the
minor jobs and contracts at the disposal of his department. In one of his
first speeches as Minister he warned the Conservatives that they "... must
not be disappointed, if under the new regime, the Liberals of Canada get
a fair chance. I am not going to make any unpleasant reference to the
regime of the gentlemen who preceded me in this department, but I must
say, that they must not be disappointed if in future, Liberals, at least get
a fair share with Conservatives. I shall make it my business to see that
they do ..."[30]

At the same time Borden set limits, imposing his own sense of justice
and business efficiency against powerful party interests. "I ... shall regret
very much if our Liberal friends are going to suffer in their loyalty to the
party because they are not allowed to take out of the Government more
than they can get from ordinary purchasers," he told a cabinet colleague.[31] Although he cancelled the three-year clothing contracts almost
as soon as he took office, Borden soon concluded that they had been in
the best interest of the department and he reopened them – with the
same Conservative manufacturers.[32]

While Borden set standards, he was also aware that the reform of his
own department depended on the co-operation of his fellow ministers,
few of whom cared much for more than the patronage aspects of the

force. To have ignored their views completely would not merely have
been out of character, it would also have robbed Borden of the bargaining power he needed. In public the Minister claimed that he would make
no distinction between the parties: a franker summary of his position
was given to his friend, John Barron, a recently defeated Liberal MP:
"As far as I am concerned, I propose to be governed by the rules of the
Department, but other things being equal, I have in every case given to
our friends the preference and shall continue to do so. I cannot promise
to do more than this nor do I think you will ask me to do so. Our friends
must not forget that in the Militia the ordinary rules applicable to the
Civil Service do not apply. I am afraid the Militia would not last long if
they did so."[33]

The Liberals came into office with no particular militia policy. Their
formal program adopted in 1893 made no mention of the subject. Their
spokesmen in opposition had often seemed opportunist and even contra-
dictory. The new Prime Minister certainly did not reincarnate Alexander
Mackenzie's zeal for military matters and would probably have been
willing to limit his interest in the Militia Department to the impact of its
patronage on his own Quebec East constituency. Disinterest in military
affairs as well as affection for a colleague helps to explain Laurier's toler-
ance of Borden's periodic absences and lapses of judgment.

Although the militia might be a peripheral concern for Laurier, his
new government found itself involved in the extensive military reforms
which followed in the wake of the Venezuela crisis. Even Colonel Lake's
purchase of modern guns, rifles, and ammunition had consequences.
Within a year nearly every rifle range in the country had been rendered
unsafe by the new high-velocity bullets.[34] The Liberals were fortunate
that their return to power was soon followed by the return of national
prosperity. Rising government revenue allowed militia reform to be
financed without any painful redistribution in public spending.

The Conservatives had always held the Liberals responsible for the
curtailment of militia camps since 1876. Borden's most radical act in
the month after he assumed office was to announce that the entire militia
would attend camp that fall. The decision led to the discovery that
although the Conservatives had also promised annual camps during
the election campaign, they had made no provision for them in their
financial estimates.[35] Another quick decision was to appoint Colonel
Aylmer as the new Adjutant General. Within six weeks of entering office
Borden had also removed General Cameron from the command of the

Royal Military College and had published the secret reports explaining why. There had been fears that the Liberals planned to abolish the college. Instead, Borden obtained a new commandant, Lieutenant Colonel Gerald Kitson of the King's Royal Rifle Corps, and authorized him to make sweeping reforms. Within a year outside examiners had demonstrated the academic limitations of the institution and Kitson had established a three-year course with a more distinctly military bias.[36]

Another of the decisions which the Conservatives had made in their last months in office had been to pay $5,000 for the patent of a new kind of equipment to replace the hopelessly obsolete and rotten buff crossbelts and knapsacks of the militia. The equipment had been invented by Dr J. W. Oliver, a British army surgeon who had retired to Halifax. Despite some pressure and many modifications the War Office had refused to adopt Oliver's invention, nor in spite of the strong support of General Luard had the equipment been seriously considered by the Canadians.[37] However, years of patient lobbying and the pressure of the Venezuela crisis were rewarded in 1896. Oliver's invention was not only necessary for an efficient, modern militia, it could also please nationalists seeking a design invented and potentially manufactured in Canada. At first the new Liberal government had second thoughts. Gascoigne had no enthusiasm for an invention rejected by the British authorities and there were competing inventors with their own political influence to bring to bear. In the end Oliver's patience was rewarded by the Liberals. The adoption of the Oliver equipment was a further small step towards military self-sufficiency for Canada.[38]

As the first Liberal minister for eighteen years in a department identified with Conservative patronage, Borden had some understandable reservations about the loyalty of his senior officials. Colonel Panet, the deputy minister, had been appointed by the previous Liberal government, but Borden found that his powers were failing.[39] Colonel Aylmer, the new adjutant general, lacked the prestige and influence of his predecessor, Colonel Powell. However, the end of Borden's honeymoon with the militia was due less to his officials than to pressure from two Liberal colleagues, Sir Richard Cartwright and Senator C. A. P. Pelletier. Both men had sons in the permanent force and largely at their behest Borden finally approved regulations giving permanent force officers a chance to achieve seniority over militia officers of the same rank.[40] Although the change met an old permanent force grievance, Borden had no intention of allowing the regulars to forget their primary role as instructors.

"[L]et the permanent force understand that their office is to teach," he told a Toronto militia banquet in November 1896, "and that we have no standing army in this country and do not intend to have one."[41]

The key departmental relationship was of course between the Minister and his General. During the election campaign Gascoigne's handling of the Hamilton case had made him the butt of Liberal criticism. The militia too was beginning to complain that the General rarely left Ottawa. In deciding to hold camps in September 1896 Borden had had to overcome Gascoigne's resistance: it was impossible, he had argued, to make such radical changes so quickly. On the other hand, Borden could be grateful that the General took public responsibility for the unpopular regulation on the seniority of permanent force officers.[42]

Inevitably, many who had had grievances against the Conservative administration of the militia now expected redress. One of them was Colonel Worsley, so abruptly dismissed by Herbert in 1891. Although Borden finally gave the unfortunate colonel his overdue gratuity, he was dissuaded from reinstating him by the strong opposition of Gascoigne.[43] It was also inevitable that a Liberal government would reconsider the case of Colonel Hamilton of the Queen's Own. Although Borden at first sought for a compromise between Gascoigne's demand for retirement and a Toronto Liberal insistence on triumphant reinstatement, he was won over gradually to the official view. Concluding that Gascoigne and Otter had been right about Hamilton in the first place, Borden admitted to Laurier: "I am disappointed and disgusted with him and those of his friends who are worrying the Government collectively and individually about this case."[44] When Hamilton refused to accept a government job at Sault Ste Marie, he was transferred to the Reserve of Officers.

The new Minister also faced larger issues of policy. His own pet project for militia reform was the creation of a medical service. The senior permanent force surgeon, Dr Hubert Neilson, was authorized to work out a plan for such a service and he soon became the department's first Director General of Medical Services.[45] An equally pressing problem to dog Borden throughout his years in the department was the need for new drill halls and armouries. The new Lee-Enfield rifles, purchased in 1896, could not be exposed to the neglect and misuse which had ruined the Sniders. Borden accepted the General's advice that the new rifles would only be issued to units with proper places to store them. In practice this meant the city corps. The rural battalions were left with the old Snider rifles and a new cause for grievance. Among the aggrieved a further debate raged. Should drill halls be built only for battalions, concentrating arms and equipment under proper supervision, or should they be built for companies, recognizing local enthusiasm and preserving both the captain's responsibility and his allowances? The political implications were quite as important as the military.[46]

On January 26, 1897, the train carrying Borden back to Ottawa from his constituency was derailed. In the accident he suffered a severe back injury and it was six months before he could return to his office. In the meantime the department was administered by Sir Richard Cartwright, the minister of trade and commerce. While Cartwright had once had a certain interest in defence policy, he had his own department to occupy him. In 1897 the national economy suffered a last spasm of difficulty. As ministers searched for savings the Militia Department became the logical target for economy. Borden's bold gesture in providing annual drill for the whole force had been expensive and now there was pressure to drop the experiment. In mid-March, with the battle at its height, Gascoigne, Panet, and Colonel Lake went down to Lakewood, New Jersey, where Borden was convalescing.[47] They easily won his approval for their policy, but they found on their return that Cartwright was unimpressed. Though he actually favoured cutting the force to twenty thousand men, the acting Minister simply declared that there would be no changes at all until Borden returned to defend them in person. The cabinet resolved its problem by cutting the estimate for annual drill by a third.

In desperation Gascoigne went directly to the Prime Minister. It was obvious to Laurier that a reversal of the policy of annual drill would do serious political harm and he was willing to compromise. Accepting the General's assurance that the money allowed by the cabinet would almost suffice if unfit men and surplus officers were ruthlessly weeded out, he agreed that the entire force would again be ordered out for training and that a supplementary estimate would cover any extra expense.[48] Other reforms approved by Borden at Lakewood were stalled. While Gascoigne was anxious to cut down the permanent staff, he could not force the retirement of some of the elderly and unfit officers until he could offer them pensions or comparable financial inducements.[49] Like other generals before him he was also finding relations with Colonel Panet and the civil branches of the department increasingly difficult.

There was also the recurrent problem of political influence, brought to a fever pitch by the arrangements for the Canadian contingent to the

Diamond Jubilee of 1897. Originally, twenty-six officers and men had been invited; almost two hundred eventually sailed. Strings had been pulled for almost every place although political pressure was most apparent in the inclusion of twelve supernumerary officers added at the last moment. Without exception they were military politicians, ranging from Sam Hughes to the Minister's own son, Harold. To the British officials who had to cope with them they were "sham warriors" and an object lesson in the corruption of military administration in the colonies.[50] For Gascoigne the Jubilee contingent simply meant a chance to be damned by those who had not been selected and abused for inadequate administrative arrangements by those who had.[51]

To Gascoigne such displays were as painful as they had been for his predecessors. Unlike Middleton he did not dissemble, and unlike Herbert or Luard he did not rebel. Instead, he hoped that "possibly in time, by gaining a kindly influence with all classes," he might "do some little good, even if only of a negative kind."[52] With Borden he sought to be accepted as the sole and ultimate professional adviser on matters of discipline: "My advice in all these matters is the same. When you have a man like myself who places his views so clearly before you, and I flatter myself, with such unanswerable arguments to back himself up; I think it is wiser for you to accept his judgements: for you have enough to go upon to defend yourself in the House and that is all you require in my opinion." At the same time, as he concluded in the same passage, "... you know by this time that you and I will not quarrel whatever view you take so you have only to express your wishes."[53]

It might be a comforting assurance to a weak minister, but it was predicated on the belief that Gascoigne's judgment was good. Borden had regular occasion to believe that it was not. In the quoted passage Gascoigne was justifying the attempt of a Liberal colonel to have his Conservative second-in-command dismissed from the militia. The colonel was James Domville, the commanding officer of the 8th New Brunswick Hussars and a foul-tempered, arrogant man with a questionable commercial reputation. The major was Alfred Markham, manager of the Saint John *Sun* and a man whom Borden was convinced had been wronged. A defector from the Conservatives, Domville had used his military position shamelessly for political purposes. To gain publicity in 1896 he had even offered his regiment for imperial service in the Sudan.[54] Inevitably, he had been one of the most troublesome of the political colonels in the Jubilee contingent. Once elected as MP for King's

County, Domville told Markham that as a political opponent he must now resign. When Markham refused, Domville proceeded to accumulate such a variety of petty charges against his subordinate that Gascoigne became convinced that Markham was in the wrong.[55] Borden had no difficulty in seeing what was happening. Indeed, Domville made his motives clear. In a letter to Laurier he explained the political importance of controlling his regiment: the corps and its connections "... cover a vote of at least five hundred now, and the votes of those that may be brought into the Regiment."[56] Borden would have none of it. Briefed by his cousin, Robert L. Borden, a new Conservative MP and the future party leader, knowledgeable himself "as one who has had long personal experience as an officer in the militia of this country," the Minister was satisfied that Markham had done no serious wrong.[57]

The Domville-Markham dispute was an instance of the role a minister had to play in the militia, an organization far more political than military in its internal relationships. Like most of his predecessors, Gascoigne found it difficult to understand the internal political machinery of the Canadian force, and assumed that it would be eliminated by a firmer application of military discipline. Yet, if he differed with Borden on such issues, Gascoigne still respected and perhaps even liked his political superior. Six months without Borden had reminded the General of the critical role a Minister played in fighting the battles of the militia within the cabinet.

Gascoigne's real difficulties were with his subordinates. He made astonishingly little attempt to become familiar with his command, never visited western Canada and never even spent a night in camp in all his time in Canada. "He has been a great failure, & is not popular either with the Minister or the people," Colonel Kitson reported from the Royal Military College to his friend, Colonel Edward Hutton. "He is so full of tact [?] you can't get a straight answer out of him & he is not dependable." Even the old general would not have been so bad were it not for his wife: "she is a terror."[58] When Gascoigne did venture out of Ottawa, the results were not always good. On his only visit to Halifax he chose to berate one of the city battalions for recruiting British army reservists into its ranks. Such enlistments were in no way prohibited by Canadian regulations and the officers of the corps demonstrated their anger by resigning in a body. Aroused by such a disturbance in his own political bailiwick, the Minister intervened, securing an apology from the General as the price of peace.[59]

By his inertia and his general failure to win the sympathy of the militia, Gascoigne found himself interposed between the discontented members of the force and the government. In the pages of the *Military Gazette* he was denounced with increasing vehemence. Even a permanent corps officer, admittedly the son of a Liberal cabinet minister, felt bold enough to criticize the General publicly. Lecturing Toronto militia officers, Captain Robert Cartwright declared that what the force really wanted at its head was: "A general who, while not necessarily insulting us will show us our faults and criticize and act without fear, favour, partiality or affection. We know our good points. We want in a general above all a critic. Also a man who will govern the force under him in a strictly military way, and be prepared to resign his command the moment he finds that injustice is being done for political or other reasons."[60] The speech seemed all the more important to Gascoigne because, as the General pointed out to Colonel Otter, Cartwright had been such a substantial beneficiary of his father's political influence.[61]

Gascoigne's bad relations with the force crystallized in his final encounter with the Fifth Royal Scots of Montreal. His intervention in the spring of 1896 had settled nothing. Within a month the quarrels between Colonel Strathy and Major Ibbotson had broken out again. After a further nine months of altercation and sensation Gascoigne came to the conclusion that both officers would have to go and the regiment reorganized. Borden, realizing that such precipitate action would merely transfer the scandal from a military to a political arena, insisted on another strategy. There would be a court of inquiry conducted by Lieutenant Colonel Houghton, now at last approaching retirement from the militia staff and, according to Gascoigne, "always more or less drunk."[62]

The court of inquiry proved to be a turbulent affair with both sides giving ample proof of their irreconcilable antagonism. Though the proceedings were officially *in camera*, the exciting details were fully reported in the Montreal press. It then took two and a half months before Houghton, somewhat assisted by Colonel Strathy himself, managed to assemble the evidence and draft a report. Gascoigne was satisfied that the evidence justified his original recommendations, particularly for the removal of Strathy: "... you Sir never in all your life saw such a mass of discreditable material brought to light ..." he commented to Lord Aberdeen.[63] At the same time, Houghton's report understandably supported the commanding officer. Since the regulations limiting tenure of command would soon oblige Strathy to retire, the General agreed with Borden to let matters lie.

They reckoned without Strathy's own continuing campaign for vindication. With the press condemning Militia Department inaction, Borden finally directed Gascoigne to go to Montreal and deliver a warning of summary dismissal for any of the participants who continued to cause trouble: "I think we should not worry ourselves over the idiosyncracies of these gentlemen, particularly as neither of them seems to have done anything demanding action, beyond perhaps the tendering of a little good advice. I think they might both read 'The Proverbs' with much advantage!"[64]

Carried away by his own indignation at their conduct, Gascoigne gave Strathy and Ibbotson a much stronger rebuke than the Minister had intended. Borden had also authorized him to tell the press how the matter was concluded. To waiting reporters the General compared the dispute to "a squabble of two washerwomen over a washtub," an image they seized on with delight.[65] Strathy was humiliated at sharing condemnation with his subordinates and he used the excuse of Gascoigne's injudicious newspaper interview to reply in kind. When the General then insisted that the threat of dismissal be invoked, Strathy mobilized his powerful Montreal friends and launched a law suit against Gascoigne for damaging his standing. As president of a large trust company, he claimed that the widows and orphans who gave him their savings would now question his reputation. As an honorary aide-de-camp to the Governor General, he also appealed to Lord Aberdeen for support.

Strathy's counterattack made impressive gains. Throughout the affair Gascoigne had proceeded with the full knowledge of both Borden and the Governor General and he should have been able to rely on their support. It was Aberdeen who backed down. Although Borden approved the strong step of removing Strathy, he used the Governor General's resistance and his own brief visit to England as an excuse to postpone action. Delay was interpreted as disavowal by Strathy and other militia officers, and Gascoigne himself felt that he had been betrayed. When he returned from England Borden used his own influence to prevail on Strathy to withdraw legal proceedings in return for transfer to the Reserve of Officers.[66]

Between them, Borden and Aberdeen had helped Gascoigne lose his last shred of prestige in the force. However, even before his last round with Strathy, the General had made up his mind to resign his Canadian appointment. The reasons were mainly financial. His own means were being used up to maintain the social position his wealthier predecessor

had established in Ottawa. During a visit to England in the summer of
1897 he had found that there was no chance that the British Treasury
would provide a supplementary allowance for the position. He had also
learned that the War Office would not be displeased if he made his salary
a reason for resignation.[67]

Since 1896 the British military authorities had been pressing Canada
to increase the pay of her General Officer Commanding. The Canadian
rate of $4,000 a year was much less than most of the Australian colonies
paid commanders of much smaller forces and only $1,500 more than the
half-pay of a British major general.[68] Canadian resistance was not solely
due to an antipathy to generals: in 1897 only six federal government
salaries were higher than $4,000. However, on March 9, 1898, the cabi-
net submitted to the pressure and agreed to amend the Militia Act to add
$2,000 in "allowances" to the General's pay.[69] On April 19 Gascoigne's
resignation was submitted and accepted.[70]

Gascoigne's resignation did not save him from further attacks. While
he remained in Canada awaiting a successor there were charges that he
was improperly retaining command of the militia.[71] The bitterest assault
occurred when the House of Commons debated the salary increase. Sir
Charles Tupper, now the leader of the opposition, had never forgiven
Gascoigne for his part in deposing his son-in-law, Major General Cameron, and the debate on the General's pay was a chance to pour a flood
of invective on the departing officer which shocked even the *Military
Gazette*.[72] Gascoigne, he charged, had disgraced his position and had
resigned to escape Strathy's law suit. When Borden and Laurier came
to the General's defence, their intervention only stirred the Conservative
leader to further flights. A fresh tirade brought him to the conclusion
that, "... tried by everything that involves manly, straightforward, independent, able discharge of public duties, General Gascoigne has been the
most signal failure ever sent to this country to occupy so high a position."
Tupper's bitterness seems to have embarrassed the regular Conservative
military critics like Tisdale and Sam Hughes and it drew few echoes from
the opposition benches.[73] For Gascoigne, however, the torrent of abuse
from Tupper was a further aggravation in a debate which had inevitably
focused on the better quality of officer a higher salary would attract.
Although he tried through the Governor General to have the Conservative leader's words expunged from Hansard, the only satisfaction the
government could offer was for Laurier to read a short statement to the
Commons from the General. By then, Tupper had left to spend the summer in England.[74]

The British had at least two reasons to welcome Gascoigne's resignation. In the first place, it had precipitated action on the long outstanding question of his salary. In the second place, Gascoigne's conception of his role made him nearly useless as an instrument for British policy as it was developing at the end of the 1890s. Gascoigne's major achievement had been to execute projects designed by Herbert. In April 1897, after complicated administrative arrangements had been approved, the permanent force infantry company at Fredericton had been exchanged with a company of the Royal Berkshire Regiment from the Halifax garrison. A year later it was the turn of one of the companies of the garrison artillery at Quebec. If Gascoigne had remained, the next step would have been to exchange the permanent force field battery at Kingston with a similar unit from England.[75] Although Gascoigne obediently told permanent force officers that their only role was to serve as instructors for the militia, he had in fact continued Herbert's policy of creating a regular army, capable of integration in the ranks of the British parent force.[76]

At the Colonial Conference of 1897 the Herbert-Gascoigne approach to military collaboration within the Empire was promoted by British spokesmen, but in military circles it had already been superseded. The sudden prospect of an Anglo-American war in 1896 had found London and Washington almost as unprepared as Ottawa.[77] In Washington and Ottawa the absence of even a vestigial planning staff meant that, even in the defence departments themselves, the hasty war plans were soon half-forgotten. In London the emergence in the previous ten years of at least a rudimentary planning machinery for colonial defence helped ensure that the vexed and insoluble problem of defending Canada from American invasion was once again open.

Early in 1896, responsibility for advising on the strategy of such a war was passed to the Joint Naval and Military Committee.[78] The committee looked at the plans Captain Lee had hurriedly prepared for Gascoigne and commended the proposed concentration on the defence of Montreal. However, the committee members had no illusions about the capacity of the militia to resist an invasion or about the dangers of plunging a British army into the heart of North America to support the Canadians. Instead, the committee asserted that the safety of Canada could best be ensured by "landing a British force on American territory and making a vigorous offensive movement."[79] Major Hubert Foster, a staff officer whose gloomy report on the state of Canadian defence had influenced the committee, was again sent across the Atlantic to report on the problems of landing on the American coast.

The Joint Naval and Military Committee had proposed a strategy which would allow Britain to discharge her obligations to Canada without being trapped by Canadian military weakness. This did not prevent a determined, if somewhat despairing, British attempt to force the Dominion to put her own defences in order. In 1892 a Colonial Office official had noted: "The Canadian Defences are an Augean Stable but it is not our business to clean it out."[80] Four years later, under the aegis of Joseph Chamberlain, the British were prepared to try.

One problem was that the Canadians had failed to respond to Colonial Office pressure to establish their own defence committee. In March 1896, apparently taking its first official look at a Canadian Militia Department report, the Colonial Defence Committee observed that it made no reference to the work of the committee Caron was supposed to have created in 1888. In a long memorandum explaining what such a committee should have been doing, the Colonial Defence Committee politely observed that since nothing had been heard of Caron's body for eight years it had to be concluded that "Canada alone of the many parts which make up the British Empire, is absolutely without organization for utilizing its splendid personnel in war."[81]

At first the British got little response. The political circumstances of 1896 left Canadians with other preoccupations and it was only in 1897 at the Colonial Conference that Chamberlain could bring direct pressure on Laurier and his colleagues. The Colonial Secretary's opening remarks to the assembled premiers made it clear that Canada was considered the most vulnerable of the colonies. Much of the subsequent discussion was devoted to impressing the Canadians with their military backwardness. Sir Wilfrid Laurier, whose public utterances contributed substantially to the imperial euphoria of the Jubilee year, was noticeably less forthcoming in the private conference sessions.[82]

If war had broken out in 1896, the man who would probably have taken charge of the defence of the Dominion was the British General Officer Commanding in North America, General Sir Alexander Montgomery Moore. While in Ottawa in 1897 as a temporary replacement for Lord Aberdeen, Montgomery Moore managed to persuade Borden that it would be valuable to develop a permanent defence plan for Canada.[83] At the Minister's suggestion he raised the matter in a formal minute to Laurier. Emphasizing that producing the plan would involve no extra cost or effort on the part of the Canadian government, Montgomery Moore suggested that a cabinet committee could work with the heads of the Militia Department, preferably under Colonel Lake, the quartermaster general, and that an expert officer should be obtained from England to act as consultant.[84] The letter was referred to Gascoigne for his comments. Perhaps piqued by Montgomery Moore's preference for Lake, the general revised the proposal by suggesting that he himself assume the presidency of a committee composed of officers from Britain, while his own staff officers, including Lake, would act as "associate members."[85] The whole correspondence was next sent off to the Colonial Office for its advice.

Montgomery Moore's initiative coincided with a fresh attempt by the War Office to get Canada to produce its own defence scheme. Under this double pressure the Canadians now made a formal request for the services of two military officers and a naval officer to help them work out a defence plan, adding that Lake, now coming to the end of his five-year term, could well be employed as a member of the group.[86] Chamberlain reacted with his usual energy. Realizing that the moment might be lost if there were a protracted correspondence with Canada about who would pay the officers, he prevailed on the two service departments to bear most of the cost. It would be undesirable, he pointed out to the Admiralty and the War Office, to have such a delicate matter as a defence scheme debated publicly, as it must be if the subject came before the Canadian Parliament.[87] Gascoigne's resignation meant that an abler, more energetic, officer could be placed in charge of the committee. Major General Leach, the former Commanding Royal Engineer at Halifax and the man who had worked with Lee at Montreal in 1896, was appointed chairman. By the beginning of August 1898 all the members of the Defence Committee were in Canada and ready for work.

Chamberlain had done for Canada what the Dominion had failed to do for itself. There would now be a defence scheme, prepared by experts. However, as a Colonial Office official pointed out, it was no longer a Canadian but a British committee. For political reasons two Canadian ministers, Borden and Sir Louis Davies, the minister of marine and fisheries, were associated with the committee but only in the final stages of its work.[88] Perhaps the real problem was one of secrecy. The direction British strategy had taken in 1896 was a matter to be concealed as carefully from Canadians as from Americans and the British had a justifiable suspicion of the capacity of the Militia Department to keep facts to itself.[89] An equally important consideration was that Chamberlain was intent on regaining the voice and influence in Canadian defence policy which Britain had given up in 1870. The basic issue in the ensuing six years of militia history was how far he would be able to succeed.

As for Gascoigne, he officially vacated his appointment on June 30, 1898. His military career was not over. He next commanded the British troops at Hong Kong with sufficient success to be knighted for his services during the Boxer rising. It was the vindication of the career of a very conventional soldier, diverted by mistake into two and a half years in a position for which neither his talents nor his experience had prepared him. In Canada Gascoigne was remembered as a failure, but when ministers had experienced his successors he would at least be recalled as a sympathetic failure.

CHAPTER SEVEN

Hutton

Imperial Agent

Chamberlain's strategy for re-establishing British influence in Canadian defence policy was apparent in the selection of Gascoigne's successor. The Canadians would have been pleased to appoint Colonel Lake to the command of the force. In almost six years in Canada he had won the confidence of both Liberals and Conservatives and, as Montgomery Moore had made apparent, had become a more trusted and influential figure in militia headquarters than the General Officer Commanding. The War Office refused to consider it. Lake's substantive rank in the British Army was major. To hold the Canadian command he would have had to be promoted to full Colonel, an unacceptable by-passing of more senior officers. Instead, the military authorities insisted that he return to regimental duties, and his recall was only postponed by his appointment as the junior member of Leach's committee on the Canadian defences.[1]

Instead of Lake the War Office offered the Canadian appointment to Colonel Edward Hutton, the officer whom Macdonald had interviewed more than twelve years before as a possible commissioner for the North West Mounted Police. Although Hutton was to hold the command of the militia for the briefest period of any of the eight British General Officers Commanding, he was also the most interesting and important of them. He was a man cast in the pro-consular mould, even down to having been a student of the redoubtable Dr Warre at Eton. He was aggressive, imaginative, and energetic, with nearly limitless self-confidence. His career had only begun to flower in 1882 when he had served in Egypt at the head of some hastily organized mounted infantry. In the ensuing desert campaigns, in the face of expert opinion, he demonstrated that British soldiers could be trained to ride and to manage camels. When he failed to get command of the Mounted Police in 1886, he went instead to the command of an experimental battalion of mounted infantry at Aldershot. As leader of some of the brightest young officers in the army and as spokesman for a novel form of military organization, Hutton acquired personal prestige and some experience of the political battles in the higher reaches of command. Lord Melgund, a lifelong friend who had tried to get him the command of the police, continued to be associated with Hutton in the mounted infantry. However, he was only one of many influential friends. Privately wealthy and having married into the Paulet family, Hutton had an easy familiarity with court, military, and political circles.[2]

What really commended Hutton for his new appointment was his success as the commandant of the military forces of New South Wales. He had spent three years, from 1893 to 1896, reorganizing the colony's military system, presiding over negotiations for an Australian defensive federation, and effectively expanding his authority over the civilian officials within the defence department. Inevitably, Hutton had also become involved in colonial politics. A government with which he had quarreled, and to some extent embarrassed, was defeated and replaced by a ministry far more sympathetic to Hutton's goals. The General greatly exaggerated his own impact on these events and the episode certainly inflated his own estimate of his considerable political skill.[3] The same judgment may have helped to persuade Chamberlain and Lord Lansdowne, now the secretary of state for war, that they had at last found the ideal man for the Canadian command. Canadians also had reason to know their new commander. An article of his on the development of mounted infantry had been printed in the *Military Gazette*.[4] In the Jubilee year Hutton's views on imperial military co-operation had gained wide publicity.[5] Hutton was the first General Officer Commanding to arrive in Canada with an established reputation.

Well before that arrival Hutton had worked out in his own mind the main lines he would follow. From the notes he kept of interviews with senior military and Colonial Office officials it is apparent too that his aggressive attitude won only qualified approval. Hutton refused to see Gascoigne when he came back to London, claiming that his predecessor had only made his own task more difficult.[6] To Chamberlain, who urged the virtues of tact and patience, he replied that he had learned in Australia how to educate public opinion.[7] With his ageing patron, Lord Wolseley, Hutton recalled the advice of their mutual friend, Sir Redvers Buller, that colonials could be led anywhere "with a silken noose." Buller, Wolseley replied, "was very sound."[8]

Hutton approached his new command with two settled policies. The first was to limit and then to eliminate political interference in the militia. The second was to create a balanced militia army for the Dominion, with the necessary staff and services to fight on its own until the British could arrive. Hutton's model was the Swiss militia, whose manoeuvres he had visited ten years before. The second policy meant an end to the series of proposals to integrate the tiny Canadian permanent force into the British regular army, the goal pursued by Herbert and Gascoigne and considered by the 1897 Colonial Conference. It also offered no encouragement for proposals to recruit Canadians directly into the British Army, schemes which Hutton dismissed as utopian.[9]

Chamberlain was determined to replace Lord Aberdeen with a Governor General who would actively promote military reform in Canada. He first considered the Duke of Connaught, the Queen's second son and a professional soldier, but then turned to Hutton's lifelong friend, the Earl of Minto, formerly Lord Melgund.[10] Montgomery Moore's successor at Halifax, Lieutenant General Lord William Seymour, was another old friend and former commander. Seymour, who developed a strong distaste for Canadian society after only a month at Halifax, strongly advised Hutton against accepting the appointment.[11]

The new GOC was not deterred. He also refused to be discouraged by what he felt to be a cool welcome from Laurier and other Canadian ministers whom he met on his arrival at Quebec. When he and his new Quartermaster General, Major Hubert Foster, reached Ottawa, the mood was still uncordial. Hutton's first duty was to open the new rifle range at Rockcliffe. The assembled militia officers listened to his speech in silence. When he prepared to fire the first shot he discovered that someone had loaded his rifle with a dummy cartridge. To offset this depressing reception there were good signs: "I never quite realized before," he wrote to Minto, "how strong the feeling of animosity to the US is in Canada!"[12]

Since he had diagnosed the ills of the Canadian militia before he left England, Hutton had little need to wait to discover a cure. Within a few days of reaching Ottawa and before he had even met the Minister, he set out on a tour of eastern Canada. In the course of two months he visited every major centre from Halifax to London, inspecting militia and permanent corps, looking into government stores, and entertaining the senior officers of the force at large receptions. Only on October 3, a month after he had reached Canada, did he meet Borden. Almost immediately he was off again. The climax of Hutton's tour was in Toronto on October 10. At the Military Institute, in the heartland of both Canadian military enthusiasm and post-Macdonald Conservatism, he proclaimed the theme of his reforms: "... the time is coming, if it has not come, when the military force of Canada, the national army of Canada, should be put upon a national basis, and as a national institution, should in every respect be above party questions of all kinds (applause). A good army, a national army, must be one which is apart from party, and which sinks all individual views, be they political or religious, in the general welfare of the country."[13]

As Hutton travelled, memoranda and letters flew out, many of them to the Minister. Lieutenant Colonel Kitson at the Royal Military College, another old personal friend, was ordered to make plans for a new militia staff training course. The artillery was reported to be hopelessly out of date and unscientific. There must be a new artillery school at Quebec and the officers to run it must go immediately to England to be trained. A British officer would be needed to restore the arm to efficiency. When Borden invited him to comment on the organization of the civil branch of the department, Hutton declared that the relationship between the civil and military branches of the department was "chaotic and pregnant with friction in peace and disaster in war or national emergency."[14] As he had warned Chamberlain, he put an end to plans for further exchanges between the permanent corps and the British regulars at Halifax. "The Militia Force of Canada is just at present in a transition stage," he explained to Borden, "and until a sound instructional system has been started it would not be advisable to make any change in the disposition of our Instructional Cadre Force."[15] An added reason was that two hundred men of the under-strength permanent force had been ordered to the Yukon as an auxiliary to the Mounted Police in coping with the Klondike gold rush and to establish a firmer stake on Canadian ownership of the territory. The administrative arrangements for the Yukon Force were simply an added concern for the General, who could justly claim that he had seen more of his command in two months than Gascoigne had seen in his entire term.[16]

The direction of Hutton's reforms was inevitably welcome to militia officers. Their self-esteem and their nationalism were cultivated by repeated references to the "Canadian Army," and by Hutton's evident determination to restore the permanent force to its instructional role. His promises about the training for the coming year were also welcome. The force had been kept in leading strings, he told commanding officers. "I propose to push forward, to rely more upon the superior intelligence and aptitude of our men, and to take to a certain extent the elementary part as more or less familiar to our men."[17] Here again was a break from the pattern established by Herbert. Hutton also included a list of the practical reforms he would stress: a simpler, more durable, uniform for training, boots to be sold to the men at low cost, dining tents to shelter the troops during their meals.

There is no record of Frederick Borden's initial reaction to his dynamic new General. In his draft memoirs Hutton later described the Minister as "a vain, weak, ignorant man,"[18] but letters written closer to the time suggest that he found Borden to be surprisingly co-operative and receptive to the condemnation of political interference. Certainly Hutton at first overestimated the degree to which Canadian ministers were willing to subordinate national goals to his own imperial vision. From his standpoint Borden could feel that he would share in the popularity the General had acquired in his first few months in Canada. If militia officers were satisfied with their new commander, their pleasure could only bring credit to the department and the government. Hutton's efforts to create a balanced army organization with its own staff and departmental corps, complemented Borden's more limited effort to create a militia medical corps. Since Hutton spoke French well he could help to create a better impression for the department in Quebec. A directive from the General that henceforth all staff officers and instructors must learn to speak French brought predictable grumbles from the department but real pleasure from French Canada.[19]

By the end of November Hutton felt that he had established firm personal control over the force. A conference of District Officers Commanding* from November 15 to 18, the first since Confederation, was a further opportunity to impress his personality and his ideas on the key

* The term "District Officer Commanding" replaced "Deputy Adjutant General" by *Militia General Order*, no. 74, September 1896.

officers in the force. By then, too, Lord Minto had arrived. Both men had
tried to work out their future relationship to prevent their collaboration
becoming too apparent to Canadians. After the conference with the district staff officers Hutton found time to send his friend a detailed account
of his plans and goals: "If Canada will only determine upon looking on
its present Militia Force as its 'National Army,' the remodelling & recon-
struction necessary for enabling a Defence Force thus designated to perform its role will become comparatively easy – moreover the political
interference and petty log-rolling which hitherto have crushed the very
life out of the Canadian troops will cease."[20]

To create a national army meant finding it a role and an appropriate
organization. This task was primarily the responsibility of the Leach
Commission. When its report was completed it fell into three parts. The
first was the defence scheme which Lansdowne and Montgomery Moore
between them had originally demanded. The plan for deploying the existing militia against an American invasion differed only in detail from
Lee's plan of 1896. The second part was in response to a British instruction to provide a "full and candid report" on the existing deficiencies of
the militia.[21] The commission managed to compile a long list, most of
which could have been found in the annual reports of the Militia Department for the previous twenty years. Canada needed a stronger permanent force with better training and career prospects. The militia
should have longer camps and better rifle training. For the new field
army there must be departmental corps under military control and a
larger headquarters staff. More artillery and enough rifles and uniforms
to equip an additional fifty thousand men in case of emergency must be
purchased. Leach's Halifax experience was evident in a strong recommendation that the General Officer Commanding the British troops in
North America should be much more closely associated with the militia
he might command in event of war.[22] A third section of the report was
intended for British eyes alone. It explained the reasoning behind some
of the recommendations, pointed out the inevitable tactical weaknesses
in the defence scheme, and considered the implications for Britain if
Canada could be prevailed upon to improve her defences as the committee had recommended.[23]

The question which now faced Hutton, Minto, and Chamberlain, in
varying degrees, was how the Leach Committee report could best be
used to persuade the Canadians to make the improvements. In reporting
the completion of his work Leach commented that the two Canadian

ministers belatedly added to his group were, "as far as my Committee can judge, prepared to endorse the majority of the recommendations made."[24] The original copy of the first two parts of the report was left with Borden, in keeping with the elaborate fiction that the Leach Commission had really been working for the Canadian government. The real sponsorship of the committee was sufficiently in doubt for a Colonial Office clerk to ask whether the two Canadian ministers would be thanked in a routine way for assisting in an "Imperial enquiry."[25] The existence of the Leach Committee had been a badly kept secret. Several militia officers had appeared as witnesses and there were newspaper reports of its activities. However, the reports themselves were secret, and in Hutton's view might never see the light of day unless some direct pressure forced the Dominion government's hand.[26]

While Lord Minto prodded his ministers directly to prevail on them to make some formal acknowledgment of the reports, Hutton prepared to publicize the major recommendations in his own way. He was not satisfied with many of Leach's conclusions. He dismissed the tactical plan, with its non-existent staffs, services, and formations, as an academic exercise. He was disappointed that there was no reference to the contribution Canada could make to imperial wars. Above all, he was utterly opposed to the suggestion that the British GOC at Halifax should have any authority over the Canadian militia.[27] However, these reservations did not cancel out the value of the reports as a whole. In order to bring them before the country in a form congruent with his own point of view, he proceeded to embody as many as possible of the practical recommendations in his report for 1898.

Hutton used a December holiday in the New Brunswick woods to draft the document. The first part consisted of a summary of the year's military events, slanted to show how much he had personally accomplished and decided. Then he turned to the short- and long-term reforms needed by the militia. His proposals were sandwiched between vigorous denunciations of existing conditions. The state of the force was "unsatisfactory in the extreme," the civil branch had "usurped" the General's powers, the militia itself was "a collection of military units, without cohesion, without staff and without those military departments by which an army is moved, fed or ministered to in sickness."[28]

Having written his report Hutton seriously doubted that the Minister would allow him to publish it. To his surprise Borden agreed to have it printed in full.[29] Why he should have done so is uncertain. He had no

desire to have himself or his department pilloried. At the same time
Borden had no quarrel with Hutton's major proposals; most of them
were to be realized during his years as Minister. He could also feel that
Hutton's prose might be persuasive in cabinet and Parliament while any
condemnation would justly fall on the Conservatives, whose administration had brought the militia to its deplorable state.

Once the report was printed, the General distributed it widely to men
whose influence might be valuable. He was flattered by their reaction.
The press, when it eventually saw the document, was also enthusiastic.
"General Hutton Scores a Bullseye," declared one Ontario daily, adding
that if his proposals were not taken up the government should "abolish
the Militia Department and put the Doukhobors on guard."[30] A Toronto
paper welcomed the report, acknowledging that Canada should not try
to escape the wave of militarism encircling the world.[31] There were
exceptions. The Toronto *Saturday Night* wondered whether it really
mattered if the forces were unready, while a columnist in the Montreal
News rephrased a more traditional argument: "The military spirit is
fatal to healthy development. We are too young. We are too hopeful.
We are agricultural by instinct and opportunity. Our business is to
conquer nature by silent, honest toil. He who encourages the passion for
militarism is no true friend of Canada."[32] Such critics mattered less
when Hutton could claim the support of both the Liberal Toronto *Globe*
and Sir Charles Tupper.[33] By early April 1899 the General reported to
Sir Richard Harrison of the Colonial Defence Committee: "I feel more
than hopeful of a satisfactory result."[34]

Hutton's tactics with his annual report showed that he was determined
to lead public opinion. He was equally anxious to unite the militia under
him and to remove any challenge to his authority. Militia political influence had developed around a number of corps and service organizations, notably the Dominion Rifle Association founded in 1869, and the
Dominion Artillery Association which the energetic General Strange had
helped create in 1876. In March 1898 a group of senior militia officers,
disgruntled by the neglect of their interests, had created a Field Officers'
Association. It was a narrow group, largely dominated by militia politicians, and it bluntly refused to associate with the United Service Club,
the latest evolution of Herbert's VRI Club. Soon after his arrival Hutton
arranged for the militia organization to change its name to the Officers'
Association and had himself elected president. He then busied himself
in negotiations to bring the two groups together.[35]

"I feel so strongly that the only possible chance of success here is by the exercise of a personal influence," Hutton wrote to the Military Secretary at the War Office.[36] Sometimes the pressure could be applied directly. The President of the Dominion Artillery Association was advised, with suitable flattery, that the annual reports of the association should be submitted to the General for his approval.[37] More often his influence was indirect. Hutton enjoyed giving speeches and the busy social life of the militia gave him ample opportunities. At a non-political dinner arranged by Israel Tarte, Laurier's erratic Quebec colleague and minister of public works, Hutton told a largely French-speaking audience that no people had ever become truly great by "the cultivation of land and pastoral pursuits."[38] The sergeants of the Toronto militia, after being reminded of their duty to defer to their officers, were told that Hutton's reforms would end the militia's state of paralysis,[39] a prediction which received wide newspaper coverage.* When militia officers were assembled at Kingston for Colonel Kitson's new staff course, Hutton was on hand to announce that their presence marked a new epoch in militia history. The formula for such speeches was consistent: appeals to national pride, condemnation of past neglect and political meddling, and promises of reform under Hutton's personal leadership.

What was more, the promises were being realized. In 1899 the government increased the sum available for annual training by a third and Hutton used the extra money to concentrate the force in fewer, larger camps. True to his promise to the commanding officers, he broke away from the old routine of squad drill and staged large-scale manoeuvres, assisted by the graduates of the staff course. Officers who had for years been granted positions on the camp staffs as minor political plums were displaced by younger, keener officers of Hutton's choice. What struck most of those who went to camp that year was the new concern for the amenities of soldiering. Hutton arranged band concerts and tattoos as well as insisting on new facilities for cooking and washing. At Lévis he won praise from French Canadians by sponsoring a choral competition and even warmer approval by arranging that the Archbishop of Quebec and the Bishop of Montreal preside over the church parades at their respective camps. Perhaps the best evidence of Hutton's success in cap-

---

* Newspapermen mistook Hutton's comment for pure denunciation. In fact he referred to plans to develop new branches and services to make the Canadian force into a mobile field army.

tivating the militia was that when he assembled the permanent force infantry for a summer camp at Ottawa for the first time since 1894, there was hardly a word of criticism.[40]

It proved easier for Hutton to win popularity and support in the militia than to establish what he felt to be his proper authority in the Militia Department. The notion of a "National Army" was a powerful emotive slogan for an organization which was finally ready for change. As a description of a balanced, self-contained force, it was a convenient summary of the reforms which both the Leach Committee and Hutton felt to be necessary. Yet, as a phrase used to describe an institution above party politics and immunized from political influence and patronage, it posed problems of authority and control which perhaps not even Hutton appreciated. If the militia was above politics, was it also above Parliament? What was the authority of the Minister if there were areas of decision in which he should not be allowed to act? It would appear that Hutton, influenced by his personal association with the British court and with two successive commanders-in-chief, was attempting to establish for himself in Canada the degree of authority that the Duke of Cambridge was believed to have exercised in the British Army. In this he was following the lead of his predecessor, General Herbert. Indeed, Herbert had insisted that British regulations governing the authority of the commander-in-chief and other staff officers applied, *pari passu*, to Canada. While the Leach Committee chose not to argue that particular contention, it approved of Herbert's proposal sufficiently to incorporate it as an appendix.[41]

Within the military branch of the department Hutton had little difficulty in imposing his authority. Foster, Lake's successor and the staff officer who had been sent spying in the United States in 1896, had been chosen in consultation with the General.[42] Hutton's authority over the few Canadians on his staff was demonstrated when he repelled an attempt by Sir Richard Cartwright to get an accelerated promotion for his son, Robert, now the assistant adjutant general.[43] Hutton also made up his mind to dispose of his Adjutant General, Colonel Aylmer. With Borden's approval the elderly staff officer was sent to England to gain more experience. Hutton then privately wrote to friends at the War Office, warning that Aylmer, "an amiable old gentleman ... of 59, without practicle [sic] experience, without natural abilities, but with the right political views," would be the likely candidate if a Canadian were chosen to succeed him. The British were asked to report on Aylmer in such terms that the promotion would be impossible.[44] With the Adjutant General gone, Foster became the Chief Staff Officer reporting directly to Hutton. The General's influence was further strengthened, although at some cost to his popularity, when he appointed a British officer, Major F. G. Stone of the Royal Artillery, to take command of the permanent force artillery.[45]

Although this kind of power would have been the envy of his predecessors, Hutton was not satisfied. He blamed many of the weaknesses of the Militia Department on the encroachments of the civil branch into what he judged to be military responsibilities. "The hopeless chaos which now exists, due to the usurpation of the Civilian Dept., of the functions of myself & the Military Headquarters Staff is too monstrous for words!" he wrote to Sir John Ardagh. "However the difficulties will soon solve themselves, & I have no reason to doubt the bona fides of the Minister and the Government."[46] As he launched his attack on the civil branch, Hutton was perhaps reliving the first major battle he had waged in New South Wales, when he had succeeded in bringing the senior civilian official in the defence department under his control rather than that of the political head. In Canada his goal was to reproduce the War Office organization, with himself as commander-in-chief and the Deputy Minister filling a much humbler role, somewhat analogous to the Financial Secretary. Like Herbert, he began to claim that the Queen's Regulations for the British Army which established the War Office hierarchy also applied to Canada.[47]

There was no doubt that there was substance to Hutton's criticisms of the civil branch's management of its affairs. The "usurpation," however, simply reflected the failure of the Canadian department to follow the War Office pattern of transferring administrative responsibilities such as the control of stores or engineering work from civil to military authority. If this had not happened in Canada it was partly due to the institutional inertia which gripped the department after 1868, and even more to the fact that it was within such responsibilities that the bulk of political patronage lay. In 1889 Sir Adolphe Caron had appointed his private secretary, Alphonse Benoit, as Director of Contracts because he could be trusted to keep track of the minutiae of political patronage, and even after a change of government Benoit held the same job.

It was a feeble system, barely able to cope with the annual routine of camps and distribution of uniforms. Civilian storekeepers and paymasters were unblushing political appointees and their force of clerks, labourers, and caretakers came and went with the shift in party fortunes. Borden himself was aware that the civilian administration was weak and had asked Gascoigne to recommend improvements.[48] There is no sign that the General ever did so.

Like so much else in the Militia Department it was the crisis of 1896 which forced reform. As the new guns, rifles, and equipment ordered by Colonel Lake began to arrive, there was no accommodation to shelter them and few trained men to unpack the crates. The Superintendent of Stores, Lieutenant Colonel D. A. Macdonald, complained that it was not only the stores branch which was at fault. The military staff not only never furnished details of its requirements but did not even tell the civilian officials when the shipments of new equipment were due to arrive. To Hutton this was merely more evidence of the need to bring responsibility for military stores under a single head. A more private reason was that it would lop off another element of political patronage in the department. "The transfer of Stores and clothing means loss of political patronage and will therefore be resisted to the last," he explained to the secretary of the Colonial Defence Committee, "I need hardly urge the absolute importance of the Military Stores being placed under my supervision and control."[49]

It was Borden who had invited Hutton to make suggestions about the reorganization of the department. It was also Borden who endorsed Hutton's scathing report and who had to defend it in the cabinet and before the House of Commons throughout the hot summer of 1899. "My Minister – Dr. Borden – is a particularly pleasant man to deal with & has a very sound grasp of the military requirements," Hutton reported in January.[50] In fact, Borden's affability was wearing thin. There had been a brief but publicized clash in November 1898 when a paymaster with the Yukon Force, a political appointee, left his post. The General, convinced that the official had merely tried to evade spending a long, dreary winter in the Yukon, insisted that he be dismissed, but political influence intervened. Before long there was a telegram from the Canadian commander of the force, praising the paymaster and explaining, a little belatedly, that he had been specially ordered to return to Ottawa.[51]

Given what Hutton was attempting to do, friction was inevitable. The General and his staff also showed little of Herbert's diplomatic skill. When Borden gave Hutton the right to make a decision on which the Minister was being subjected to considerable political pressure, he was rewarded by the somewhat condescending rejoinder: "I much appreciate the manner in which you have dealt with this case. It is one which I am so pleased to see you acknowledge falls solely within my jurisdiction."[52] When Captain Clive Bell, Hutton's aide-de-camp, called at the Minister's office and found him engaged, he left with the audible comment: "some more boodling business, I suppose."[53] Borden was not amused.

As long as Colonel Charles Panet remained as Deputy Minister, Hutton had an unconscious ally in his struggle with the civil branch. Borden was convinced that his Deputy would have to go. "The old man's heart is in the right place," he told Laurier. "He is a loyal and true friend ... But he is not the man he was, and he has failed lamentably during the two years which I have been his chief."[54] In the summer of 1897 Panet had taken leave in hope of recovering his failing eyesight. Assuming that he would not be coming back, Borden had approached Major L. F. Pinault, a prominent Quebec City Liberal, newspaper manager, and militia officer, to become the new Deputy. When newspaper reports began to circulate about the forthcoming change, Panet went to his powerful patron, Senator C. A. P. Pelletier, a veteran of Mackenzie's cabinet and now Speaker of the Senate. Panet returned to the department, and in the summer of 1898 there was an embarrassing scene in the Quebec Garrison Club when the Deputy Minister encountered Pinault and announced that he would be a long time waiting for the office. As it happened, the embarrassed Pinault had only to wait a few months. On November 22 the old Colonel died in office and Pinault was appointed in his place.[55]

In his new Deputy Borden gained a powerful ally. Pinault had the political experience and the business ability to save his Minister from some of the difficulties he had encountered in his first years in the department. In the undefined authority structure of the Militia Department, he was an alternative to the General as a source of advice and support.

By the time the General discovered that the forces against him had been strengthened, he was engaged in what he soon regarded as the ultimate battle against political interference.

Borden had strengthened the regulations imposing a five-year tenure of command by making them retroactive. There were also rules to allow a brief extension of command. The fact that the new regulations affected about half the commanding officers in the militia demonstrated their necessity.[56] The changes had considerable long-term significance. Many of the senior militia officers who now found themselves displaced were among the ranks of the militia politicians. Their military eminence was merely an aspect of the community leadership which had qualified them for election to Parliament or to provincial legislatures. The officers in the next generation seem to have lacked the political involvement and sometimes even the social eminence of their elders, but they were also more keenly identified with the force as such. Borden's regulations did not change the political complexion of the force – many more generations would pass through the Canadian militia before partisan affiliations were irrelevant – but they did alter the way politics worked in the organization.

The change of generations occurred with surprisingly little resistance. Most of the colonels affected were Conservatives but they included two Liberal MP s. Lieutenant Colonel Joseph Tucker of the 62nd Saint John Fusiliers cheerfully gave up his command but his fellow Liberal, Colonel James Domville, proceeded to use every excuse to cling to his position at the head of the 8th Hussars. To Hutton the case was simple. Domville had commanded his regiment for seventeen years, he had a reputation for drunkenness and commercial sharp practice, and he had not called out his regiment for training for the past two years. His term was up in the summer of 1898 and as soon as Hutton found time to write he invited the colonel to resign. Domville took no notice of the request. Hutton, none the less, made arrangements to hand over the regiment to Domville's hated rival, Major Alfred Markham.

When Domville, who had been absent in England, discovered what had been done he was furious. Borden had no personal fondness for Domville, but he was aware of the political implications of the colonel's position. Domville's election in 1896 had been a personal victory over the Minister's most merciless parliamentary critic, George E. Foster. That may have created at least a slight bond of sympathy between the two men. Borden therefore agreed to postpone the announcement of Domville's retirement until after the forthcoming New Brunswick provincial elections. He also intervened personally to get Domville to retire, pointing out that he was now the only officer affected by the regulations who had not done so. It was to no avail. Domville's next excuse was that he could not resign while there were charges outstanding against him. Contrary to the regulations Domville had kept and spent the allowances intended for his troop commanders. He had used the money quite reasonably to pay for a store and caretaker for regimental equipment, but George Foster, perhaps at Markham's behest, had laid charges

against him before the Public Accounts Committee. It was next Hutton's
turn to intervene, privately, tactlessly, and unsuccessfully, trying to persuade Foster to withdraw the charges to clear the way for Domville's
resignation.[57]

The Domville affair had now reached an impasse. Hutton had failed
to get Foster's charges withdrawn and had damaged his standing with
the cabinet by his unauthorized attempt to negotiate with the opposition.
Domville made no haste to appear before the Public Accounts Committee. The regimental stores had been transferred to Markham but Domville, although on leave, continued to command the regiment. To Borden
the solution was to start afresh, undoing some of the General's more
arbitrary acts.[58] To Hutton this meant a crucial challenge to his authority. In a long memorandum he reviewed the history of the affair and
proceeded to warn that if he had to withdraw his orders he would resign:
"I need hardly bring to your notice a fact which, unfortunately, is too
well known throughout the Empire, that Canadian troops have been
subjected to the criticism that political influence has been allowed to
interfere with the discipline and good order of the Force. I understood
from you when assuming command, that political influence would not
be allowed under the new Government, to weigh against the discipline
and good order of the Force."[59]

It was rather an uncompromising document to lay before a political
superior. Borden took Hutton's letter to the cabinet and Laurier in
turn took it to the Governor General. It was the first occasion on which
Minto had formally been involved on behalf of his friend and he had
clearly not been consulted about all the steps Hutton had taken. He
insisted that Hutton's memorandum was a purely personal and friendly
message to the Minister and he acknowledged that Hutton had been
wrong to negotiate with Foster and to place Domville on leave without
the Minister's approval. In return Minto won a written promise that
Domville would be made to retire at the end of the session when his
chance to justify himself before the Public Accounts Committee would
have expired.[60]

Hutton believed that he had won a real victory. The Governor
General was assured that his stand had "done more to restore discipline
& real efficiency into the Canadian Army than all the humble efforts
of myself & others."[61] To Sir Redvers Buller he claimed that Minto had
backed him "like a hero."[62] In fact, the triumph was far from complete.
Domville still had influence enough to make sure that the change of

command was postponed until Markham, nearing the age limit, could hold it for only a week. The command of the regiment then passed to a less politically sensitive officer.[63]

Hutton had also opened a permanent breach with Borden which Minto's conciliation could not fill. Of this the General seems to have been largely unaware. Borden was welcomed at the big camps at Niagara and Laprairie during the summer. In August Hutton suggested to him that they would both be protected if a regulation were adopted preventing militia officers from serving actively when they became MPs. "This will prevent the scandal of officers actually serving under my command availing themselves of their Parliamentary priviledge [sic] to abuse the Minister of Defence & their superior officers."[64]

In making this proposal Hutton had Domville in mind, but he had already clashed with another of the "parliamentary colonels," Sam Hughes. In general Hutton had been successful in cultivating Canadian imperialists. While some of them, like George Parkin and Principal Grant of Queen's, had supported the Liberals in 1896, most of them were Conservatives. Hutton's contacts with the opposition were sometimes an asset. When he had to reorganize the highly Conservative and inefficient 7th Fusiliers of London in 1899, he was able to call on local Conservatives like Sir John Carling for their help. To Liberals it sometimes seemed that Hutton foresook political neutrality in pressing for extensions of command for Conservative colonels or in placing the organization of the new medical unit in Toronto in the hands of Conservative doctors.[65] It might not be predictable, therefore, that his staunchest political antagonist in Canada would be the Conservative, imperialist colonel from Lindsay.

In fact, since 1896 Hughes had fallen from strict party loyalty. For his part Borden had helped Hughes obtain command of the 45th Battalion by the aid of some judicious transfers and reorganization.[66] When Hutton arrived Hughes had expected a fellow spirit and had presented him with sixteen pages of advice on how to reform the militia.[67] Within months one arrogant reformer had clashed with another. According to Hughes, Hutton had tried to forbid him to present his reform notions to Parliament. According to Hutton, Hughes was simply insubordinate. At the camp at Niagara in 1899 the two men continued their quarrel.

Hutton was not particularly worried by such enemies as Domville and Hughes. By the summer of 1899 he was riding on a wave of success. He had won his point in the Domville affair. The summer camps had been a brilliant success. Public opinion was massing behind him. In August he took two weeks for a holiday and then received the highest honour in Canadian summer oratory by being invited to open the Toronto Exhibition. His speech caught the spirit of that climactic year of imperial sentiment:

Our pastimes, our cricket, our football, and our manly games may, and undoubtedly have done much for the manhood of the Empire. There is, however, something greater, higher, nobler, in a nation's life which athleticism does not teach. It is the profession of arms when undertaken upon its true lines, which inculcates the spirit of discipline of mind and body, the subordination of self to a noble end, the love of country and honour to God. These are the qualities which constitute the warlike strength of a people and become the true reflexes of their moral and mental vigour.[68]

From an imperial standpoint Hutton had accomplished far more than anyone could have expected a year before. It was paradoxical that one of the few additional worries Hutton acquired in that triumphant summer was a bitter dispute with his old friend, Lord William Seymour, the British general at Halifax. At first the two generals had worked in harmony. One of the few policies of his predecessors which Hutton had warmly endorsed was the integration of the local militia into the garrisons at Halifax and Esquimalt. In Nova Scotia the local force was reorganized and largely handed over to Seymour for training and supervision. While the old general regarded the Halifax militiamen with thorough contempt, he was also pleased by the extension of his absurdly small command.[69] The two men also agreed on the folly of attempting to recruit Canadians for the British regular army, an experiment then in progress at Halifax through the Leinster Regiment, the old 100th Royal Canadians.[70]

The dispute between Hutton and Seymour broke out quite unexpectedly in June 1899. The fault lay almost entirely with the older man. Colonel Foster, the quartermaster general, had shown his highly secret report on the United States to the Governor General, but when Seymour asked to see it he insisted on prior War Office authorization. Hutton endorsed Foster's scruples. Seymour was incensed at this apparent insubordination and warned Hutton that he did not intend to be balked: "I do not wish to proceed at once to order him to do so through you, but by a letter I have lately received from the War Office, placing my authority over all Imperial officers in Canada beyond doubt, I could do this without hesitation."[71]

Seymour's evidence for believing in his authority over all British officers in the militia was based on a War Office request to forward confidential reports on them. A small-minded, unbalanced man, frustrated by the limits of his tiny command, Seymour had seized on the unthinking act of a War Office official as justification for commanding the obedience of all British officers in the service of the Canadian government.[72] Already made sensitive by the recommendations of the Leach Committee, Hutton refused to accept the claim. After trying to argue the case directly with Seymour, Hutton referred the dispute to the man he actually regarded as his direct superior, the Governor General.[73]

There were precedents for Seymour's claim but they had been firmly countered by successive Governors General. In 1871 Sir Hastings Doyle had claimed authority to prepare confidential reports on Colonel Robertson Ross, and in 1874 Lord Dufferin had had to remind Sir William O'Grady Haly that Selby Smyth was not his subordinate.[74] Hutton's dispute with Seymour would probably have ended very quickly if it had been referred to his own Minister. Instead, he had taken it to Minto. Although the Governor General had no doubt that the two commands were entirely separate in peacetime, neither he nor Hutton wished to involve the Canadians in what they saw as an embarrassing British dispute. Indeed, both men were afraid that Seymour, his fury rising, might appeal to the Canadian politicians and so give them a chance to pronounce on the proper chain of military authority. The aged Lord William had already criticized Hutton's public speaking and what he regarded as excessive reforming zeal.[75] Nothing would undermine Hutton's authority in Canada more quickly than a public dispute between the only two British generals in the country. When Minto was in Halifax in August he sought without avail to mediate. He found that Seymour now insisted that he must be the Governor General's sole military adviser. Only a truce could be arranged while the dispute was referred to the War Office in London.[76]

The friction with Seymour was a reminder of the cross-pressures which could be exerted on a British officer in command of the Canadian militia. Seymour's claim was groundless, as the War Office quickly admitted. At the same time, Seymour could be a powerful and influential enemy. Hutton was only a colonel in the British army, a relatively junior officer, as Seymour took pains to remind him. With Minto's support Hutton had no difficulty in winning his case while he was in Canada. The dangers, both for him and Foster, were to lie ahead, when Seymour's presence at the War Office was to affect both their careers.[77]

Within the limits of his Canadian mission, far more urgent difficulties were beginning to encompass Hutton than the future influence of Lord William Seymour. Despite his high confidence in the summer of 1899 it seems hardly possible that Hutton could have continued to surmount the antagonism he was creating in political circles for the further two years he had agreed to serve in Canada.[78] His departure was only hastened by the disputes surrounding the organization of the Canadian contingents for South Africa.

The approach of the South African War gave Hutton an opportunity to test his solution to the problem of imperial defence. In Australia he had helped to form two military components in the local forces: volunteers for fixed defences and militia able to be sent to the aid of other colonies. This division had not seemed appropriate for Canada where the basic military problem, for Hutton as for Leach, had been to meet an American invasion across a long and virtually undefended frontier. Still, the idea had remained at the back of Hutton's mind. On July 3, 1899, Chamberlain asked Minto to discover whether the Canadian government would "spontaneously" agree to send a contingent to South Africa if war broke out. Although Laurier refused to give any such prior commitment, he led Parliament in a resolution of support for Britain and the Uitlanders.[79]

Quietly, at Minto's suggestion, Hutton and Foster spent part of July working out a detailed plan for a contingent of twelve hundred Canadians, organized as infantry, field artillery, and mounted rifles. Although the General himself informed Chamberlain of the existence of the plan, his own minister was not told about it for a further two months.[80] By then an effective campaign to push the government into sending a contingent to South Africa was already well underway. Borden, fully on the side of the imperialists in the cabinet, was delighted to find that a scheme for a suitable contingent was available.[81]

Laurier and many of his colleagues were less pleased. Six months before, the Prime Minister had astonished Lord Minto by asserting that the British government had a perfect right to move Canadian troops in or out of the Dominion, thanks to Section 79 of the Militia Act.[82] Minto's surprise was due to his own experience of Sir John A. Macdonald's attitude at the time of the Sudan campaign, when the Conservative leader

had insisted that Britain could only obtain troops from Canada by persuading them to enlist under her own Army Act. Of course there was a
difference between the two positions but it was of less significance than
Minto may have realized. What neither Canadian premier had offered
and what Chamberlain now wanted was action on the part of Canada
herself. If Britain ordered out Canadian militia or recruited volunteers,
that would be her initiative. The Canadian government would be spared
a decision which, as Laurier already appreciated, might split the country
between the imperial enthusiasts and those, largely in French Canada,
who wanted no part in Britain's wars.[83] It was also true that in previous
crises Britain had rejected offers of colonial troops and it did not seem
likely that she would need them to defeat the Boers.

Hutton was aware of the views of the Prime Minister and of the divisions in the cabinet. He was also aware that what Chamberlain wanted
from Canada was neither professional efficiency nor unofficial enthusiasm but official commitment. He therefore set out to fulfil the Colonial
Secretary's wishes.

The most serious threat to Chamberlain's hopes was that enthusiasm
would be channelled into a private offer to raise troops, like those of
Laurie or Domville in previous crises, thus allowing the Dominion government to offer no more than an informal blessing. Precisely such an
offer was being made by no other than the irrepressible imperialist, Sam
Hughes. In fact, Hughes made three simultaneous offers: to Hutton
through militia channels, to Laurier in his capacity as an MP, and to
Chamberlain directly as "a citizen of the Empire."[84] Although Hutton
had destined Hughes for an important post in his planned contingent,
he was annoyed at the presumption of the offer and ignored it. Laurier
for his part planned to tell Chamberlain of the gesture but he was dissuaded by Minto who was well aware of what the Colonial Secretary had
in mind.[85] It was only through the offer to Chamberlain and its fulsome
acknowledgment that Hughes won the congratulations and publicity to
which he felt entitled.

Hutton was indignant. Hughes had nearly upset his strategy; besides,
he had signed himself to Chamberlain as commanding officer of the 45th
Battalion. As a lesson in discipline and perhaps to discourage other
colonels from similar acts of public patriotism, Hughes was delivered a
sharp rebuke for offering troops without authority. The Colonel replied
in a flood of memoranda, couched in his characteristically passionate
prose. It was a new version of the old battle between MacDougall and

Hughes, but this time it had to be waged amidst the preoccupations of war and of organizing the Canadian contingent.[86]

Besides discouraging private volunteers, Hutton had another political concern: to escape identification with the agitation to send an official contingent:

I was well aware that there existed in Canada a small coterie of eminent men who had banded themselves together for the purpose of enforcing through the Press, the policy of intervention, and of forcing the Laurier Government into co-operating with the Mother Country in a crisis involving Imperial affairs. It was obviously desirable that this movement should emanate from the Canadians and Canadian public opinion and that any appearance of an Imperial officer such as myself having a hand in such coercion of the existing Government could only be most detrimental to its successful issue.[87]

To avoid any appearance of influencing policy Hutton deliberately spent most of the summer and fall away from Ottawa. He returned in September only long enough to present his scheme for a contingent and to make the final amendments (including the deletion of Hughes' name from the proposed officers) so that Foster could put it into effect in his absence. At the end of the month he was called back to see the cabinet, to be asked by Richard Scott, acting prime minister and one of the few English-speaking opponents of intervention, whether a few hundred volunteers might be got together. "[N]ot a few, but five thousand men, without any difficulty," Hutton replied, adding that he had already warned Borden that if war came public opinion "would be so expressed as to force any Government into sending Troops."[88] It was a rash comment, inferring a familiarity with the impending campaign for Canadian participation which undid the General's attempts to appear uninvolved. It was certainly recalled a few days later when war was declared and the Ministers found themselves engulfed in a well-organized and successful press barrage. By that time Hutton had left for an extended tour of western Canada, determined not to return until the contingent had been authorized and at least partly organized.

Hutton's presence was not needed. On October 3 the regular issue of the *Canadian Military Gazette* appeared, carrying an accurate description of the contingent Hutton had worked out the previous July. On the same day a telegram from the Colonial Office reached Ottawa and was simultaneously released to the press, thanking the Canadians for a contingent they had yet to offer. In fact, the message was a carelessly drafted circular to all the self-governing colonies, but in Canada it undid the effect of spontaneity it was supposed to acknowledge. On the following day, in an unprecedented interview with a reporter from the Toronto *Globe*, Laurier announced firmly that there were no plans for a contingent.[89] The apparent confusion was fuel for the campaign to force Canada to participate. From the west Hutton wrote somewhat disingenuously to Borden: "The hydra-headed newspaper staff show a curiously accurate perception of much that would be necessary if you and the cabinet decide upon sending troops."[90]

On October 14 the government's nerve broke. Laurier hurried home from the Chicago World's Fair and announced that Canada would be sending a thousand infantry to South Africa. Four days later the offer was defined more precisely as a battalion of infantry under the command of Lieutenant Colonel William Otter.

Two political storms now moved out to meet Hutton, then delivering patriotic speeches on the Prairies. The first was the mood of the cabinet, furious at having been coerced to act against its will and convinced that Hutton was at least partly responsible. Chamberlain's message of October 3 was associated with the leak in the *Military Gazette* and with Hutton's earlier remarks to the cabinet. When Ministers demanded an explanation, Hutton, remote in the west and aggressively innocent, treated their suspicions with scorn.[91]

The other storm was Sam Hughes, determined at any price to secure a prominent position in the contingent. The first storm had to blow itself out, leaving the cabinet ruffled and deeply mistrustful of its General. The second lasted much longer and acquired some of the force of the first. In his original organization Hutton had planned to divide a small infantry battalion into two wings, giving command of one to Lieutenant Colonel Oscar Pelletier, son of the French-Canadian Speaker of the Senate, and the other to Hughes. However, having come to the conclusion that Hughes's "want of judgement and insubordinate self-assertion" made him unsuitable, Hutton replaced him by Lieutenant Colonel Lawrence Buchan, a permanent force officer for whom Hughes nourished a particular hatred.[92]

In the cabinet there was considerable support for Hughes, and Borden himself championed the Colonel's cause. Minto, sensing the swelling anger of his ministers, pressed Hutton to give way. Only on October 25, less than a week before the contingent was due to sail, did Hutton return to Ottawa. On the following day he was summoned to the cabinet and subjected to considerable abuse, particularly from Richard Scott, for his alleged role in the agitation for the Canadian contingent and for his treatment of Hughes. Hutton stood firm, convinced that no officer would be accepted by the British without his approval. By October 27 he had apparently won. Not only were all his nominees for commissions confirmed but he had had the satisfaction of a letter of abject apology from Hughes. The Colonel had come, Hutton boasted to Minto, "full of tears and contrition," to beg a place in the contingent.[93] That night, travelling to Quebec City with Borden to see the troops off, Hutton agreed to let Hughes go with the force as a civilian, although he promptly wrote to the British commander at Capetown to warn against giving the troublesome officer any employment.[94]

Once again Hutton believed that he had successfully asserted his authority over political interference. Again it was an illusory victory. His stubbornness had strained the good will of the Governor General; it had embarrassed Borden and exasperated the rest of the cabinet. There were ministers who would have been delighted to have the political problem of the South African contingent solved by Hughes leading off his private army. When Hughes demanded to know what right Hutton had to control his correspondence with a British official, they could sympathize.

At Quebec City Borden and Hutton found further reasons to complain of each other. At one of the dinners for contingent officers, Hutton spoke pointedly of the need to abolish political influences in the militia. It was an awkward beginning for an evening which ended, according to Hutton's account, with Borden being carried drunk to bed. When the contingent sailed on October 30 the Minister arrived late and ill-tempered at the quayside. When Hutton approached to ask about a detail of the officers' pay, he was loudly told to go and mind his own business.[95]

The arrangements for the first contingent had reopened the breach between Hutton and Borden; the preparations for the second made it irreparable. The British had at first refused a Canadian offer of more troops but after a series of reverses in South Africa in early November, and because additional troops had been accepted from New South Wales, a second contingent was belatedly welcomed. After more indecision both at the War Office and in Canada, it was agreed that Canada should organize three batteries of field artillery and two small battalions of mounted rifles. This time the Militia Department had no prepared plan. The political pressure for commissions in the contingent was far fiercer than in October and the difficulties of mobilizing and training troops in the depth of a Canadian winter created a series of administrative problems.

Hutton began his part in the organization of the contingent by quarreling with Lord Minto. His own intention had been to raise three squadrons of mounted rifles in eastern Canada, trusting that many of the best western horsemen would come east to join. When the regiment had been sufficiently strengthened he would then begin to recruit a fourth squadron in the west. The Governor General, perhaps a little vain about the knowledge of the North West he had acquired in 1885, deplored the scheme as ignoring the real military need for mounted scouts. So strongly did he feel about the issue that he complained directly to Lord Lansdowne, the British war secretary, and even to Laurier. Hutton, he suggested, was merely seeking popularity among the eastern militia officers by trying to give them a cavalry regiment. "The artillery & other (mounted) troops cannot possibly represent a high standard of efficiency," he wrote to Lord Roberts, the British commander-in-chief in South Africa. "I am disappointed in the way the organization has been undertaken, but of course cannot do more than advise strongly."[96]

Minto finally arranged that separate battalions were organized in the two regions of the country, but his struggle with Hutton gave him some sympathy with the growing indignation of his Canadian ministers. In his letter to Lansdowne the Governor General had gone on to criticize Hutton's persistent use of public speaking and newspaper interviews to spread his influence. In a letter to Chamberlain he wrote in evident impatience: "... he speaks very well, but far too much & I have told him so, & it has given offence as he has been accused of touching too much on political subjects." The Governor General had detected warning signals from Liberal ministers, growing restive as an election year approached and increasingly annoyed by the comfort Hutton was giving to their Conservative critics.[97]

Since September Hutton had vainly sought an opportunity to go to the war, preferably as the commander of all the colonial contingents. His request had been refused by the War Office. In December, when Hutton renewed his application, Borden cheerfully endorsed it, seeing a chance to be rid of his difficult subordinate. When the General suggested that Colonel Kitson could take temporary command in his absence, the Minister made it clear that the departure would be permanent: "I have to say that we do not share your apprehensions as to the improbability of the Imperial Government being able to find a competent successor in case you offer to serve in South Africa and your offer was accepted." And, he concluded pointedly, "I can only repeat that the Government cannot think of putting any obstacle in the way of Her Majesty's Government receiving the benefit of your skill and experience."[98] To go on these terms would be to leave the hopeless Colonel Aylmer in command and to endanger all that Hutton felt he had accomplished in Canada.

In January, however, came insults he could not accept. Colonel Kitson, sent to Toronto to buy horses for the second contingent, was accused by local Liberals of showing favour to Conservative dealers. Hutton promptly went down to Toronto to support his officer. Without consulting him, Borden also sent his own agent, Robert Beith, a prominent horse dealer and Liberal MP. Hutton, furious at this check on his integrity, refused to allow Beith to examine the horses already purchased. When the Liberal obtained confirmation of his authority direct from the Minister, the General immediately returned to Ottawa. Borden, a little embarrassed, apologized for his action and Hutton, making allowances "for the ignorance of Colonial politicians in matters requiring delicate treatment ...," accepted the apology. A few days later, however, the Minister raised the matter again by demanding to see the horse purchase book. This time Hutton's patience was exhausted. His personal honour, he claimed, was being challenged. Full of indignation he took his grievance to the Governor General.[99]

Immediately afterwards Hutton left for Halifax to supervise the embarkation of troops of the second contingent, leaving Minto to make peace between him and the government. In the event, it was Laurier who took the initiative. On January 17 he called on the Governor General to explain that either Borden or Hutton would have to go. Since no other Liberal minister would put up with Hutton, it was plainly the General who would have to depart.[100] At first Minto toyed with the idea of forcing his government to resign to save Hutton but he soon retreated to the more modest, if only slightly less dangerous, task of using the conflict to expose the evils of political meddling in militia affairs.

The first step in the Governor General's campaign was to write a long, passionate, and sometimes intemperate, defence of Hutton's position, insisting that a fundamental imperial issue was at stake. Could a British officer of standing hold the command of the militia as it was then administered? Was it right at a moment of imperial crisis to remove so distinguished a soldier as Hutton? To Minto's chagrin and annoyance, Laurier presented this document to the cabinet and had his Minister of Justice, David Mills, draft an even longer and much more formal reply. Its theme, repeated in various terms, was that if Hutton could not accept that a Canadian minister was in every way supreme in his department, he was obviously unfitted for his position.[101]

At the end of January Hutton returned from Halifax where he had patched up his social relations with Seymour but aggravated their military quarrel. During his absence he had found new grounds for conflict with Borden. On January 13 the British government had accepted an offer by Lord Strathcona, the wealthy Canadian high commissioner in London, to raise and equip a regiment of mounted rifles at his own expense. Strathcona clearly intended that Hutton should be personally responsible for organizing the unit and selecting the officers and Hutton was delighted by the responsibility. It would be a chance to show the Canadians how such things should be managed.[102] However, Borden had interpreted the High Commissioner's message to apply to the department as a whole and not merely to its chief military officer. "Lord Strathcona's corps will be organized under direction of myself as Head of Militia," Borden telegraphed, "The respective officers of the service including yourself will take their instructions from me."[103]

The Strathcona affair was fresh fuel for Hutton's indignation. In Ottawa he settled down with a lawyer to prepare a long statement of his grievances against the Minister. The lawyer's professional restraint did not prevent the portrayal of Borden as a weak, unscrupulous, and corrupt figure who had broken promises and impeded the General at every stage of his important imperial work.[104] Sharing an illusion common among men with a grievance, Hutton believed that publication of his account would be enough to arouse an outcry which would sweep the Liberals from office. Indeed, it was apparently alarm at the prospect of a Liberal defeat (as well as the moderating influence of Minto) which dissuaded him from publication. Like Middleton before him, Hutton had now developed a fervid hostility to "disloyal" French Canadians, but he was politician enough to believe that it was better for them to be in office under the control of an English-speaking minority than to send them into disloyal opposition. He yielded, he later claimed, "on the higher, broader, vastly more important issue of Imperial expediency."[105]

It is also likely that Hutton considerably overrated his own popularity. He had inevitably shared in the general devaluation of the prestige of

British generalship following the disastrous first months of the South African War. In his case the devaluation could be specifically related to his treatment of Colonel Sam Hughes, left stranded, if far from silent, at Capetown. It was Hughes who had warned Hutton in August that "the old plugs of Boer farmers" would beat the British if they did not change their tactics.[106] The prophecy had been borne out, and at this stage of the war public acclaim was largely reserved for unconventional irregulars like Hughes. In Canada, Colonel Domville was already demanding the papers in the Hughes-Hutton dispute. Hutton told officers of the second contingent that publication of the papers would put Hughes in "a pitiable position" and he later told reporters that the Colonel "could not have been exactly in his right mind" when he had written some of the letters.[107] Hutton had already made a serious mistake in underestimating Hughes's political influence; by making further personal attacks he aggravated his error. A little too late to retrieve his position he quietly sent word that Hughes was now recommended for an appointment. To Borden's astonishment the General even suggested Hughes for a captaincy in Lord Strathcona's new regiment.[108]

The Minister had meanwhile been uncovering further and unexpected evidence to substantiate his case against Hutton. Without consulting Borden, Hutton had selected the candidates for the second militia staff course and published them in General Orders. This was the first notice the Minister had had of the names and he chose to strike out two of them. Letters were sent to the two officers at Hutton's direction explaining that their places had been cancelled for "having recently taken an active part in politics by public speaking." A few days later one of them was informed that his name had been removed from the list "... by the Honourable the Minister on the grounds that you had of late taken some active part in politics on behalf of the Opposition."[109] Both of the officers were prominent Conservatives; one of them had recently told a Guelph audience that he looked forward to going to war with the French Canadians as soon as the Boers were beaten.[110] It is likely that Borden had political reasons for acting, but he could also claim that both men were elderly and had recently retired from their commands. (It was equally true that both men were only in their fifties and both had commanded excellent militia units.) What really concerned Borden was to discover how such deliberately mischievous letters could have emanated from his department.

He first sent for Colonel Foster, author of the embarrassing letters, only to be told that the Chief Staff Officer could not see him without the General's permission. An angry and perplexed Borden set off in person for Foster's office. When he found him he was told that a year before Hutton had ordered that neither Foster nor Aylmer were to see the Minister without his approval. If they did meet Borden by chance, they were to report on their conversation at their earliest opportunity. The Minister had this surprising information substantiated in writing by both officers and reported the facts to the Prime Minister. He also ordered Pinault to write to the General to find out why "entirely erroneous and misleading" explanations had been sent to the two staff course candidates.[111]

That day, February 3, was the climax of the Hutton crisis. For ministers wavering in the face of Minto's resistance, Borden's discovery of the General's secret order was evidence enough. For Minto it was the day on which he submitted a second, more restrained memorandum of his position, withdrawing the earlier version. In the afternoon Fred White, the comptroller of the Mounted Police and an old friend, called on the Governor General to warn him not to overestimate Hutton's popular following. In the evening there was a letter from the General himself promising to fight "à l'outrance" against "the party political interference with the functions of my military command."[112]

Then, quite suddenly, it was over. On the next day Hutton took to his bed with a bad cold. Four days later, when he had recovered sufficiently to get up, he found that Minto had capitulated. Embarrassed by his own earlier memorandum, disconcerted by Laurier's steady pressure, the Governor General had finally signed the order-in-council demanding Hutton's immediate recall.[113] On the following day the General's spirits revived and he announced to Minto that he was making plans to force the government to grant a royal commission inquiry into the Militia Department. The plans were short-lived. On the evening of the ninth he received orders to report to South Africa for special service. Accordingly, he resigned.

Neither the British nor the Canadian governments had wished to press the issue to the point of dismissal. By the beginning of February both would have been glad to see Hutton leave for South Africa without provoking a public outcry.[114] It was Minto, with his determination that the Canadian ministers would be brought to account for their sins, who had forced the issue to the point of dismissal. When the order-in-council had finally been signed on February 7, he waited expectantly for a public reaction. Hutton was asked to delay his resignation for, as Minto explained, "... the object of the line I have taken is to ensure an opportunity for public opinion to express itself. If your resignation goes in before the govt.'s action is announced, such an opportunity may to some extent not occur & I might be asked to cancel the request for recall."[115]

In fact, although the appointment to South Africa had come too late to forestall the order-in-council, Minto found that his government did insist on replacing it with another on February 12, merely recommending that Hutton's resignation for service in South Africa be accepted. The next day, when a Conservative MP tried to adjourn the House of Commons to debate Hutton's departure, Laurier refused to be drawn beyond the explanation that the General was leaving on a patriotic duty.[116]

Given Ottawa's notorious incapacity to keep political secrets it was unlikely that the real reason for Hutton's departure would have been long unknown. However, robbed of his chance to bring down the government or even to expose Borden before a royal commission, Hutton refused to wait on time for his vindication. Instead, he used his two last speeches in Canada, both to hastily organized farewell banquets, to give generous hints of the real reasons for his going. At the Rideau Club, flanked by two Conservative MPs, he spoke of his struggle to create a national army. "I should have felt more confident of the ultimate success of this national effort if the government had ever indicated its approval of my schemes or had shown interest in their evolution." To militia officers he explained that "no petty misunderstanding with the minister of militia" had led to his resignation, but "broader, wider, vastly more important issues." What they were he failed to specify, but repeated references to the need to eliminate political interference from the force made his meaning clear.[117]

On February 15 the Huttons left Ottawa for the last time. For the General, feeling the bitterness of personal defeat, the large crowds which gathered to see them off must have been some consolation. So were the letters from well-wishers, among them Theodore Roosevelt.[118]

Edward Hutton was the ablest of the British officers sent to command the Canadian militia. His predecessors had largely accepted the militia as they found it, carping at its failings and tinkering with its reform. Even the best of them, General Herbert, had sought reform through the artificial application of British models and by trying to rescue only a small component, the permanent force, from the hopeless mass. Hutton's contribution was to see the force as a whole and to see it as it might be. Individually, his reforms were not original: put together, they were the basis for a self-confident, unified, military institution.

Hutton's other contribution was not merely to demand a military ethos

of pride and discipline from the militia but to make it popular as well.
In terms of his own standing, the battles with Domville and Hughes
proved to be pyrrhic victories, but they forced through a change of era.
He helped bring to the top a new generation of militia officers, less evidently using their positions as political stepping stones. It was these men,
and the few from an earlier generation who had already conscientiously
attempted to adopt a military style, who now most sincerely mourned his
departure. To Colonel Otter, one of the few senior staff officers who had
no partisan ties, Hutton's resignation was a crushing blow. Writing to
the General he declared that he was seriously considering leaving the
militia and remaining as a settler in South Africa: "I have worked hard
for very many years, nay all my life for the force and your advent seemed
about to bring rewards at last. Now in the general scramble that will take
place my chances are pretty sure to be I very much fear nil."[119]

There was another side to Hutton: the man who could find Otter's
desolate letter "very cheering," the man whose brilliant skill as a practical politician was undermined as much by his own arrogance as by his
enemies.[120] If Hutton had attempted to co-operate with his Minister and
to appreciate his political difficulties, he might have found that Borden,
with all his own limitations in imagination, energy, and judgment, was
the most powerful force for reforming the military system in the entire
cabinet. Instead, Hutton insisted on being his own political master, on
building his own constituency across Canada, and on treating his ministerial superiors as slightly disreputable meddlers. Thanks to the students
of his papers, Hutton's characterization of Borden as a vain, weak,
drunken figure, as a "vacillating, unprincipled fool,"[121] has had a popular currency. Borden's final judgment on Hutton also deserves to be
heard: "Since the time of Alexander I doubt if a more ambitious and
unscrupulous warrior ever lived. His whole aim seems to be to destroy
existing conditions and substitute others, with his own impress upon
them, regardless, apparently, of consequences. He was always playing
to the galleries, always thinking about the possible effect of any move
upon his own name and fame. It was Hutton first and devil take whoever came afterwards."[122]

Yet, with all his shortcomings Hutton had succeeded more than he
knew. There would be a Canadian Army and the condemnation of influence and patronage in the Militia Department was firmly entrenched
as a political issue.

CHAPTER EIGHT

O'Grady Haly

Transitional Commander

Lord Minto had manoeuvred hard to make sure that Hutton's departure would be the occasion for a public debate on the position of the General Officer Commanding. By forcing the cabinet to present a formal request for the General's removal, he gave himself the right to prepare a covering despatch which would oblige the British government to reply. In his despatch to Chamberlain, Minto not only invited a response, he also asserted a British right to intervene in Canadian defence policy: "It appears to me that considering to what an extent the defences of Canada depend upon Imperial aid, Her Majesty's Government has some claim to share in directing the efficiency of the Military Forces of the Dominion, for good as the material composing them is, they are in many ways most inefficient, whilst the social and official surroundings besetting the force would render it quite impossible for one of its own officers to undertake its reorganization with any hope of success."[1]

The public debate Minto had sought began in Parliament on February 13 and continued at intervals throughout the session. From the outset, Conservative MPs and newspapers tried to enrol the General as an absentee supporter.[2] It was a claim complicated by the well-known views of the equally absent Colonel Sam Hughes. That discord was at least softened when Colonel Domville, Hutton's other victim and Hughes's self-appointed spokesman, succeeded in having the Hughes-Hutton correspondence published as a parliamentary return. "The journals which imagined that Col. Sam Hughes was a victim to General Hutton's prejudice against colonial officers must feel like asking the earth to open and swallow them when they read those awful letters ... ," admitted one of the offenders.[3]

Hutton's stock rose with Hughes's humiliation, but by April, when a full debate was arranged, Borden had prepared his own careful counter-attack. Even Colonel Tisdale, as a former minister of militia, had to admit that Hutton's order barring his staff officers from access to the Minister was indefensible. Borden also stood by his decision on admissions to the staff course. In the administration of a force in which ninety per cent of the officers were known Conservatives, he claimed, "nothing more than justice has been done to the Liberal Party."[4]

It was easier for the Canadian government to cope with its domestic critics than to win acceptance for its view of the Hutton case in Britain. On his return to London Hutton had been delighted to find that both Chamberlain and Lansdowne shared the belief that crude political interference had been at the root of his troubles with the Canadian government. The Colonial Secretary even blamed Laurier rather than Minto for forcing matters to a dismissal.[5] His viewpoint was quickly absorbed by Lord Strathcona, the Canadian high commissioner and already one of Hutton's admirers. On February 22, after he had agreed to an opposition demand for the papers in the Hutton affair, Laurier wrote to Chamberlain to explain his position. By his two farewell speeches Hutton had compelled the government to reply to his allegations. The Prime Minister defended Borden: "I am justified in saying that he has been fair, impartial, just to all shades of opinion, and that his administration has been singularly free of 'party political interference.' "[6] To Strathcona he wrote in even stronger terms: "It is impossible to understand the conduct of General Hutton except by the assumption that being an officer of the Imperial Army, he was superior to the Minister of Militia, that he was the supreme authority in the Department, and that the Minister was his subordinate."[7]

Laurier's viewpoint had little weight in London. When Chamberlain finally replied to Minto's despatch, he delivered a firm reprimand to the Canadian ministers. After praising Hutton's services in Canada, he pointed out that neither of his two predecessors had been able to finish their terms. There had to be some permanent cause since it could hardly be the fault of the officers themselves, "experts in Military administration and of course absolutely removed from political influence." Chamberlain concluded with some curt advice: "... it is desirable that the Officer in Command of the defensive forces of the Dominion should have a freer hand in matters essential to the efficiency of the Militia than would be proper in the case of an ordinary civil servant even of the highest position."[8]

It would have been difficult for the Canadian government to accept such a rebuke without reply, particularly as the Colonial Office despatch was clearly intended for publication. In a memorandum designed as a basis of reply Borden hotly denied that the interests of the militia had been subordinated to politics: "Such a state of affairs, the Minister wishes to say most emphatically, has not within his knowledge prevailed and does not prevail in Canada. The causes of difference between the Minister and the Major General were in no sense political." Instead, they stemmed from Hutton's assumption that he could dictate to his Minister, his disobedience of orders, his indiscreet speeches and interviews, and above all his secret orders to cut the Minister off from contact with the military staff.[9] This long statement, stronger in debating points than historical accuracy, was included in a cabinet minute which went on to deny that Hutton deserved the credit for Canada's contingents in South Africa. The Canadian ministers concluded their rebuttal on high constitutional ground: "They are quite prepared to concede a very free hand to the General in all matters affecting the discipline of the Militia, but they cannot for a moment yield to claims which practically would make the General the controller of the policy of the Government in Militia matters."[10]

Borden's warm self-defence drew the scorn of the Governor General. In his covering despatch Minto observed: "My Government would appear to assume that the actual military command rests with the Minister, who is justified in interfering in every military detail, however small, and that the General Officer Commanding is merely the equivalent to the Chief Clerk of a civilian Department ..."[11]

The doctrine both Minto and Chamberlain were pressing on Canada was plausible enough but what were its limits? Hutton had accused his Minister of political meddling but he himself had been engaged in an essentially political campaign from the moment he landed in Canada. In dealing with George Foster during the Domville affair he had used his influence in a directly political way. Political considerations as well as pique had governed his treatment of Sam Hughes. Hutton would have been naïve indeed if he had failed to realize that his programme of military imperialism and of cleansing the Militia Department of political influence-mongering were not also useful supplements to the armoury of the Canadian Conservatives. Certainly the General took a lively interest in the state of the party battle and of his own potential role in it. As GOC, Hutton might pretend that the men with whom he dealt had no party affiliation. Borden could not. There were begging letters on the Minister's own files from some of the very men who were applauding Hutton's anti-political sentiments.

Like his predecessors after similar crises over the command of the militia, Lord Minto had now to secure the succession for a British officer. As after most of the previous resignations, there was again talk of appointing a Canadian. In the debate immediately following Hutton's resignation, Borden had cautiously suggested that perhaps the time had come to enlarge the field from which the generals were selected.[12] There was unexpected, if tentative, support for the idea from the veteran Sir Adolphe Caron (now the member for Trois-Rivières), but the frail chance of bipartisan unity was lost when Domville, in an intemperate outburst against Hutton, declared that he would rather have a Boer than a British general at the head of the militia.[13] On March 26 an alarmed Governor General warned the Colonial Office that Borden had actually prepared a bill to open the command of the force to militia officers and asked for Chamberlain's support in opposing it. "I am convinced," he wrote, "that circumstances might easily arise when irresistible party pressure might be brought to bear on a Minister to nominate a Canadian officer no matter how incapable he might be."[14] Both Chamberlain and Lansdowne agreed: to the latter, such an appointment would be "little short of disastrous."[15] In fact, Minto had been mistaken. The rumoured bill was only another of the works of Colonel Domville.

It was now necessary to find a replacement for Hutton. To Minto's intense displeasure Colonel Aylmer took up the temporary command of the militia, although as long as Section 37 of the Militia Act was not amended, a British officer was still needed for the permanent appointment. Colonel Kitson, the commandant at the military college, was qualified for the post and anxious to have it. "... [I]f I started with a clear understanding with the Minister," he suggested to Minto, "I think I could keep things going for a time without serious difficulty & I might be of a great deal more use to Canada & the Empire than I am here."[16] Neither Minto nor the government were anxious to promote Kitson. Perhaps hoping to restore good feelings with the Governor General, Laurier then proposed Major Lawrence Drummond, his military secretary who was then serving in South Africa. Minto was embarrassed by the suggestion, particularly when it became public knowledge, but in any event the War Office decreed that Drummond was too junior in rank to be promoted.[17] Instead, after considerable efforts of its own, the War Office decided to bring an elderly officer out of retirement to fill the appointment for a year.[18]

Their choice fell on Colonel Richard O'Grady Haly, a fifty-nine-year-old infantry officer, the eldest son of Lieutenant General Sir William O'Grady Haly, who had commanded at Halifax from 1873 until 1878. The new GOC had had an unexciting career in India and Egypt, with his last years of service spent in unimportant staff appointments in England. A more distinguished contemporary recalled him as an officer of competence whose career had been limited by too many children and too few means.[19] Hutton, who had been his contemporary at Staff College, regarded his successor with contempt. "I much fear that old O'Grady Haly & his pomposity will first amuse & then disgust my Canadian comrades," he wrote to Minto. "He is an ass & I fear will not be persona gratissima to you & Lady Minto."[20]

Hutton's opinion may have revealed more about his own damaged pride than about O'Grady Haly. Colonel Foster reported the new general to be "a pleasant, genial Irishman with a lot of common sense & will be very easy to work with," although he also predicted that nothing more than routine administration could be expected.[21] The Canadian government had asked that whoever accepted the appointment should be asked to study the various memoranda on the dispute with Hutton. O'Grady Haly appears to have taken their lessons to heart. He had personal reasons for wishing to keep the good will of his Canadian employers. If he could keep his rank long enough, he could be confirmed in his temporary rank of major general and return to retirement with his pension suitably increased.[22]

The new general did far more, however, than bide his time. In his first public statement he called for the establishment of a musketry school for the Dominion. Within a year the government, mindful of the lessons of the South African War, had established one at Ottawa. During the summer of 1900 O'Grady Haly visited the camps and systematically consulted with commanding officers. The results of his findings were presented as a special memorandum to the Minister and were published with his annual report. In addition to the well-established recommendations for an extended training period, the new general also suggested that bush camp cooks should be employed to teach the men how to prepare their food and that rough shelters should be built to protect the horses from the elements. Since the animals normally belonged to the men themselves, better conditions for the horses would also encourage recruiting. The General's chief concern was with the rapid turnover of men in the ranks of the rural militia. Over sixty per cent were new each year, implying that a large number of recruits broke their engagements. "To me it appears degrading to the moral sense of the people that annually a large number of intelligent and fairly well educated young men should enter into a three year contract with their country, and deliberately break it with impunity." Although he recommended the deterrent effect of a few convictions, the new General pressed even harder for a system of graduated pay for each additional year of training, with a gratuity at the end of the engagement.[23] Borden consented to "make an example" of some of the offenders and to improve the amenities of camp life.[24] Graduated pay would come later.

O'Grady Haly's experience in Canada suggests that there were alternative ways of achieving improvement than Hutton's bustling, abrasive style. Instead of reacting with indignation to directions and suggestions from his Minister, the General gave at least the impression of accepting political necessities. He also accepted instruction in political tact. "I beg to suggest to you," Borden wrote, "... that it would be undesirable to give one of the reasons, at any rate, mentioned in your memorandum, viz. that the Field Battery at Sydney has been dispensed with in order to enable a Field Battery to be established at or near Ottawa. I am sure that you will easily see that, even though the reason be the best in the world from the military point of view, to publish such a reason would be exceedingly awkward for me in the Province of Nova Scotia."[25]

By the end of 1900 Borden had won peace in his department and a marked improvement in his relations with Parliament. The 1900 elections brought the defeat of his bitter critic, George E. Foster, and of his troublesome colleague, Colonel Domville. Soon after the elections his first cousin, Robert L. Borden, became Leader of the Opposition.

In securing his position the Minister had won a fierce political battle, but at a cruel personal price. As a doctor, with an eye for commercial innovation, he had been interested in food concentrates. At his own initiative he provided the men of the second contingent with a special emergency ration, apparently of Canadian design. In fact, an investigation forced by the Conservatives revealed that the substance was nearly worthless. Borden and his Director General of Medical Services had been swindled by the son of a former Liberal MP. The "Emergency Food Ration Scandal," with its implications of corruption and mismanagement at the expense of gallant fighting men, promised real benefits for the Conservatives in an election year.[26] Suddenly, the issue turned sour. Only a few days after the report of the parliamentary committee had been released in Parliament, news reached Ottawa that Borden's only son, Harold, had been killed in action. For Borden it was a bitter personal tragedy. A handsome, athletic, third-year medical student, Harold was the hope of his father's life. With Borden's help he had risen to be a major in the militia by the age of twenty-four, commanding his own cavalry troop in Nova Scotia. His father could not refuse to let him go to war as an officer in the 1st Canadian Mounted Rifles and Hutton, under whose command he came, found him to be a keen, adventurous, if somewhat undisciplined, officer.[27] Harold's death killed something of his father's buoyancy and good nature. Broken in spirit, the Minister and his wife set out for England, making the journey they had earlier planned as a reunion with their son.

The younger Borden's death was more than a personal tragedy. It also helped to influence Borden's view of British officers and military administration. Borden became convinced that his son's military exploits – swimming the Vet River under fire and leading the counter-attack in which he met his death – were the equal of those which won the Victoria Cross for other Canadians during the war. When Harold was denied the posthumous award of even a lesser decoration, Borden concluded – quite unfairly – that it was due to the resentment and hostile influence of Hutton and his friends.[28]

Borden's mixture of pride and grievance was an acute example of a more general feeling among Canadians, a tendency to exaggerate the significance of their contribution to the war. The schoolchild who allegedly explained Britain's early reverses in the war by the fact that the Canadians had not yet arrived, helped to symbolize the prevailing mood of military self-congratulation.[29] Canadians went to South Africa as imperialists; they returned, for the most part, as nationalists.[30]

One consequence of this new pride in Canada's military performance was a willingness in Parliament to treat the country's professional soldiers more reasonably. In 1901, after years of false starts, a pension system for the staff and permanent corps was adopted with the support of both parties. Another result was growing pressure for Canadian officers to fill appointments now held by British officers. Even before the war the selection of Major Stone to command the Canadian artillery had provoked sharp resentment. In July 1900 Stone resigned. His grievance was that Borden would not promote him to full colonel to safeguard his precedence over Canadian officers, but it was apparent that he had not adjusted to colonial conditions.[31] His place remained vacant.

Two other appointments also seemed appropriate for Canadians with experience in command and on the staff in South Africa, those of Quartermaster General and of Commandant of the Royal Military College at Kingston. Borden had correctly identified Foster as a partisan of General Hutton and made no secret of his desire to see him go.[32] However, it was Colonel Kitson of the Royal Military College who was the first to resign, seizing an opportunity to become British military attaché in Washington. Automatically, the War Office found a replacement, Major R. N. R. Reade, and accordingly notified Ottawa.

The British were premature. No request for a replacement for Kitson had been sent and Borden was making his own plans to fill the position. Soon after the 1900 elections he proposed to Laurier that the position should go to the commander of the first contingent in South Africa, Colonel Otter, "an excellent administrator and disciplinarian," while Lieutenant Colonel Pelletier from the same contingent "could do the work of the Quartermaster General's office better and more acceptably than it is being done by Foster."[33] The officers themselves were also making their plans. Foster was anxious to get command of the military college; he persuaded Otter to advise Minto that if the Quartermaster General went to Kingston, Otter would happily replace him.[34] Reade's nomination came unwelcomed into all these calculations. It was left to Minto to devise a solution. Neither he nor the British had forgotten the disastrous consequences of General Cameron's appointment. The War Office suggestion was unhelpful: the aged Lord Aylmer, already the only senior Canadian officer, might be retired to make room for others, leaving the British share of senior positions unchanged.[35] Minto's alternative was to offer appointments to selected Canadian officers on the staffs of the British garrisons at Halifax and Esquimalt.

By February 1901 the Minister had withdrawn his objections to Major Reade and thus the command of the military college was retained by a British officer. By June Foster left, resigning prematurely on the promise of an attractive staff position in the War Office. The promise may perhaps have been a decoy, for when he returned to England he found that the vacancy had not materialized and he was obliged to accept an obscure regimental position.[36] His successor was neither Otter nor Pelletier but Colonel William Henry Cotton, an elderly permanent force gunner whose only active service had been with the militia in the Fenian raids, thirty-five years before.

A more general grievance in the Canadian militia was the automatic seniority accorded to British officers. Two sections in the militia's *Regulations and Orders* had been cancelled by Hutton because he claimed that they infringed on the principle. In July 1900 the Minister had them restored. Borden also obtained new powers to promote militia officers to the rank of full colonel and used his new authority to reward senior Canadian officers for their services in South Africa. To Lord Minto and Colonial Office observers, however, these attempts to give Canadians added status in their own force were dismissed as the wish of "one or two Parliamentary Colonels."[37]

British officials complained partly because they believed that Canadians were neglecting more substantive military responsibilities. The reports of the Leach Committee, for all Minto's efforts, had not brought forth a clear statement of defence policy from the Canadian government. Three months after the report was handed to Borden an official copy was finally forwarded to the Governor General with the statement that it was "under consideration."[38] In July 1901 the War Office asked for a progress report. Another year passed before any reply was forthcoming. In his usual fulsome style, Borden expanded on his achievement in building departmental corps, expanding the staff, and creating a Reserve of Officers. There was now even a prospect of transferring the old Stores Branch to military control. More would have been done but for the work of preparing the contingents for South Africa. The report was forwarded under Minto's sour minute that it was "extremely plausible and in some points entirely misleading."[39]

At the Imperial Conference in the summer of 1902, St John Brodrick, the secretary of state for war, used the occasion to subject the state of Canadian defence to its customary condemnation, using O'Grady Haly's annual reports as his ammunition. Borden (knighted in the Coronation honours) was present to reply. Pointing out that the British criticisms had been based on observations extending over only a few years, he insisted, with some justice, that there had been a dramatic improvement in the Canadian militia since 1896.[40]

The wider goal of the conference was to arrange for permanent mili-

tary contributions from the colonies for imperial defence. Since neither
Laurier nor Borden had much sympathy for such schemes, their intransigence was glossed over in a conference memorandum stating that, as the
defence of Canada would be the most difficult military problem the Empire could face, the primary duty of Canadians would be to provide their
own efficient militia.[41]

In his address Brodrick had sharply condemned the only Canadian
military reform he did mention, the adoption of the Ross rifle. Steadily
since 1870 Canada had been making herself self-sufficient in military
supplies. Uniforms, cartridges, artillery shells were now joined by the
rifle. During the South African War Borden had found it impossible to
persuade either the War Office to make more Lee-Enfields available or
to prevail on a British firm to manufacture them in Canada. He was
therefore highly susceptible when Sir Charles Ross, a Scottish sportsman,
offered to manufacture his own pattern of rifle in Canada. Borden
formed a committee under Colonel Otter to test the weapon. Although
the tests found most of the defects which were to plague the weapon
throughout its life, the glib Sir Charles was able to persuade the committee members to endorse his rifle rather than the official Lee-Enfield.
It was particularly fortunate for Ross that Borden had included Sam
Hughes on the committee. Between them, Borden and Hughes were to
be the most powerful men in determining Canadian military policy for
the next fifteen years and both men's reputations were inextricably linked
with the standing of the Ross rifle. From the beginning, Hughes was a
passionate advocate of the weapon. In time, the rifle was to prove a tra-
gically expensive experiment in military and economic nationalism. To
Canadians in 1902 it was a self-confident rebuff to British industrial
domination.[42]

O'Grady Haly had not been consulted about the Ross rifle. He attended the trials unofficially and was invited to offer his comments only
four weeks after the contract had been signed. He was critical of the
competence of the committee and his observations on the rifle's failings –
the difficulty in extracting the spent cartridge and its lack of robustness –
were to be fully justified by time. However, his advice came too late and
would almost certainly have been suspect as coming from a man bound
to sustain the British arms industry against colonial initiative.[43]

O'Grady Haly's modest role in the adoption of the Ross exemplified
the small part he played in the Militia Department. So did the fact that
he now corresponded with Borden largely through the Deputy Minister,
Colonel Pinault. Yet, like his predecessors, O'Grady Haly could not en-

tirely escape from the battles of political colonels. In October 1900 troops were sent from Montreal to Valleyfield to guard a factory against striking workers. For reasons of protocol, not politics, Lieutenant Colonel J. P. Cooke, the only Liberal commanding officer in Montreal, refused to accept the orders of Lieutenant Colonel Minden Cole to call out his regiment. The refusal led to a sensational altercation on the floor of the Montreal drill hall, ending when Cole placed Cooke under arrest. Since Colonel Cole was also a friend and financial adviser of the minister, the political hazards of the case were considerable. The General's solution – to release Cooke from arrest but to deliver a reprimand as well – proved sufficiently judicious to win the Minister's approval.[44]

O'Grady Haly's success in escaping destruction in the ensuing legal battle between Cooke and Cole was a tribute to his luck and dexterity and to his skill in adapting to Canadian conditions. The *Military Gazette* treated him with conspicuously more sympathy than any of his predecessors, praised his annual reports, and even gave him the credit for a more tactful tone in correspondence emanating from militia headquarters.[45] When his first year was up Borden was happy to obtain an extension. "In many respects he has done excellent work," the Minister wrote to Minto, "& I firmly believe that at the present juncture it will be for the best interests of the Militia to retain him."[46] With a further brief extension in December 1901, O'Grady Haly managed to spend a total of two years in command of the Canadian militia.

Nevertheless, when he again retired in the summer of 1902, it was as a disappointed man. Despite his loyal service and the evident satisfaction he had given his Canadian superiors, the War Office was impatiently waiting with a new candidate for the appointment. The imperial policies interrupted with the departure of Hutton were now ready for a new impetus. In hope of being confirmed in the rank of major general, O'Grady Haly had remained in Canada until the last possible moment. It was to no avail. Probably the fact that he was "acceptable in high places" in the Dominion helped to tell against him in British circles. To Lord Minto, indeed, the elderly officer had become a roadblock for reform: "He is a very good fellow & socially popular but I cannot honestly consider him the man to command the Militia which with all its great faults of administration has certainly now some keen soldiers who want to see it improve & who are critical of the ability & energy of an Imperial officer sent to command them."[47] O'Grady Haly's claim for promotion was rejected and it was as a colonel that he returned to the obscurity of retirement.[48]

Dundonald

Last Struggle for Authority

If the British had been in a somewhat indecent haste to get rid of O'Grady Haly it was because, after considerable difficulty, they had found a successor fit to take up Hutton's work. Major General Douglas Mackinnon Baillie Hamilton, twelfth Earl of Dundonald, had already added a respectable chapter to the history of a distinguished political and military family. As an officer in the Life Guards he had played an heroic part in the Desert Column of the Gordon Relief Expedition of 1885. In the South African War he had gained distinction as a cavalry general and wide fame as the first commander to enter beleaguered Ladysmith. During the war Canadian troops had come under his command and had felt the impact of his personality. Dundonald was more than a professional soldier. Like some of his ancestors he was also an inventor and a politician. A tent of his design was demonstrated in Canadian militia camps in the summer of 1901. As a peer he had taken his place in the House of Lords as a Liberal. Dundonald had also become an enthusiast for "citizen armies," an interest which led Brodrick to appoint him to an important committee to reform the English yeomanry.[1]

These seemed impressive credentials for a difficult post, but it was also true that Dundonald was a second choice. When Minto asked Colonel Kitson, the former commandant of the military college, to suggest suitable generals, he was told that the best man would be Major

General Horace Smith Dorrien, who had commanded the first contingent of Canadians in South Africa. However, Smith Dorrien had been given a more attractive position elsewhere.² Minto himself made it clear to Lord Roberts, now the commander-in-chief, that a great deal would depend on the capacity of the officer chosen:

On present conditions the position of the GOC here is undoubtedly a difficult one. I have often said it is impossible, but if the conditions of the appointment even in its present lines could be made clear I should not take such a pessimistic view provided the right man is appointed, and as to him it is absolutely necessary that a distinguished soldier with a recognized reputation not only as a fighter but as thoroughly up in his profession should be selected, there are such men that Canadian troops have served under who would be received here with enthusiasm and whose reputation would nullify corrupt opposition.

Minto went on to make it clear that his first choice would be Major General E. A. Alderson, who had not only commanded Canadians during the war but whose social assets "would do much for his popularity."³

As for Dundonald, Canada was not even his first offer. He had been suggested for the command in the new Commonwealth of Australia but had rejected it for family reasons. It was Hutton, who had also done well in South Africa, who went there instead. Interestingly, the former GOC regarded Dundonald with scorn: "No really good man of experience or with aspirations elsewhere will look at such a difficult and ill-paid job!"⁴ Hutton may have been jealous that others would try to succeed where he himself had failed, but he was not alone in having reservations about Dundonald. Few of those who had served in Canada knew much about him but Kitson's observations were hardly hopeful: "... he has the reputation of being a good fellow though rather of the dismal order."⁵ In the circumstances, he concluded, Canada would probably do as well with him as with other candidates still in the field and Minto, also swallowing his reservations, concurred. To Laurier the Governor General reported that Dundonald was known to be able: "He used to appear to me rather quiet and reserved – not undesirable qualities possibly."⁶

The Canadian ministers did their best to make sure that Dundonald would understand in advance his status in Canada. Like O'Grady Haly he was asked to study the series of memoranda which had emerged from the Hutton dispute. Canadian newspapers were initially sceptical that the new General would fare much better than his predecessors. Opposition journals predicted that political interference would soon make his position untenable. The Brantford *Courier*, summing up many arguments about the difficulty of the command, predicted that it would be a miracle if Dundonald succeeded:

In the first place the advisability of appointing an Imperial officer to the position is very much open to question. He is of necessity not in touch with Canada or Canadian feeling and he brings with him notions which do not successfully apply to the control of volunteers.

In the second place, such an officer does not have full command. He is subordinate to the Minister of Militia and on every hand his best efforts are thwarted by the circumstances that for political reasons this, that, or the other move cannot be made despite the fact that they should be made in the best interests of the force.[7]

The new GOC reached Canada on July 24, 1902, leaving his invalid wife in London. "I quite see the difficulty or rather the difficulties for these appear to be many, of the post I am about to fill," he wrote to Minto, " – but after all one can only do one's best and this I am prepared to do ..."[8] Excited crowds met Dundonald on his arrival, anxious for a glimpse of a famous war hero. Their reception was in contrast with the cool and practical advice the new General received from Laurier soon after his arrival in Ottawa. "You must not take the Militia seriously," the Prime Minister told him, "for though it is useful for suppressing internal disturbances, it will not be required for the defence of the country, as the Monroe doctrine protects us against enemy aggression."[9] This was disconcerting advice for a man who, like Hutton, had come to Canada with the intention of preparing the country against American invasion. Dundonald was also anxious to apply his own ideas of a "citizen army" to his new command. He had spoken in England of "a well-instructed skeleton to be filled up in time of war with those who had been able to give less time to military pursuits but were physically sound and good shots ..."[10] The actual volunteer militia in Canada, with its disproportionate ratio of officers to other ranks, would provide the skeleton while the flesh would be formed by men with a limited knowledge of drill and a chance for regular rifle practice. As Dundonald inspected the militia during the summer and fall of 1902 he saw how his "citizen army" scheme could be applied to the Dominion. He also found most of the problems his predecessors had noted. The rural militia battalions were still largely armed with the useless Snider. Since fifty cents a day was even more inadequate pay in times of prosperity than during a depression, militia captains were having desperate difficulty in filling the ranks of their companies. Annual camps meant that they had to face the problem twice as often. The city corps still spent no time in camp. During the grand reviews for the Duke of Cornwall in the summer of 1901, O'Grady Haly had been shocked to find that the splendidly drilled city battalions were unable to cook their own meals or even to put up their own tents. Yet to suggest that the city corps should go to camp was still treated as a defiance of the rights of employers.[11]

The new General also rediscovered the deplorable state of the permanent corps. Inevitably, the South African War, with its demonstration of the effectiveness of an irregular force against a large professional army, had raised the self-esteem of militia officers and reinforced their prejudice against the permanent schools. The schools had also deteriorated. The perennial problem of desertion was aggravated by rising wages and the failure of the government to repair or replace unsanitary barracks. O'Grady Haly had helped to win his officers and men a pension scheme but his efforts to raise their pay had been unavailing.[12] Men who would enlist for the forty cents a day of a permanent force private were not likely to become competent instructors for the militia. As the schools deteriorated, an increasing proportion of militia officers obtained their certificates from local, provisional schools.

The mood of the militia was expectant and critical. Perhaps Lord Dundonald had advantages in dealing with such a situation which not even Hutton had had. The new GOC had enjoyed a sufficiently varied career and enough financial independence to escape from some of the military stereotypes which had inhibited even his abler predecessors. Like Hutton, he planned to take his command by storm. At Toronto on September 1 he delivered the opening day speech at the Exhibition before the largest crowd in the fair's history. That evening, in the more subdued surroundings of the National Club, he called for officers "so thoroughly trained that there should be no need for them to learn their lessons on the dead bodies of the men who followed them in time of war."[13] It was an appropriately earnest sentiment and it won wide approval. The Conservative *Mail & Empire* reported that Dundonald was a man of "refined and attractive personality," while the Liberal *Globe* simply observed: "Lord Dundonald will do."[14]

One of Dundonald's admirers was Colonel Sam Hughes. The Con-

servative colonel had by his own account performed astonishing feats
of daring as soon as he had been granted a military appointment in
South Africa. These deeds had been reported in detail to friends in
Canada. It was all the more aggravating to Hughes, therefore, to find
himself suddenly ordered home. The real reason was that some of his
indiscreet letters, full of criticism of his British superiors, had been
published in the Capetown papers. Hughes preferred to believe that it
was due to the malevolence of General Hutton. Back in Canada the
Colonel soon recovered his public standing as his warlike feats with
Turpin, his servant, passed into legend or oblivion.[15] Borden, anxious to
keep him as an ally, made him a member of the Ross rifle committee and
appointed him to the Board of Visitors of the Royal Military College.
When the time limit would have forced Hughes out of the militia,
Borden promoted him to full colonel and created the nominal post of
Staff Officer for Railway Intelligence for him.

Minto was furious when Dundonald responded to Hughes's overtures,
claiming that he was now really a man without influence.[16] Dundonald
saw matters differently, recognizing the weight Hughes could exert on
both sides of the House of Commons and perhaps overlooking the erratic
qualities of his ally. To Roberts, Dundonald predicted that Hughes
"... may be either the strongest supporter or the most effective enemy of
the Imperial side of the matter."[17]

When Dundonald returned to Ottawa after his preliminary inspection of the militia, he warned the Minister that he would be asking for
trained personnel from England to set up a proper Engineer Branch, to
provide qualified musketry instructors and to set up a school of signalling. A few months later he presented Borden with plans for an intelligence department and a Corps of Guides. In the absence of satisfactory
maps, the Guides would be available with knowledge of their own
vicinity, a valuable asset in meeting an American invasion.[18] In a speech
to Toronto militia officers on November 19, 1902, he denounced those
who suggested that Canada had reached a millennium where no defences
were needed and then turned to more practical problems of the force.
Too little was done for the private soldiers in the militia. Better men
would be recruited, he suggested, if they could at least be provided with
facilities to take a bath in camp.[19]

These suggestions were all ancillary to the plans for a new approach
to militia organization which had been taking shape in Dundonald's
mind. His "citizen army" plan would offer Canada a force of a hundred

thousand men. The cadres of key officers and instructors would be trained at a central camp with the permanent force. Then, at district camps, this training would be passed on to the "skeleton," the rest of the militia officers, non-commissioned officers, and a few privates. For the "flesh and blood," Dundonald wanted compulsory military training for all boys between the ages of fourteen and eighteen. One feature of his plan would be company armouries built not merely to store uniforms and arms but to serve as lecture halls and centres for military activity throughout the year.

The skeleton scheme demanded some major new spending. Arms and equipment for an army of a hundred thousand men and uniforms of "greenish brown" would have to be purchased and stored. There would have to be a few officers and non-commissioned officers in each militia unit who would be paid to give most of their time to militia work. The permanent corps would have to be extended to provide training facilities throughout the country. Land would be needed for a big new central camp and for several local camp sites.[20]

If the government had really seen its militia policy in terms of providing protection against American invasion, Dundonald's plan would have offered as cheap a military organization as could be had. In fact, as Laurier had tried to make clear to the General on his arrival, and quite to the contrary of a series of minutes from imperial and colonial conferences, Canadian defence policy had no such basis.

Dundonald had ignored the advice. Instead, he prepared his annual report for 1902 to publicize his own views. Part I would consist of observations and criticisms of the existing militia; Part II would compare militia deficiencies with the Leach Committee recommendations and give an account of his skeleton army proposals, with all their implications of mobilizing for war against the United States. Once the report was published, public opinion would coalesce behind him and he could defy the government not to carry out his programme.[21]

In 1899 Hutton had been astonished by Borden's willingness to publish a damning report. By 1903 the Minister had lost his innocence. Hutton's second report had been severely edited after his departure and those of O'Grady Haly had been closely examined.[22] Borden had no difficulty in divining Dundonald's intentions and he refused to allow Part II to be published. Even Part I was mildly edited.[23]

Dundonald was indignant. Rumours of the suppression of part of the General's report were soon circulating in Ottawa. So was a report that

Dundonald had recommended changes that would cost the country over twelve million dollars. Although the estimate was remarkably close to his own private calculation, Dundonald angrily repudiated the rumour.[24] In Parliament and in the press there were predictable demands that the whole report be published, pressures nourished by the General through occasional, oblique, public references to its contents. Borden insisted that it remain a confidential document which he would show to the Leader of the Opposition and to members selected by him.[25] The Minister's offer was not accepted.

Rumours of conflict in the Militia Department had barely been laid to rest before Dundonald was again the centre of news. At Hamilton on April 23 the General, William Mulock, and F. D. Monk, a French-Canadian Conservative MP, were all speakers at a St George's Day banquet. By some accounts Mulock's speech, describing militarism as "the enemy of true liberty," was received with markedly less enthusiasm than Dundonald's declaration that the "northern nations of the world must be the dominant nations" or his assertion that what he sought in the reform of the militia was "a condition in which when he pressed the button, the regiments throughout Canada would turn out at once."[26] This disturbing notion, together with reports of interviews Dundonald had granted on his way to Hamilton, gained wide publicity. Henri Bourassa, the French-Canadian nationalist, used the press reports as a text to warn his former Liberal colleagues that control of military policy in Canada was slipping out of their hands. Illustrating his contention with quotations from a number of Dundonald's speeches, Bourassa pointed out how far the General's publicly expressed views differed from official government statements: "The gentleman who leaves the other side to take command of our militia has no intentions of becoming one of our own, and does not come here to take his responsibility as a Canadian officer. He comes here to introduce into the military organization of Canada such reforms as may be pointed out by the head of the War Office in the mother country."[27]

During the ensuing parliamentary debate, Bourassa's speech goaded some English-speaking imperialists to proclaim their full support for the General's views. His defenders included Sam Hughes and even a number of Liberals. Neither Laurier nor Borden accepted Bourassa's particular charges against Dundonald but both men used the debate as an opportunity to reiterate their insistence on the subordination of the military command to the government. "Do not let us misunderstand this point," said Borden, "that although he is an imperial officer, that fact does not give him any additional power or authority in this country."[28] Laurier's warning was even sharper: "If the General Commanding the Militia has advice to tender, it is not his right – I say it deliberately – to offer advice to the public, but it is his duty to offer it to the minister, and for that policy the minister shall be responsible."[29]

Dundonald felt no apparent need to heed the warnings. He took comfort from the speeches of the English-speaking MPs and believed that his position had been strengthened by their support. He also found that Borden was willing to allow him to proceed with a long list of reforms which had previously been delayed. Like Hutton in the summer of 1899, Dundonald believed that a major political battle had been won, although he was sensible enough to see that there were still difficulties ahead. Writing in June 1903, Dundonald recorded his impressions of the government's attitude to defence: "The mainspring of the difficulty is this confessed belief of some members of the Government that military expenditures and preparations are in themselves mistaken and unnecessary. In their eyes, the Militia is merely a make-believe to keep the Jingoes and ultra-loyalists quiet: and this belief as to military preparations is not confined to politicians. It is widespread among the people and is commonly expressed both in conversation and in the press."[30]

By the end of the year Dundonald should have had little reason to complain of the progress being made. Within the department the stores and engineer branches had at last been transferred from civil to military control. Units of medical and army service corps had been organized and had attended the annual camps. Dundonald had been able to try out the first instalment of his skeleton army scheme by calling to camp only the officers, non-commissioned officers, and a small proportion of the privates. It had not been a great success. In MD 2, normally the heart of military enthusiasm in the Dominion, almost half the allocated places were unfilled. Even the arrangements for baths were not as popular as Dundonald had expected: a reporter for the Toronto *News* observed that "the infrequent spectacle of a militiaman armed with soap and towel making his way to the 'bath tub' line is greeted with howls of derision from his comrades."[31] Other reforms, such as better medical and cooking facilities, were better received and Borden was persuaded that poor attendance was due to inadequate drill pay rather than the new system of training.[32]

In the autumn of 1903 the Minister brought in large supplementary estimates for his department, asking for money to buy enough arms and equipment for a wartime militia strength of a hundred thousand. Another long-standing issue was apparently resolved by a cabinet minute of October 29, 1903 establishing the respective responsibilities of the officers of the military staff. The General Officer Commanding was not given exclusive access to the Minister: the Quartermaster General, Director General of Ordnance, and Director General of Medical Services were also advisers in their own fields, but neither was there any notion of collegiate responsibility:

The General Officer Commanding shall be charged with the military command and discipline of the militia, shall issue General Orders and hold periodic inspections of the militia.

He shall be the principal adviser of the Minister of Militia and Defence on all military questions and shall be charged with the control of the branches of the Adjutant General, the Director-General of Military Intelligence and Military Secretary and the general supervision of all other military branches.

He shall be charged with the general distribution and localization of the militia and with the selection and proposal to the Minister of Militia and Defence of fit and proper persons to be recommended for commissions in the militia, of fit and proper officers for promotions, for staff and other military appointments, and for military honors and rewards ...[33]

The year 1903 saw many long-awaited changes in the militia. Borden planned one more: the first thorough overhaul of the Militia Act since 1883. His plans went beyond the elimination of obscure passages and obsolete phrases. The new act would recognize the Canadian mood of self-confidence in military affairs by wiping out provisions which gave automatic seniority to British officers over militia officers of the same rank. In future, the wartime command of the force would not automatically pass to the British general in command at Halifax. The section which delegated royal authority over the militia to the Governor General would be omitted. Above all, the new version of the Militia Act would meet a demand intermittently expressed since 1875: the command of the Canadian militia would henceforth be open to Canadians.[34]

The Governor General reacted to Borden's proposed changes with predictable dismay. Some of them were inevitable. It was no longer possible to justify the rule that wartime command would go to the senior British officer at Halifax. In July 1900, after a voluminous correspondence had failed to win War Office support for his battle with Hutton and Minto, Lord William Seymour had resigned.[35] When the Governor General arranged that the administrator in his absence would thereafter be the Chief Justice of the Canadian Supreme Court, the British demoted the Halifax command to a colonel's vacancy.[36] Other changes had to be resisted. Although Minto was annoyed that his own official relationship with the militia was so unceremoniously cut off, his main battle had to be waged against the possibility that a Canadian might get command of the force. Not only was no Canadian officer remotely qualified for the position but he was certain that "some utterly incompetent public favorite or political supporter" would be pushed into the post. Even if good men could be found, "they would necessarily be so crippled by political and social influence as to render their position useless."[37]

After persuading his ministers not to go ahead with the bill during the current session of Parliament, Minto began hunting for some means to preserve British influence while satisfying Canadian ambitions. He was convinced that the real motive for the change was the pressure of some Canadian officers for professional advancement. To meet their demands he returned to his old suggestion that places might be found for Canadians on the staffs of the British fortresses at Esquimalt and Halifax. He also revived the old suggestion that the British and Canadian commands might be united under a British lieutenant general at Ottawa, serving both governments at once.[38] Lord Dundonald, who had now been promoted to the rank of lieutenant general, warmly endorsed the idea: it would liberate him from an unsatisfactory subordination to Canadian politicians. With paternal firmness the General assured Minto that the majority of good militia officers wanted no one but a British commander: "They dread the appointment of a Canadian General picked from the politician class, from those who have the 'pull,' one who could show no qualifications at all adequate to the post. The desire of the Militia at large is to be well-governed, to be commanded by one who is a soldier, one who knows his work, one who is moved by a sense of justice, and one who is not the mere register of the Minister's will."[39]

At the Colonial Office, Minto's reports on the intentions of his government made "dreary and most unsatisfactory reading."[40] Rather more than the Governor General or Lord Dundonald, the British officials remembered that it was the Canadians who had the ultimate power to control their defence policy. While the Colonial Defence Committee drafted long memoranda with elaborate schemes for a command structure in Canada, more realistic officials began to conclude that, as an instrument of British policy, the GOC was in fact largely ineffective. The point had been underlined in the Bourassa debate on Dundonald's "educational efforts." One senior Colonial Office official, Sir John Anderson, commented perceptively:

If the Minister is weak, inefficient or obstructive, we have no means of proving it, except by means of private and confidential communications which we cannot use. The Governor General may, of course, dismiss him, but a Governor General is as helpless as regards justifying his action as we are. We have no legitimate means therefore of letting the Canadian public know that things are altogether wrong and rotten except through a Minister who may be the real cause of the whole mischief and over whom we have no control whatever.[41]

The British were not totally without means of influence. Their standing pledge to come to Canada's defence implied a right to some voice in its military affairs. Canadian governments were still sensitive to unfavourable publicity released in London.[42] Canadian ministers were susceptible to flattery. One condition for delaying the 1903 Militia Bill was that Borden would be invited to London for special consultation with the British authorities. It was December before the arrangements could be made. Sir Frederick Borden found himself invited to participate in a session of the Committee of Imperial Defence, the first colonial statesman to be so honoured.[43]

By December 1903 the British had largely reconsidered their position in Canada. Anderson's viewpoint that the power of the GOC was largely illusory had come to be shared more widely. It would be better to secure formal military commitments from Canada than to risk friction by supporting Minto's anguished protests. When Borden attended the meeting of the committee on December 11 he found that the changes of imperial significance in his draft legislation were quickly conceded. Perhaps carried away by the ease of his victory the Canadian Minister stayed to discuss a wide range of British proposals for which he carried no brief. Canada was invited to take over the defence of Halifax and Esquimalt, provided that she would keep them up to British standards. Canadians should consider raising a battalion to serve in India. The disadvantages of losing the British GOC would be alleviated if Canada would invite senior British generals to inspect her militia periodically. To all these ideas Borden apparently gave a reserved consent.[44]

Borden may have left the meeting with a sense of accomplishment but he soon had reason for second thoughts. In Canada his participation in the Committee of Imperial Defence provoked suspicion, particularly in French Canada. Those sections of Canadian opinion which might have welcomed signs of imperial consultation were equally inclined to deplore Borden's errand. The Prime Minister was displeased that the supplementary propositions had been considered and at least tentatively approved by Borden. Most dissatisfied of all was Lord Minto for the British had surrendered ground which he would have defended to the end. By now the Governor General had lost the capacity to judge the question objectively, forwarding extracts from strongly Conservative and pro-imperial newspapers as "fairly to indicate public opinion in Canada."[45] Dundonald, who tried to strengthen the Governor General's case with his own memoranda, was equally dismayed.[46] As for Borden, he was obliged to write a formal letter disowning any suggestion that Canada should add to her military responsibilities. In Britain, where the precise decisions reached at the meeting had also become a matter for dispute, Borden's letter was added to the official minutes, a forlorn footnote to what had otherwise seemed an inspiring imperial occasion.[47]

Borden could hardly regard his venture into diplomacy as a great success. Still, he had won British approval for his Militia Bill in the face of Minto's open and Dundonald's secret resistance. Early in the 1904 session it was presented to Parliament. Most of the new provisions were welcomed, even by the opposition. There would be higher pay for the permanent corps, graduated drill pay of up to a dollar a day for militiamen, and the chance for officers to rise to the rank of brigadier general and to retire as a militia major general. The maximum time allowed for annual drill was increased from sixteen to thirty days. The perennial grievances surrounding the militia obligation to serve in aid of the civil power were at least partially relieved by a new provision that henceforth the permanent force would do the bulk of the work. The Minister could congratulate himself that in an election year he had presented a generally popular bill. One Ontario Conservative demanded that MPs be allowed to consult their constituencies before approving such expensive legislation.[48] Henri Bourassa tried in vain to have a ceiling of fifty thousand men applied to militia strength, an obvious challenge to Dundonald's plan for a hundred thousand–man army.[49] Such critics were in a minority.

The real issue was Section 30, allowing a Canadian to command the militia. Dundonald's success in winning the support of Sam Hughes was demonstrated by the Conservative Colonel's total opposition to the change. If a Canadian were wanted, Hughes insisted, it must be a Canadian who had risen to a suitable rank in the British Army.[50] Colonel Tisdale, Hughes's fellow Conservative, offered the kind of arguments that had already been presented by Lord Minto: "It does not matter what party is in power, once you get this law upon the statute book, the politicians are not going to be easy until they force upon the country some friend of theirs whether he be fit for the position or not."[51]

Borden's reply to the Conservatives was one which had already failed to placate the Governor General: he had no intention of appointing a Canadian for the time being. Instead, hoping to put his imperialist adversaries on the defensive, he suggested that the command of the militia should be as open to an Australian or a South African as to a Canadian or British officer.[52]

By then Borden's thinking was already moving beyond the problems of appointing a General Officer Commanding. On April 15, 1904, three weeks after he had introduced his bill, he reported to Lord Minto that he was planning to create a Militia Council, with a Chief of the General Staff who would, "for the present & probably for some time to come," be a British officer, and with three other military members. The Minister, his Deputy, and the Secretary of the department would represent the civilian interest. Borden also suggested that an Inspector General would be appointed, a British officer to be paid and selected by Canada on terms analogous to the appointment of the General Officer Commanding.[53]

The proposals can have come as no surprise to Minto. They were modelled on the Esher Committee reforms in the British Army which had recently swept away the appointment of commander-in-chief and created a new Army Council, resembling the Board of Admiralty. However remotely Canadian practice resembled the British command system, the War Office had always been a distant model for the Militia Department. Borden may have had a first hand opportunity to consider the British changes when he was in London for the Committee of Imperial Defence. He may also have been influenced by a memorandum submitted to Lord Minto by Sir Charles Parsons, the latest British commander at Halifax. Parsons proposed the creation of a "Defence Council," uniting the British and Canadian commands under the chairmanship of the Governor General. While Borden would have had no sympathy for the overall structure of such a system, his own Militia

Council bore a close resemblance to the staff structure proposed by Parsons.[54]

At first Minto had little fondness for Borden's new plan. Even if the Chief of General Staff were a British officer he would be too junior in rank to possess real influence. Somehow, he urged the Colonial Secretary, the Canadians had to be prevented from gaining unimpeded control over their own military forces.[55] However, before either Minto or the opposition could do more to save the British position, it had been hopelessly jeopardized by Dundonald himself.

Far from being satisfied by his achievements in 1903, the General had continued his campaign to win influence over the government's military policy. The idea of his hundred thousand–man army was expounded on a variety of platforms, regardless of the absence of real ministerial approval. In November 1903 Dundonald set out for British Columbia, announcing the formation of new militia units along the way in the style of a barn-storming politician. On the Pacific coast he toured the area in dispute between Canada and the United States and later in Vancouver told a largely Conservative audience that the Liberal government's complaints about the boundary settlement were almost groundless.[56]

The General also continued to cause friction in the Militia Department. When the military stores were transferred to a new Ordnance Stores Corps, Borden insisted that five of the former superintendents should become lieutenant colonels, a rank they had previously held as militia officers. Dundonald attributed the demand to political influence. The same motive was held to underlie the Minister's refusal to grant a Conservative colonel an extension of his term in command. When Borden refused to allow the General to reprint a set of instructional placards, it was taken as a personal affront. Finally, there was a battle over Dundonald's second annual report. Determined to frustrate ministerial censorship, he kept his draft until well after the deadline for submission. Instead of putting his recommendations together in a special section he spread them through the text, deliberately making reference to the suppressed Part II of the previous year. Undeterred by his General's tactics, Borden revised the report even more ruthlessly than he had the year before.[57]

The creation of a Militia Council, which Dundonald naturally opposed, would have left him little place in the militia system. The appointment of Inspector General, for which he might have been destined, did not include membership of the Council. He did not wait to bring matters to a head. For some time the General had been increasing the number of cavalry regiments in the Eastern Townships of Quebec as a safeguard against American invasion. In March 1904 he announced that a defunct local infantry regiment would be turned into the 13th Scottish Light Dragoons. Lieutenant Colonel R. W. Smart, a Montreal businessman, was appointed commanding officer and told to work with the local cavalry brigadier, Lieutenant Colonel Fred Whitley. The expansion of militia cavalry in the townships meant that qualified officers were hard to find. To fill the gaps Smart decided to appoint a number of local dignitaries, among them Dr Wilfred Pickel, mayor of Sweetsburg, warden of Missisquoi County, and owner of the local rifle range.

Sydney Fisher, the minister of agriculture and cabinet spokesmen for the Eastern Townships, soon learned that the new corps, like others in the area, was being officered by strong Conservatives. At least five of the men proposed for commissions, including Dr Pickel, were related to the local Conservative leader, Senator George Baker. Accordingly, Fisher warned Whitley and Smart of the political implications of their selections and tried with only limited success to find them some Liberal alternatives. As the drill season approached Whitley and Smart grew anxious about the progress of their organization. Finally, they submitted a list of their proposed officers, including the influential Dr Pickel as major. Fisher, who conveniently happened to be acting for Borden in his absence, examined the list, deleted Pickel's name, and allowed the remainder to go forward for publication.[58]

When he learned from the Governor General what Fisher had done, Dundonald was furious. In Montreal on June 3 he learned from Whitley and Smart that the Minister of Agriculture was still interfering with the regiment. That evening Dundonald spoke at a banquet given by Montreal militia officers: "Political intrigue, intrigue for personal advancement, other than that deserved by military efficiency, is dormant in times of national peril. But when peace comes and the vigilance of a nation is at rest, political wiles are active and political schemers begin to weave their nets." To illustrate his text Dundonald went on to tell his audience how the Minister of Agriculture had prevented Dr Pickel from serving his country:

I feel certain that had Mr. Fisher's life led him to soldiering instead of to agriculture, he would feel annoyed, perhaps on personal grounds, by the extraordinary lack of etiquette involved in scratching out the name of a gentleman put forward

by a man whose business it is to find efficient officers for the Militia. (Applause)
But on personal grounds, I don't mind in the least. Lack of etiquette affects me
little; I have been two years in Ottawa. (Laughter) It is not on personal grounds
that I inform you of this but it is on national grounds. (Hear, hear) I feel anxious,
profoundly anxious, that the Militia of Canada may be kept away from party
politics.[59]

Dundonald's outburst had a slightly delayed reaction. A Liberal officer, Lieutenant Colonel Fred Hibbard, tried to answer Dundonald's
allegations on the spot and, perhaps to protect the General from his
indiscretion, persuaded the only newspaper reporter present not to report the speech.[60] It was June 8, five days later, before details were
widely known and June 9 before the Montreal *Gazette* published the
authoritative account. Dundonald, who had been waiting for the publicity, proudly acknowledged his words when challenged by Borden.[61]

On June 10, to a packed House of Commons, Sydney Fisher formally
denied the allegation that he had meddled with Smart's regiment for
political reasons. His sole concern had been to eliminate an unqualified
officer. Sir Frederick Borden had barely ended his own speech supporting Fisher when Sam Hughes unveiled the opposition's secret weapon.
It was a statement from Dundonald, full of names, dates, and details
and prepared for Hughes to read. Borden, who had received a copy only
as the House was assembling, was completely unprepared. After hearing
the damning charges Fisher could only protest that he had intervened
to prevent the regiment from becoming a Conservative machine. A tired
Laurier joined the debate to explain that Dundonald was a stranger
to the townships, slipped on the English translation of *étranger,* and
called the General a foreigner. The opposition clamour rose. If Dundonald had sought to make his case a major issue in the 1904 elections,
he seemed to have succeeded in the first round.[62]

Having placed his case in Hughes's hands, Dundonald ignored Borden's suggestion that he should remain in Ottawa and hurried away to
the militia camp at London. He would defy the government to dismiss
him. After the disastrous debate on June 10 the Liberal cabinet soon
recovered its composure. It was Lord Minto who was in a terrible
dilemma. However anxious he might be to condemn political interference in the militia, he could not support Dundonald's action. "He
was absolutely in the wrong," he wrote later to George Parkin, "... and
not only that but he had put himself absolutely in the wrong by the

course he was pursuing before things came to a head in his Montreal speech."[63] Over a year before the Governor General had warned the British Secretary of State for War that Dundonald might not stay long in Canada and that if he went it would not be entirely the Canadians' fault.[64] Minto was well aware that the General had been playing politics against his employers:

His vanity is beyond bounds. No doubt if he meant to sacrifice himself with the idea of making known to the Canadian people a great scandal in their public service there is much to be said for it – but in all his conversations with me he has been entirely carried away by the idea of his own popularity and the fact that he is posing as the popular saviour of the position. He has worked the press and opposition members in a way in which no Govnt. could stand – and he has taken this line for a long time.[65]

Moreover, at a period when many Canadians including the Prime Minister seemed to be questioning the imperial tie, Dundonald had chosen the wrong moment to force his issue. Minto was not even certain that Fisher could be fairly condemned, at least by Canadian standards. Despite the arguments of his Military Secretary, Major Stanley Maude, and the editorial advice of the Conservative press, Minto signed the order-in-council dismissing Dundonald with scarcely an argument.[66]

Since Dundonald had chosen to leave Ottawa, the news of his dismissal reached him at London late on the night of June 14. Returning at once to Ottawa he cleared out his office at militia headquarters and distributed another statement of his case, this time directed against Borden. It was a feeble document. Major grievances were mingled with personal complaints; trivial incidents were the sole evidence for serious charges.[67] An Ottawa which had already been offended by Dundonald's reference to the capital's "etiquette" as implying a disdain for local society, began to have second thoughts about his case as a whole.

The Conservatives had also recognized that Dundonald's position was indefensible. On June 23, when the opposition censure motion was presented, it was limited to a denunciation of the Minister of Agriculture. The ensuing debate revealed the Liberal resilience. In a fighting speech Fisher defended his right to be concerned about the regiment and demonstrated that he had worked as hard for qualified Conservative officers as for Liberals. His speech so delighted the Liberal backbenchers that they crowded around him when he had finished to sing "He's a Daisy."[68] Sir Frederick Borden's self-defence was equally self-confident and on the following day Hughes was neutralized by the able mockery of Benjamin Russell, a Liberal MP and professor of law at Dalhousie University. Laurier, in concluding the debate, resolved the question with satisfying simplicity into an issue of civil or military supremacy and announced: "... so long, at all events, as there is a Liberal government in Canada, the civil power shall rule over the military."[69]

Dundonald remained in Canada. His address before a large audience at Toronto on July 15, although ostentatiously directed above the party conflict, gave rise to reports that he would be a candidate in the forthcoming elections. Having reverted to British half-pay, Dundonald believed that he was his own master and the excitement of running his own campaign was engrossing.[70]

In Canada the General was rapidly becoming as much an embarrassment to Lord Minto as to the government. Even in Britain, where his case aroused the transient support of service periodicals and the more Conservative sections of the press, his subsequent attacks on the Dominion government brought reaction in Parliament. Liberals like Lloyd George and Winston Churchill demanded that the War Office control its "raging myrmidon." [71] Even former GOCs were critical. Ivor Herbert, campaigning in Wales for his own election, was reported as claiming that he for one had always respected the constitutional supremacy of his Minister. Hutton, writing from his remote command in Australia, agreed with Minto that Dundonald had put himself "entirely in the wrong."[72] The British government forestalled further criticism by bluntly ordering Dundonald to report to the War Office and reminding him of the regulations against political speaking.[73] Major Maude was sent to persuade the General not to issue a parting statement and after many hours of argument he was successful. When Dundonald finally left Ottawa on July 26 he contented himself with crying out to the huge crowd gathered to see him off: "Men of Canada, keep both hands on the Union Jack!"[74] On the following day he left Montreal in a driving rainstorm and so passed out of Canadian history.

For about a month Laurier's correspondence included echoes of the Dundonald affair but by October he could assure a prominent Toronto supporter that it had seemed "quite dead some two weeks ago."[75] If Dundonald affected the 1904 elections, he gave little comfort to the Conservatives. They suffered a net loss of six seats and received exactly the same percentage of the popular vote they had received in 1900 – forty-seven per cent.

Dundonald's experience in Canada had duplicated that of Hutton.

Like his predecessor he had set out to eliminate political interference in the militia administration and to impose his own military policy on the Canadian government. Like Hutton, he had found that to supplant the authority of political superiors, he himself had to engage in political activity. And, as Minto had observed of both men, he had used tactics of pressure and subterfuge which no government could have tolerated for long. Unlike Hutton, he had chosen to force a public confrontation on his government. When it came, it proved to be a futile emotional indulgence.

Even without Dundonald, the limitation of the command of the Canadian militia to a British general was becoming an anachronism. So was the system of having a single commander for the military branch of the department. Dundonald's defiance of the government merely ensured that the change would come with greater certainty and added turbulence.

CHAPTER TEN

Militia Council

Conclusion and Beginning

On July 11, 1904, even before Lord Dundonald had left Canada, Sir Frederick Borden introduced the amendment to the Militia Bill creating the Militia Council. "I think I may say without fear of contradiction that the system which has been in existence in this country since Confederation has not worked well," he explained.[1] The council, as Borden had already indicated to Lord Minto, would consist of three civilian members: himself, the Deputy Minister, and the Secretary as financial representative; and four soldiers: the Chief of the General Staff, the Adjutant General, the Quartermaster General, and a new Master General of Ordnance.[2] Related to the Militia Council plan was an idea earlier advanced by Dundonald: major administrative decentralization to the commanders of the military districts. In eastern Canada the nine old military districts were to be reorganized into four large commands.[3]

Inevitably, the change in organization was considered in the light of the Dundonald affair. "The doors of political interference are thrown open," declared an Ontario Conservative, A. B. Ingram. Through the council, Borden had explained, the Minister would be in direct contact with all aspects of his department. To some opposition members this seemed in itself a criticism of the change. "He is the master; he is the dictator"; announced Colonel Tisdale, "but I warn them to look out; he may become the tyrant." Inevitably, there were also the claims of imperial sentiment, again expressed by an Ontario Conservative: "It seems to me that in doing away with the requirement that the General Officer Commanding shall be one of His Majesty's colonels, the Minister is weakening the ties – and there are very few of them left – that bind us to the mother country."[4]

Before the Militia Bill passed Borden had managed a coup which diluted a good deal of opposition criticism. Of all the British officers who had served in Canada, few had been more popular with Canadians than Colonel Percy Lake, the former quartermaster general. In 1898 Borden had tried in vain to retain him as GOC. Now he again asked for Lake to fill the new post of Chief of the General Staff. As before, the War Office objected that Lake was too junior to be promoted even to the necessary militia rank. It now added that the proposed position was not sufficiently defined and that the financial return was inadequate. Some of the resistance seems to have come from Lake himself.[5] Making his last intervention in Canadian military affairs, and recognizing that Lake's appointment might be the last chance to insert a British officer in the Dominion's military hierarchy, Minto backed up his Minister's appeal with his own considerable influence. Under the pressure both the War Office and Lake relented. As a compromise he was sent out for six months with the rank of acting brigadier general, merely to get the new Militia Council organized. He was to remain for six years.[6]

Ironically, the authority for the new Militia Council was the last order-in-council Minto was to sign as Governor General of Canada. The man who had regarded Canadian military affairs with such unremitting disapproval for five years finally confessed himself to Borden as favouring the new system of command.[7] The council was to operate without significant difficulty during the remainder of Borden's long service as Minister of Militia. With many variations, a comparable system of command, with the service and civilian heads of the Department of National Defence in regular and direct contact with the Minister, has continued in Canada to the present time.

It would be easy to exaggerate the degree of change which the Militia Council introduced. Contrary to both British and Canadian expectations, it did not lead to a monopoly of staff positions by Canadians. Except for the period between 1908 and 1910 when the post was held by Brigadier General Sir William Otter, the appointment of Chief of the General Staff was held by British officers until 1920. Even the brief Canadian interlude might have been avoided if Otter had preferred to accept the command of a British infantry brigade at Aldershot.[8] Nor did the change eliminate British officers from more subordinate positions. By 1912 more British officers were serving in key positions in the Canadian militia than ever before, although their proportion of the expanded number of permanent force positions was naturally much smaller.

Not even the quarrels of Ministers and Generals were at an end. In 1913 Colonel Sam Hughes, Sir Frederick's successor as Minister of Militia, forced his Chief of the General Staff, Major General Colin Mackenzie, to resign on grounds which would have been familiar enough ten or twenty years before.[9] In his years as Minister Hughes also demonstrated that the Militia Council system was as adaptable to gross political favouritism as any system that went before, even if the politics were more personal than partisan.

The most substantial change in Canada's military position after 1904 lay less in the alteration of a system of authority in the Militia Department than in the *de facto* end of the 1865 defence partnership. After years of pressure on Canada to build her defences against a possible American war, Britain quite suddenly found herself adopting the Canadian point of view. Given British military and naval resources, an Anglo-American war was not only a remote and appalling contingency, it was not even physically possible for her to make adequate preparations against the possibility.[10] This realization was one of the early achievements of the Committee of Imperial Defence. The new and prolonged contact between the British service ministries exposed the contradictions of their policies. The Army had been expecting the Royal Navy to perform a vital role in the defence of Canada. The Admiralty, in an unusually frank memorandum, confessed that if such an unlikely and potentially disastrous conflict broke out, it was unlikely to play any role at all and certainly not the part the Army had planned for it.[11] Confrontation led to rationality and in turn to a second and more complete British withdrawal from Canada than in 1870.

The practical consequence of this withdrawal was the British abandonment of their fortresses of Esquimalt and Halifax. At the Admiralty, Admiral Sir John Fisher's policy of concentrating the British fleet in home waters to meet a growing German naval menace meant that such outlying bases were no longer needed. The fact of withdrawal was, however, concealed by a fortuitous Canadian willingness to replace the British garrisons with their own troops. Lord Minto had been dismayed at earlier proposals that Britain consign strategic fortresses to careless and corrupt Canadian hands.[12] Once the bases had lost their strategic importance, it no longer really mattered. The true reasons for the withdrawal, like the belated conclusion that the fortification of Esquimalt had been a mistake, were secrets not to be shared with Canadians. Instead, prodded by a peculiar mixture of national and imperial sentiment, the Dominion not only took over the defence of Halifax and Esquimalt during 1905 and 1906 but even consented to maintain a higher scale of defence at the Atlantic port than the British had furnished during the previous thirty-five years.[13]

On November 4, 1905, the liner *S.S. Kensington* sailed from Halifax for Liverpool, carrying home the main body of the British garrison. It was a less dramatic occasion than the departure of the *Orontes* from Quebec thirty-five years before but it was of equal significance in the development of Canadian nationhood. It was the end of a British military presence in Canada. As was to become apparent in two world wars, Halifax had not lost her strategic significance for Britain. The British withdrawal was more than a logical last step of Cardwell's policy of 1870. Instead, it was evidence that the defence commitment of 1865 had been superseded by history. Henceforth, Canada would have to guard her frontiers alone.

By 1905 Canada had completed a significant, if almost unconscious, step towards self-government. Militarily, Canadians were now on their own in their own continent for the first time. The odd, ill-defined, defence arrangements stemming from the 1865 meetings were now at an end. Thanks to the Committee of Imperial Defence, the long-standing Canadian contention about the unreality of preparing for war with the United States had finally been accepted: the consequence was the second and final British withdrawal from Canada. That Canadians were now ready to accept the military responsibility for the two British fortresses in the Dominion was a demonstration of maturity which would have been inconceivable thirty-five years before.

A rational re-examination of the North American defence problem had been forced on the British government by many considerations, chief among them the expansion of American naval and military strength after the Spanish-American War. However, a significant factor had been the realization that Britain had no effective influence on Canadian defence policy. Efforts to apply that influence through Colonial Office circulars, the 1898 Defence Committee, and successive Governors Gen-

eral had had only a transient effect. The most sustained channel for
pressure had been through the British officer commanding the militia.
As the chief military officer in the Dominion, the General Officer Commanding had seemed the natural agent for British policy. It took the
experience of eight officers during thirty years to demonstrate that Canadians would not accept imperial policies simply because they were
channelled through their own military commander.

In fact, that such pressures came through a British general created
obstruction. In 1872 Macdonald had argued that the Dominion needed
a British officer not merely for his professional knowledge but because
Canadians needed an impartial and external authority in their military
administration to save them from the misdeeds of their political masters.
Whether or not Macdonald was serious in his argument, thirty years of
experience had proved that no government would accept such an inter-
mediary authority. When Conservatives suggested in 1904 that a British
officer could be trusted to defy his Minister to prevent abuses and that
a Canadian could not, their contention was historically absurd. Experience had repeatedly demonstrated that no minister of either party
would accept any general's defiance, whatever his origins or affiliations.
The fact that the generals between 1874 and 1904 were outsiders seems
to have made it easier for Canadian ministers to arouse national antagonism against them.

While British officers at the head of the militia were helping Canadians learn lessons of civil-military relations, they were serving a less
conscious and less recognized function. In the development of a modern
rational-bureaucratic system of public administration, the Militia Department had a central, if unappreciated, role in Canadian government.
Alone among federal departments, it had a conscious model in the
British War Office. While in Whitehall the War Office might appear a citadel of old-fashioned methods, in terms of the elimination
of patronage and influence, it was a generation ahead of its Canadian
counterpart. By imitating its model, the Militia Department could play
a modernizing role. The sometimes absurd aping of British military
customs and costume by Canadian militia officers was not merely an in-
fantile aberration; it was also the visible sign of the striving to match the
model. The conflicts between the Ministers and Generals were the symp-
toms of the strain inherent in the confrontation of two different sets of
institutional values.

The agent for transmitting the more advanced system to Canada was the British GOC. Sometimes, as with Herbert and Hutton, the General was seeking an explicit transfer of institutional patterns from the War Office to Canada. More persistently, a general principle was involved: the divorce of the army from party politics. It was apparent to successive British commanders that politics, in all its manifestations, detracted from the military character of the Canadian force. Their task was to combat it. The path to their downfall lay through their attempts to fight a political battle without the means or the position to sustain it.

Each successive general faced the same hazards. Militia officers who preached fidelity to British institutions could be among the first to resort to political influence, even against a British general. Ministers gave priority to military considerations only when the claims of colleagues or constituents were not pressed too hard. For British generals, the supposed assets of independence and aloofness from the political struggle could also be liabilities. Generals lacked any firm base of support. Caron was content to retain Middleton until he attracted opposition criticism; he was opposed to accepting Laurie as GOC because of the personal influence he would bring with him from the Tupper connection. Not even all Governors General backed their military compatriot at a critical juncture, as Gascoigne found with Aberdeen and Dundonald with Minto.

Some generals did appreciate that the extent to which politics penetrated militia administration was itself a political question which they could attack with political weapons. Herbert's success in manipulating two ministers, Bowell and Patterson, was one kind of achievement. Hutton and Dundonald, with their speeches, interviews, and secret manoeuvring, demonstrated another approach, although their tactics really only produced ammunition for party warfare.

Not all generals wanted to be reformers. One observation about the eight men who commanded the militia between 1874 and 1904 is that each was a contrast to his predecessor. Age and youth, reforming zeal and complacency, alternated as the British vainly sought a combination of qualities which might succeed in the position. Each general sought to compensate for the weaknesses of his predecessor, but neither reformers nor time-servers could escape their fate. Borden concluded that the fault lay with the system of authority within the Militia Department: "I believe it is an impossible system. I believe that it is absolutely and entirely impossible to get on with the system which we have attempted to work in this country since Confederation. We have had abundant examples not confined to the Liberal administrations alone, in which it has been found unendurable."[14]

Borden had a strong basis for his belief. The system was at fault not simply because of an inherent conflict in the goals of Minister and General but because it concentrated all the strains of modernization on the General. Whether he was aggressive or easy-going in imposing outside values, the GOC was too obviously the target for disgruntled soldiers or politicians. As a man with apparent authority but without political power, he was easily blamed and easily jettisoned.

Borden also contended that his generals failed because they had no experience of the War Office or of appointments where they would have learned more of the practical relationship between ministers, civil officials, and senior officers:

They come here as Imperial officers, having lived for a very long time in a narrow sphere where they have learned nothing but to command, being also under the command of a superior officer, not even ever having had the opportunity to serve in a permanent position in the War Office where they could be brought into contact with the executive government, with the War Minister. They come to this country, therefore, without this experience which would fit them for a position directly under a minister who is directly responsible to the Parliament and people of Canada.[15]

Borden's claim was not completely accurate. Herbert, Hutton, and Dundonald were sufficiently close to the central figures in the British Army of their era, the Duke of Cambridge, Lord Wolseley, or Sir Redvers Buller, to know a good deal about the conflicts which affected British civil-military relations in the late nineteenth century. Hutton's appointment in Canada was largely due to his apparent success in working with the government of New South Wales. What was significant was not that these officers were inexperienced in the politics of the high command but that they were *engagé*. Followers of Lord Wolseley could be depended upon to be not so much removed from politics as bitterly hostile to politicians. Queen Victoria described the anxiety of her cousin, the Duke of Cambridge, to do what was best for the Crown, "and to maintain the office of Commander-in-Chief so that it should never become Parliamentary."[16]

A prejudice against politicians, particularly when it was fortified by a disdain for the "tone" of colonial society, was hardly useful baggage for a GOC. It was certainly apparent in the relations between Sir Frederick Borden and his two ablest generals. Borden was not opposed to military reform. His private papers show that he fought the grosser forms of political influence and even Lord Minto came to admit as much.[17] The fact that so many of his generals' suggestions were carried out in due course suggests that fruitful co-operation was possible. The career of General Lake after 1904 confirms it. Much of the explanation of conflict must lie in the instinctive hostility of officers like Hutton and Dundonald to the working of politics in Canadian society as they found it.

What particularly embittered Hutton and Dundonald after their ex-perience in Canada was the sense that evil had triumphed. Political influence, the "Upas tree" as Hutton repeatedly called it, still apparently flourished. In fact, their perspective was too narrow. What is far more apparent in the period between 1870 and 1904 is how far the campaign against political influence had succeeded. The evidence must be impres-sionistic. No calculus exists to quantify political pressure. However, by 1904 there were not only guaranteed vacancies for Royal Military Col-lege graduates in the permanent force but there were more positions than qualified cadets wanted to fill. By the turn of the century the number of parliamentary colonels had declined to insignificance.* Perhaps the best evidence of the decline was the fact that it was at last being publicly de-bated and condemned. That, at least, was the conclusion of Lord Minto as he looked back on his five years in Canada: "the political influence which has been so injurious to it [the militia] is decidedly on the decline; its evil effects are becoming more clearly recognized ..."[18] If this were indeed so, successive General Officers Commanding deserved substantial credit.

Individually and collectively, the Generals had been defeated. Their cause, in large part, had succeeded. With, and sometimes without, their help, Canadians had developed their own military institutions. They had come with reluctance to accept defence as a legitimate responsibility of self-government. By 1904 there was a Canadian Army in all but name. Above all, Canadians had begun to come to terms with the place of political party influence in a mature and democratic administrative system. It was no small achievement.

* See Appendix B.

APPENDIX A

TABLE I

CANADIAN MILITIA STRENGTH
AFTER REMUSTERING AND
RE-ENROLMENT, 1868 AND 1869

Province	Active Militia	Reserve Militia
Ontario	21,816	293,536
Quebec	12,637	202,597
New Brunswick	1,789	53,833
Nova Scotia	928	69,946
Total	37,170	618,896

REFERENCE: *Militia Report*, 1868, pp. 3, 4–17.

TABLE 2

THE MILITIA LOBBY: MEMBERS OF THE CANADIAN
HOUSE OF COMMONS IDENTIFIED WITH THE
CANADIAN MILITIA, 1874–1900

Category	Party	Parliament elected in						
		1874	1878	1882	1887	1891	1896	1900
Officers in the Active Militia	C	8	15	15	8	13	7	3
	L	16	5	3	6	1	3	2
	Total	24	20	18	14	14	10	5
Retired Officers	C	4	11	9	7	7	2	1
	L	3	—	1	1	2	2	2
	Total	7	11	10	8	9	4	3
Reserve Militia Officers	C	6	8	4	4	2	—	—
	L	6	1	4	2	1	—	—
	Total	12	9	8	6	3	—	—
Total in the House of Commons	C	18	34	28	25	22	9	5
	L	25	6	8	9	4	6	3
	Total	43	40	36	34	26	15	8
Total membership of the House of Commons	C	73	137	139	122	122	88	81
	L	133	69	71	93	91	118	132
	Total*	206	206	211	215	215	213	213

*includes Independents and others.

REFERENCES: Parliamentary Guides and Companions for 1875, 1880, 1885, 1889, 1891, 1898–9, and 1901. MPs have been included only if they indicated their military affiliation in the *pro forma* biographical sketch submitted to the editor.

TABLE 3

CHANGES IN THE MILITIA ORGANIZATION: THE
NUMBER OF COMPANY-SIZED UNITS, 1875–1904

Arm	Sub-unit	1875	1885	1895	1903
Cavalry	troop*	40	41	44	32*
Field Artillery	battery	13	18	17	16
Garrison Artillery	battery or company	55	41	30	32
Engineers	company	4	3	2	4
Infantry	company	622	611	614	691

*for 1903, squadrons of approximately two troops.

REFERENCES: *Militia Lists* for 1875, 1885, 1895, and 1903.

TABLE 4

THE COMPOSITION OF THE STAFF AND THE
PERMANENT CORPS OF THE CANADIAN MILITIA
BY ORIGIN, 1886–1912

Rank	British Officers			Canadian Officers *English-Speaking*			*French-Speaking*		
	1886	1899	1912	1886	1899	1912	1886	1899	1912
Major General	1	1	1			1			
Brigadier General						3			1
Colonel		1	2	1	1	9			3
Lieutenant Colonel	2	2	3	15	14	27	5	4	3
Major	3		9	8	11	52	3	3	5
Captain	1		2	4	13	68	1	4	12
Lieutenant	3			18	12	67	6	1	3
Totals	10	4	17	46	51	227	15	12	27

REFERENCES: *Militia Lists* for 1886, 1899, and 1912.

TABLE 5

FEDERAL GOVERNMENT EXPENDITURE ON MILITIA AND DEFENCE
1868–1905

Budgetary year beginning	Defence spending ($ million)	Per cent of revenue	Per cent of expenditure	Per capita (dollars)
1867	.8	5.8	5.8	.23
1868	.9	6.2	6.2	.25
1869	1.2	7.8	6.7	.34
1870	.9	4.6	4.8	.25
1871	1.7	8.2	6.7	.46
1872	1.3	6.2	3.9	.35
1873	1.3	5.3	3.9	.34
1874	1.1	4.4	3.4	.27
1875	1.1	4.8	3.5	.27
1876	.6	2.6	1.9	.15
1877	.6	2.7	2.0	.15
1878	.8	2.9	2.7	.19
1879	.8	3.4	2.4	.19
1880	.8	2.7	2.5	.19
1881	.9	2.6	2.7	.21
1882	.8	2.2	1.9	.18
1883	1.1	3.4	1.9	.25
1884	2.8	8.4	5.9	.62
1885	4.5	13.5	7.5	.99
1886	1.6	4.5	4.0	.35
1887	1.9	5.3	4.4	.41
1888	1.4	3.6	3.4	.30
1889	1.4	3.5	3.5	.30
1890	1.4	3.6	3.5	.29
1891	1.4	3.8	3.5	.29
1892	1.5	3.9	3.7	.31
1893	1.4	3.9	3.6	.28
1894	1.7	5.0	4.2	.34
1895	2.2	6.0	5.2	.44
1896	2.6	6.9	6.4	.51
1897	1.8	4.5	4.2	.35
1898	2.6	5.6	5.3	.50
1899	3.6	7.0	7.2	.69
1900	3.2	6.1	5.7	.60
1901	2.8	4.5	4.6	.52
1902	2.6	3.7	4.4	.47
1903	3.7	5.2	5.3	.66
1904	4.2	5.9	5.5	.72
1905	5.7	7.1	7.0	1.00

REFERENCES: Buckley and Urquhart, *Historical Statistics of Canada*, Tables G-21, G-42, and A-1.

APPENDIX B

MINISTERS OF MILITIA AND GENERAL OFFICERS COMMANDING THE CANADIAN MILITIA

I *Ministers of Militia and Defence, 1868–1911*

George Etienne Cartier, July 1, 1868 – May 20, 1873 (created baronet, 1868) (c).
Hugh McDonald, July 1, 1873 – November 4, 1873 (c).
Lt. Col. William Ross, November 7, 1873 – September 29, 1874 (L).
William Berrian Vail, September 30, 1874 – January 20, 1878 (L).
Lt. Col. Alfred Gilpin Jones, January 21, 1878 – October 16, 1878 (L).
Lt. Col. Louis F. R. Masson, October 19, 1878 – January 15, 1880 (c).
Sir Alexander Campbell, January 16, 1880 – November 7, 1880 (c).
Adolphe Caron, November 8, 1880 – January 24, 1892 (knighted, 1885) (c).
Mackenzie Bowell, January 25, 1892 – December 4, 1892 (c).
James Colebrooke Patterson, December 5, 1892 – March 25, 1895 (c).
Arthur R. Dickey, March 26, 1895 – January 6, 1896 (c).
Alphonse Desjardins, January 15, 1896 – April 30, 1896 (c).
Lt. Col. David Tisdale, May 1, 1896 – July 12, 1896 (c).
Frederick W. Borden, July 13, 1896 – October 9, 1911 (knighted, 1902) (L).

II *General Officers Commanding the Canadian Militia*

Major General Edward Selby Smyth, April 20, 1875 – May 31, 1880
(knighted, 1877).
Major General R. G. A. Luard, July 1, 1880 – April 30, 1884.
Major General F. D. Middleton, July 12, 1884 – June 30, 1890 (knighted, 1885).
Major General I. J. C. Herbert, November 20, 1890 – August 1, 1895.
Major General W. J. Gascoigne, September 19, 1895 – June 30, 1898.
Major General E. T. H. Hutton, August 11, 1898 – February 12, 1900.
Major General R. H. O'Grady Haly, July 19, 1900 – July 19, 1902.
Major General the Right Honourable the Earl of Dundonald,
July 20, 1902 – June 14, 1904.
Colonel the Right Honourable Matthew, Lord Aylmer,
June 15, 1904 – October 31, 1904.

Notes

CHAPTER ONE

1 On the British role in the defence of Canada, see Kenneth Bourne, *Britain and the Balance of Power in North America, 1815–1908* (London, 1967); J. Mackay Hitsman, *Safeguarding Canada, 1763–1871* (Toronto, 1968); C. P. Stacey, *Canada and the British Army, 1846–1871* (rev. ed., Toronto, 1963).

2 *Report on the Defence of Canada and of the British Naval Stations in the Atlantic by Lieut.-Col. Jervois ...* (February 1864), PAC, RG 8, II, vol. 20.

3 *Report on the Defence of Canada* (November 10, 1864) wo 33/15 (and in MP, vol. 100, pp. 39484–9).

4 *Confederation Debates*, February 8, 1865, p. 106.

5 "Memorandum by the Defence Committee on the Report of Lieutenant Colonel Jervois ..." (May 17, 1865), wo 33/15 (also in MP, vol. 100, pp. 39487–9).

6 Cardwell to Monck, June 17, 1865, *Papers Relating to the Conferences which have taken place between Her Majesty's Government and a deputation from the Executive Council of Canada ...*, CO 42/693, pp. 380–1.

7 George Brown to Anne Brown, June 3, 1865, PAC, Brown Papers, vol. 6, pp. 1282–7.

8 *Confederation Debates*, February 16, 1865, p. 257.

9   Sir Joseph Tassé, *Discours de Sir Georges-Etienne Cartier* ... (Montreal, 1893), p. 572; John Boyd, *Sir Geo.-Etienne Cartier; His Life and Times* (Toronto, 1914), p. 293.

10   J. M. Hitsman, "The Militia of Nova Scotia, New Brunswick and Prince Edward Island" (unpublished report in CFHS), pp. 13–15, 21–4.

11   Province of Canada, *Report of the Commissioners ... upon the Best Means of Re-organizing the Militia of Canada* ... (Toronto, 1856), p. 1. On the pre-Confederation Canadian militia, see G. F. G. Stanley, *Canada's Soldiers* (rev. ed., Toronto, 1960), and J. M. Hitsman, "The Canadian Militia Prior to Confederation" (unpublished report in the CFHS).

12   Parliamentary Debates as reported in the Toronto *Globe*, March 31, 1868.

13   *Report of the Department of Militia and Defence*, 1869, p. 24. Drill pay was a sufficient issue to be mentioned prominently by Liberal speakers in 1872: see Owen Carrigan, *Canadian Party Platforms, 1867–1968* (Toronto, 1968), p. 9.

14   31 Vict., c. 40, s. 18(3).

15   Macdonald to Sir John Young, July 14, 1868, CO 537/100, pp. 78–9.

16   31 Vict., c. 41. On negotiations for the guarantee, see Hitsman, *Safeguarding Canada*, pp. 207–8.

17   Granville to Young, April 15, 1869, "Correspondence with the Imperial Authorities since Jan. 1, 1869 ... ," Canada, Parliament, *Sessional Papers*, 1871, no. 46, pp. 2–4.

18   Cambridge to Cardwell, December 20, 1868, with memorandum, PRO 30/48, Cardwell Papers, box 3/11.

19   Windham to War Office, June 4, 1869, CO 42/680, pp. 471–3.

20   C. P. Stacey, "The Garrison of Fort Wellington: A Military Dispute during the Fenian Troubles," *CHR*, XIV, 2 (September 1933).

21   Granville to Young, February 12, 1870, "Correspondence with the Imperial Authorities ... ," pp. 8–9.

22   Lindsay's correspondence with the Canadian government is in WO 32/813/058/316, on microfilm in the CFHS.

23   A Canadian [Lt. Col. W. F. Coffin], *Thoughts on Defence from a Canadian Point of View* (Montreal, 1870).

24   Col. B. H. Martindale, *Report on the Withdrawal from Quebec*, WO 33/24. See also correspondence in WO 32/7025.

25   *Militia General Orders*, no. 24, October 20, 1871.

26   For the early years of "A" Battery, see Maj. Gen. Sir Sam Steele, *Forty Years in Canada* (Toronto, 1915), pp. 47–8, and for "B" Battery, see Maj. Gen. T. B. Strange, *Gunner Jingo's Jubilee* (London, 1893), pp. 351–2.

27   On military schools, see *Militia Report*, 1870, pp. 33–5; 1872, p. lxxix, 1873,

p. 1. On deterioration in the force, see report by Col. Henry Fletcher, June 5, 1872, CO 537/103, pp. 297–300.

28 Annual militia spending may be found in an abstract in *The Department of Militia and Defence under the Honourable Sir Adolphe Caron, K.C.M.G.* ... (Ottawa, 1887), pp. 10–12.

29 Gladstone to the Queen, April 9, 1872, PRO, Cab. 41/4/15; Gladstone to the Queen, November 28, 1872, Cab. 41/4/51.

30 Comment by Col. Patrick MacDougall, cited in Jay Luvaas, *The Education of an Army: British Military Thought, 1815–1940* (London, 1965), p. 108.

31 Kimberley to Gladstone, December 9, 1870, Cardwell Papers, box 5/31. For British strategic considerations, see C. P. Stacey, "Britain's Withdrawal from North America, 1864–1871," *CHR*, XXXVI, 3 (September 1955).

32 Parliamentary Debates as reported in the Toronto *Globe*, April 23, 1868. The Jervois plan envisaged the sacrifice of southern Ontario and a retreat to the main British stronghold at Quebec.

33 See *supra*, n. 8.

34 *House of Commons Debates*, April 16, 1878, p. 2052.

35 Maurice Ollivier, *The Colonial and Imperial Conferences from 1887 to 1937* (Ottawa, 1954), vol. I, pp. 38–44. An even more laborious effort at self-justification was the report of the Minister of Militia and Defence, January 23, 1888, CO 42/795, pp. 292–333; it represented, Sir Robert Herbert of the Colonial Office minuted, "a great amount of labour" (p. 287).

36 Caron to Macdonald, January 31, 1884, MP, vol. 200, p. 84640.

37 On Halifax, see "The Adequacy of the Existing Garrison and Defences of Halifax to Resist an Attack by Land" (secret), December 11, 1903, Cab. 38/3/83. On Esquimalt, see Sir Anthony Hoskin to Sir Robert Meade, February 17, 1893, and minutes of February 8 and 17, 1893, CO 42/819, pp. 122–7.

38 *Report on the Canadian Militia by the Inspector General of the Forces* (London, 1910), in Cab. 11/27, p. 23. The reference to war with the United States was omitted from the version of the report printed in Canada (Canada, Parliament, *Sessional Papers*, 1910, vol. 21, no. 35a).

39 Canadian attitudes to the United States are discussed in S. F. Wise and R. C. Brown, *Canada Views the United States* (Toronto, 1967), especially pp. 98–120.

40 *House of Commons Debates*, February 15, 1875, p. 153.

41 Walker Powell memorandum, n.d., MP, vol. 100, p. 39747.

42 *House of Commons Debates*, April 21, 1896, pp. 6931–3 (James McMullen, MP).

43 Toronto *Globe*, March 24, 1898.

44 *House of Commons Debates*, February 25, 1875, p. 156; Toronto *Globe*, February 27, 1875.

45 *House of Commons Debates*, April 19, 1877 (Hon. Peter Mitchell, MP).

46 Parliamentary Debates as reported in the Toronto *Globe*, May 16 and 17, 1868.

47 Denison memorandum to Macdonald, n.d., MP, vol. 332, pp. 150174–6; Two Militiamen, "A Plea for the Militia," *Canadian Monthly*, February 1879. The two authors, to judge from a copy of the article in the library of the Royal Canadian Military Institute, Toronto, were probably Denison and Lt. Col. Thomas Scoble, later editor of the *Nor'Wester*.

48 George T. Denison, *Soldiering in Canada* (Toronto, 1900), p. 186. A more balanced commentary on the election is in Robert Rumilly, *Histoire de la Province de Québec* (Montreal, 1941), vol. II, pp. 219–28.

49 *Canadian Military Gazette*, July 12, 1904.

50 *Ibid.*, November 8, 1904. It might be conjectured that any self-conscious militia vote would have been so committed to the Conservatives in 1900 that it no longer had a "swing" in it.

51 Caron to Macdonald, August 14, 1881, MP, vol. 200, p. 64377. Caron was referring to a possible general election in 1883. It came in 1882.

52 Caron to Lt. Col. John B. Taylor, December 6, 1886, CP, l.b. 17, p. 135.

53 J. C. Patterson, MP, to Caron, February 22, 1889, CP, file 10729.

54 *Canadian Military Gazette*, March 1, 1896.

55 Toronto *Mail & Empire*, November 27, 1896.

56 On the appointment of Col. Henry Pellatt, see Lord Minto to George Parkin, September 26, 1904, PAC, Parkin Papers; Borden to Minto, April 16, 1902, NLS, Minto Papers, box 210, case C. For evidence of Pellatt's services, see Sen. G. A. Cox to Borden, August 21, 1900, BP.

57 John Small, MP, to Caron, October 24, 1889, CP, file 13623.

58 Amos Rowe to Bowell, April 13, 1885, CP, vol. 199, p. 263.

59 Caron to Lt. Col. G. A. Kirkpatrick, MP, April 28, 1882, CP, l.b. 2, p. 260.

60 G. E. McPherson to S. R. Hesson, MP, April 12, 1888, CP, file 12098.

61 31 Vict., c. 40, s. 28.

62 Powell to Lt. Col. W. D. Otter, October 20, 1880 (private collection).

63 Toronto *Daily Telegraph*, March 21, 1872.

64 Lt. Col. W. H. Forrest to Caron, September 10, 1887, CP, file 11309; Forrest to Caron, February 4, 1891, *ibid.*, file 13388.

65 Caron to Capt. John Peters, June 5, 1888, CP, l.b. 24, p. 263. Peters wrote a number of articles satirizing the militia in the *Canadian Militia Gazette* and is the most likely author of the anonymous pamphlet, *How Not To Do It: A Short Sermon on the Canadian Militia* (Quebec, 1891).

66 H. H. Dewart to Sir Richard Cartwright, June 9, 1897, BP, p. 2263.

67 On the appointment of Lt. Col. J. H. Gray, see CP, files 10157 and 10899; Caron to Macdonald, July 21, 1887, MP, vol. 200, pp. 84373–4.

68 Hutton to General Sir Evelyn Wood, February 23, 1899, HP, p. 52.

69 Lord Wolseley, *The Story of a Soldier's Life* (London, 1904), vol. II, pp. 230–1.

70 MacDougall to Cartier, May 10 and 18, 1868, RG 9, IC I, vol. 290.

71 Canada, Parliament, "Return to an Address of the House of Commons dated 10th May 1869 for a Copy of Colonel MacDougall's letter resigning his office of Adjutant-General" *Sessional Papers*, 1869, no. 31.

72 Sir James Lindsay, "Memorandum on the Report of the Canadian Department of Militia and Defence for 1870," May 17, 1871, in CFHS file "Withdrawal of British Troops, 1865–1871."

73 Dufferin to Carnarvon, November 19, 1875, PRO 30/6, Carnarvon Papers, vol. 25, p. 173.

74 Toronto *Daily Telegraph*, March 14, 1872.

75 Lindsay to Young, July 26, 1870, WO 32/813/058/316.

76 Lindsay to Cardwell, August 19, 1870, CO 42/693, p. 382.

77 *Militia Report*, 1870, pp. 37–8.

78 The original despatch has not been found but it was almost certainly based on War Office to Colonial Office, September 11, 1871, in CFHS file "Withdrawal of the British Troops ..." For Cartier's comments see Cartier to Macdonald, January 2, 1873, MP, vol. 202, pp. 85650–1.

79 Robertson Ross finally received the honorary rank of major general on his retirement in 1880. *The Times*, July 25, 1883.

80 Macdonald to Lisgar, February 17, 1871, CO 537/102, pp. 45–8.

81 Dufferin to Carnarvon, n.d., Carnarvon Papers, vol. 28, p. 69.

82 Lt. Col. Henry Fletcher, *Memorandum on the Militia System of Canada* (Ottawa, 1873).

83 Toronto *Globe*, January 19, 1874. On Mackenzie's military views, see D. C. Thompson, *Alexander Mackenzie: Clear Grit* (Toronto, 1960), p. 331.

84 Cambridge to Dufferin, January 22, 1874, RAW, Cambridge Papers.

85 Dufferin to Mackenzie, February 18, 1874, PAC, Mackenzie Papers, M-197, pp. 317A-B.

86 Dufferin to Cambridge, March 27, 1874, Cambridge Papers.

87 Dufferin to Carnarvon, March 26, 1874, C. W. de Kiewiet and F. H. Underhill, *The Dufferin-Carnarvon Correspondence* (Toronto, 1955), pp. 17–19.

88 The negotiations are described in "Memorandum on Services of British General," Colonial Office to War Office, September 22, 1874, CO 537/105, pp. 84–8.

CHAPTER TWO

1 Carnarvon to Dufferin, July 30, 1874, C. W. de Kiewiet and F. H. Underhill, *The Dufferin-Carnarvon Correspondence* (Toronto, 1955), pp. 58–9.

2 Carnarvon to Cambridge, August 5, 1874, RAW, Cambridge Papers.

3 Dufferin to Carnarvon, November 12, 1874, de Kiewiet and Underhill, *Dufferin-Carnarvon Correspondence*, p. 100.

4 Dufferin to Cambridge, December 11, 1874, Cambridge Papers.

5 Toronto *Globe*, January 13, 1875.

6 Mackenzie to Blake, January 4, 1874, Ontario Archives, Blake Papers. On the difficulties Mackenzie faced, see Sister Teresa Avila Burke, "Mackenzie and His Cabinet, 1873–1878," *CHR*, XLI, 2 (June 1960).

7 Jones to Mackenzie, June 7, 1874, PAC, Mackenzie Papers, M-197, pp. 555–6.

8 *House of Commons Debates*, February 25, 1875, p. 325.

9 *Ibid.*, p. 326.

10 R. J. Wicksteed, *The Canadian Militia* (Ottawa, 1875), p. 21.

11 Col. Fletcher's report is in Dufferin to Kimberley, July 5, 1872, CO 537/102, pp. 297–300. The staff officer was Lt. Col. W. H. Jackson, DAG, of MD 4.

12 Lt. Col. Henry Fletcher, *Memorandum on the Militia System of Canada* (Ottawa, 1873), p. 5.

13 R. H. Davis, *The Canadian Militia: Its Organization and Present Condition* (Caledonia, Ont., 1873), p. 6 (italics in the original).

14 Dufferin to Kimberley, July 5, 1872, CO 537/102, pp. 297–300. The conditions in the militia camps are apparent from the very frank reports of local staff officers published in the annual departmental reports, as well as from newspaper reports of local camps.

15 *Militia Report*, 1874, pp. xi-xx passim. Selby Smyth's first impressions are in an undated memorandum, PAC, Dufferin Papers, A-420, no. 30.

16 *Militia Report*, 1874, pp. viii-x, and in memorandum (above).

17 Toronto *Globe*, February 24, 1875.

18 Wicksteed, *Canadian Militia*, p. 17. G. H. Perry, a strong Conservative critic of Wicksteed, agreed entirely on this point: Selby Smyth's report "would have the effect, if carried out, of destroying the whole force." MP, vol. 203, pt. II, p. 138289. See *Militia Report*, 1875, pp. xi-xii.

19 *House of Commons Debates*, February 25, 1875, p. 326.

20 Selby Smyth to Cambridge, June 2, 1876, Cambridge Papers.

21 "Historical Notes on M.D. 3," CFHS, file 959.013, p. 28.

22 *Militia Report*, 1877, p. 1.

23 *Ibid.*, p. xi.

24 J. J. C. Abbott to Caron, July 13, 1891, CP, file 15276; *House of Commons Debates*, July 13, 1891, pp. 2146–7. On the other cases, see *Militia Report*, 1876, p. 43; 1878, p. xlviii; MP, vol. 83, pp. 32267–98; CP, file 3937.

25 One description of the ambiguities in the act is Lt. Col. H. R. Smith, "Military Aid of the Civil Power," *Selected Papers of the Canadian Military Institute*, vol. XI, 1899–1900.

26 Maj. Gen. T. B. Strange, *Gunner Jingo's Jubilee* (London, 1893), pp. 365–7; Dufferin to Mackenzie, June 18, 1878, Mackenzie Papers, M-199, pp. 1948–50.

27 Toronto *Mail*, January 5, 1877.

28 *House of Commons Debates*, April 4, 1877, p. 1155.

29 The Belleville affair is described (from the militia standpoint) in the Toronto *Mail*, January 3, 1877. See also Ernest Chambers, *History of the Queen's Own Rifles of Canada* (Toronto, 1901), pp. 81–2.

30 Toronto *Globe*, October 4, 1875.

31 *Ibid.*, June 28–July 15, 1878; Henry J. Morgan, *Dominion Register and Review for 1878* (Montreal, 1879), pp. 182–4; D. C. Thompson, *Alexander Mackenzie: Clear Grit* (Toronto, 1960), pp. 335–6.

32 Leonid Strakhovsky, "Russia's Privateering Projects of 1878: A Page in Russian-American Relations," *Journal of Modern History*, VII, 1 (March 1936).

33 Mackenzie to Charles Mackenzie, May 12, 1878, Mackenzie Papers, M-199, pp. 1914–16.

34 Dufferin to Colonial Office, May 11, 1878, CO 537/167, p. 1; Privy Council minutes, RG 2, 7a, vol. 16, pp. 642–3; vol. 17, p. 34.

35 Irwin memorandum, May 27, 1879, MP, vol. 229, pp. 98665–7; J. F. Cummins, "A Distinguished Artillery Officer," *Canadian Defence Quarterly*, January 1928; "Notes from the Diary of a Staff Officer," *V.R.I. Magazine*, November 1894. On the defence of British Columbia, see R. H. Roy, "The Militia and Defence of British Columbia, 1871–1885," *British Columbia Historical Quarterly*, January and April 1954.

36 Privy Council minutes, RG 2, 7a, vol. 17, pp. 108–9.

37 Mackenzie to Dufferin, June 11, 1878, Dufferin Papers, A-411.

38 Dufferin to Hicks Beach, n.d., *ibid.*, M-1140, p. 215.

39 T. B. Strange, "The Military Aspect of Canada," *Militia Report*, 1879, pp. 293–5.

40 Privy Council minutes, RG 2, 7a, vol. 17, pp. 108–9.

41 Minutes by Pennell and Kimberley on Sir John Adye to Colonial Office, May 8 and 31, 1882, CO 42/773, pp. 618, 622.

42 On Palliser's negotiations, see Draft Report, November 20, 1884, RG 9, IIA1, vol. 600; Caron to Macdonald, March 7, 1885, MP, vol. 200, p. 84723; and CP, files 4349, 5406, 6630, and 6633.

43 Privy Council minutes, December 22, 1879, RG 2, 7a, vol. 19, p. 55; *Militia Report*, 1879, pp. xli–xliii; 1879, pp. xiii–xxiv; *House of Commons Debates*, April 13, 1880, pp. 1364–5.

44 Deputy Minister of Militia to Governor General's Secretary, November 4, 1880, CO 42/763, p. 380. For the development of the factory, see *Militia Reports*, 1881, p. 276; 1883, pp. 247–52; 1885, p. xii. See also Arthur Penny, *The Dominion Arsenal at Quebec* (Quebec, 1947), pp. 24 ff.

45 "General MacDougall's memorandum on raising a Division in Canada," WO 32/120. See Adrian Preston, "Canada and the Russian Crisis of 1878: A Proposed Contingent for Imperial Defence," *Dalhousie Review*, XLVIII, 2 (Summer, 1968).

46 Selby Smyth memorandum, May 29, 1878, *ibid.*, and RG 7, G-19, vol. 30.

47 MacDougall memorandum, n.d., WO 32/120, and MP, vol. 80, pp. 31464–70.

48 For example, Lt. Col. T. C. Scoble, *The Utilization of Colonial Forces in Imperial Defence* (Toronto, 1879); see also R. A. Preston, *Canada and "Imperial Defense"* (Toronto, 1967), pp. 134–5.

49 Selby Smyth memorandum, November 12, 1879, MP, vol. 306, pt. II, pp. 13974–88; Selby Smyth memorandum, March 27, 1880, WO 32/120.

50 Alice R. Stewart, "Sir John A. Macdonald and the Imperial Defence Commission of 1879," *CHR*, XXXV, 2 (June 1954); Macdonald memorandum, November 10, 1879, WO 32/120.

51 War Office to Colonial Office, December 10, 1880, CO 42/765. See also minutes to WO 32/120.

52 Mackenzie to Robert Mackenzie, January 31, 1878, Mackenzie Papers, M-199, p. 1854.

53 The correspondence is in Mackenzie Papers, M-198, pp. 1651–79 and 1845–9.

54 *Militia Report*, 1877, p. xxiv; *House of Commons Debates*, April 16, 1878, pp. 2042–4.

55 *Militia Report*, 1879, p. xxxi.

56 *House of Commons Debates*, April 30, 1879, p. 1632.

57 Desmond Morton, "The Canadian Militia and French Canada," *Histoire Sociale/Social History*, no. 3 (June 1969).

58 Doyle to Sir John Young, November 26, 180, *Correspondence with the Imperial Authorities* (withdrawal), p. 63. Also Robertson Ross to the Military Secretary at Halifax (Col. Luard), May 10, 1873, RG 8, C series, vol. 1772, p. 354.

59 Masson to Lorne, February 5, 1880, PAC, Lorne Papers, vol. 4, p. 108. Lord

Dufferin disposed of an earlier and similar proposal: Dufferin to Carnarvon, November 22, 1877, de Kiewiet and Underhill, *Dufferin-Carnarvon Correspondence*, p. 384.

60 J. F. Cummins, "General Sir Edward Selby Smyth," *Canadian Defence Quarterly*, July 1928.

61 George T. Denison, *Soldiering in Canada* (Toronto, 1900), pp. 242-4.

CHAPTER THREE

1 Cambridge to Lorne, August 9, 1879, RAW, Cambridge Papers.

2 Privy Council minutes, March 26, 1880, RG 2, 7 a, vol. 19, pp. 304-5. Mackenzie had nothing to say about the "vetting" service provided by Lord Carnarvon.

3 Ponsonby to Cambridge, n.d. (E 61-43), Cambridge Papers. On attitudes to the appointment, see Colonel Stanley to Cambridge, February 28, 1880, *ibid*.

4 Lorne to Colonial Office, March 16, 1880, CO 42/760, p. 421; CP, file 2956; R. A. Preston, *Canada and "Imperial Defense"* (Toronto, 1967), p. 141.

5 Lorne to Colonial Office, March 26, 1880, CO 42/760, p. 450.

6 W. S. MacNutt, *Days of Lorne* (Fredericton, 1955), p. 188.

7 Lorne to Colonial Office, June 7, 1880, and minute, CO 537/107, pp. 11-13. Macdonald later believed that Luard had been appointed because British colleagues wanted him out of the country for a time: Sir Joseph Pope, *Correspondence of Sir John Macdonald* (Oxford, n.d.), p. 474.

8 *Militia General Orders*, no. 16, August 5, 1880; Luard to Cambridge, August 4, 1880, Cambridge Papers.

9 Luard to Cambridge, September 12, 1880, *ibid*.

10 Luard to Minister of Militia, September 8, 1880, RG 9, II A 1, vol. 604, pp. 183-5 and n. 8.

11 Privy Council minutes, May 16, 1879, RG 2, 7 a, vol. 18, pp. 94-5.

12 A. S. Woodburn ("Centurion") in *Canadian Military Review*, August 1877, p. 23.

13 *House of Commons Debates*, April 13, 1880, pp. 1359-61.

14 *Ibid.*, p. 1362. Strange won sympathetic attention in the Toronto *Mail*, April 14, 1880.

15 Draft order-in-council, October 30, 1880, RG 9, II A 1, vol. 604, pp. 193-201; Luard to Cambridge, November 25, 1880, Cambridge Papers.

16 Mackenzie to Dufferin, August 5, 1878, PRO, Northern Ireland, Dufferin Papers.

17 Dufferin to Mackenzie, August 31, 1878, PAC, Mackenzie Papers, M-199, pp.

2062–5; Dufferin to Lorne, n.d., MP, vol. 79, p. 31074. The solution was to provide a small guard from an Ottawa militia battalion which had bought uniforms modelled on the Coldstream Guards: Lt. Col. J. G. Baylay, ed., *The Governor General's Foot Guard* (Ottawa, 1947), p. 8.

18 Macdonald to Sir Stafford Northcote, May 1, 1887, MP, vol. 79, pp. 31056–9.

19 Privy Council minutes, October 5, 1880, RG 2, 7 a, vol. 20, pp. 123–4. Consideration of the change may have predated Luard's arrival. The policy had been urged by Lt. Col. G. A. Kirkpatrick, MP, an influential Conservative, earlier in the year: *House of Commons Debates*, April 13, 1880, p. 1362.

20 T. H. Gault to Caron, April 14, 1884, CP, file 3989.

21 Worsley to Macdonald, March 9, 1881, MP, vol. 200, pp. 84359–62. See also CP, files 3650 and 5258.

22 Lorne to Sir Ralph Lingren, March 28, 1881, and enclosures, CO 42/770, pp. 550–71.

23 Preston, *Canada and "Imperial Defense,"* p. 171.

24 Henry J. Morgan, *The Canadian Annual Register for 1880* (Montreal, 1881), p. 127; Masson to Macdonald, November 2, 1880, MP, vol. 229, pp. 98728–9. See also pp. 98712–15.

25 The *Shareholder*, November 12, 1880.

26 Privy Council minutes, December 14, 1881, RG 2, 7 a, vol. 21, p. 608.

27 Macdonald to Caron, June 21, 1881, CP, vol. 191, pp. 3987–9; *House of Commons Debates*, March 4, 1881, pp. 1227–8.

28 *Militia Report*, 1881, p. x.

29 Lorne to Macdonald, June 29, 1881, MP, vol. 81, pp. 31888–9. On Colonel Campbell's resignation, see George T. Denison, *Soldiering in Canada* (Toronto, 1900), pp. 246–8; Caron to John Mackenzie, July 23, 1881, CP, l.b. 1, p. 276.

30 For example, Luard to Caron, July 24, 1883, RG 9, II A 1, vol. 605, pp. 659–64.

31 *Militia Report*, 1880, p. ix.

32 W. T. Barnard, *The Queen's Own Rifles of Canada, 1860–1960* (Don Mills, Ont., 1960), pp. 47 ff.

33 Horatio C. King, *An Account of the Visit of the Thirteenth Regiment, N.G.S.N.Y., to Montreal, Canada, May, 1879* (Brooklyn, 1879).

34 Toronto *Globe*, February 22, 1879. See also G. H. Perry to Macdonald, July 10, 1875, and enclosures, MP, vol. 200, p. 138282.

35 Lt. Col. R. G. Dawson to Macdonald, January 22, 1890, CP, file 14014.

36 *Canadian Militia Gazette*, December 1, 1885.

37 The affair is summarized in the Toronto *Mail*, January 20, 1879. See also

House of Commons Debates, April 21, 1880, pp. 1629–32; Thomas E. Champion, *History of the 10th Royals and of the Royal Grenadiers* (Toronto, 1896), pp. 86–92.

38 Sherbrooke *Gazette,* February 24, 1882.

39 *Militia General Orders,* no. 27, November 25, 1881.

40 *House of Commons Debates,* May 3, 1882, pp. 1292–1301.

41 Note by Caron on John Barwick to Macdonald, November 28, 1881, MP, vol. 200, pp. 84392.

42 Lt. Col. S. S. Lazier to John White, March 15, 1882, CP, file 2643. Brown, a Liberal MP, commanded the neighbouring battalion.

43 Note by Caron on Lt. Col. J. Cole to Macdonald, May 20, 1882, MP, vol. 200, pp. 84483.

44 Luard to Otter, March 22, 1882, PAC, Otter Papers.

45 Cambridge to Lorne, June 24, 1882, and Lorne to Macdonald, June 9, 1882, MP, vol. 82, pp. 32065–77. On Caron's efforts to obtain Strange, see Caron to Macdonald, March 6, 1882, *ibid.,* vol. 200, pp. 84452–3. (Strange was promoted to major general on retirement.)

46 Macdonald to Lorne, July 21, 1882, PAC, Lorne Papers, vol. 4, pp. 273–6.

47 Major E. G. Scott, memorandum, etc., case 19013, RG 9, II A 2, vol. 35; Luard to the Adjutant-General, September 7, 1882, RG 9, II B 1, vol. 554, p. 428; CP, files 5563 and 11018; Toronto *Mail,* September 10, 1882; Montreal *Star,* September 12, 1882.

48 Montreal *Witness,* September 12, 1882.

49 Caron to Pentland, March 11, 1884, CP, l.b. 7, pp. 318–9.

50 Lorne memorandum to Council, March 7, 1883, MP, vol. 83, pp. 32251–7. See also Lorne to Macdonald, *ibid.,* p. 32259.

51 Caron to Luard, May 8, 1883, CP, l.b. 5, p. 100.

52 Caron to Luard, May 14, 1883, *ibid.,* p. 110.

53 Caron to Macdonald, August 25, 1883, MP, vol. 200, pp. 84586–8.

54 46 Vict., c. 11. For the debate, see *House of Commons Debates,* April 10, 1883, pp. 526–30; April 19, 1883, pp. 721–8; April 26, 1883, pp. 830–4.

55 On Otter, see Powell to Otter, October 19, 1882, Otter Papers. On the commandants of the schools, see Ernest J. Chambers, *A History of the Canadian Militia* (Montreal, 1897).

56 Caron to Sewell, March 12, 1883, CP, l.b. 4, p. 576.

57 Luard to Lorne, June 21, 1883, MP, vol. 83, p. 32469; Lorne to Macdonald, June 23, 1883, *ibid.,* p. 32465; Macdonald to Lorne, July 10, *ibid.,* pp. 32473–6.

58 Luard to Otter, August 21, 1883, Otter Papers.

59 Luard to Caron, July 25 and August 3, 1883, RG 9, II B 2, vol. 8, file 22.

60 *Militia General Orders*, no. 4, February 7, 1884; no. 20, October 16, 1884. For a more personal account, see Capt. Thomas McKenzie, *My Life as a Soldier* (Saint John, 1896), pp. 174 ff.

61 Williams to Caron, September 25, 1883, CP, file 6246.

62 Lorne to Colonial Office, October 6, 1883, CO 537/108, p. 93.

63 Caron to Macdonald, October 24, 1884, MP, vol. 200, pp. 84610–11.

64 Lansdowne to Macdonald, February 4, 1884, MP, vol. 84, p. 32703. (See also *ibid.*, pp. 32663, 32689–92.) Lorne to Cambridge, March 24, 1884, Cambridge Papers.

65 Lansdowne to Cambridge, February 4, 1884, *ibid.*

66 Russell to Cambridge, July 2, 1884, *ibid.*

67 *House of Commons Debates*, March 10, 1884, pp. 748 ff.; Lansdowne to Cambridge, March 12, 1884, Cambridge Papers.

68 The problem is analysed in the Montreal *Witness*, February 12, 1884.

CHAPTER FOUR

1   Laurie to Tupper, October 6, 1883, CP, file 3411. See also file 3820.

2   J. B. Taylor to William Wright, March 21, 1884, *ibid.*, file 3820.

3   Middleton to Caron, September 11, 1883, *ibid.*, file 3283; Lt. Col. J. F. Turnbull to Caron, February 15, 1884, *ibid.*, file 3644.

4   Middleton to Caron, n.d., *ibid.*, file 3820.

5   Caron to Macdonald, April 25, 1884, MP, vol. 200, pp. 84663–7. See also CP, file 3820.

6   Lansdowne to Cambridge, May 11, 1880, RAW, Cambridge Papers.

7   Lansdowne to Cambridge, May 19, 1884, *ibid.*; Lansdowne to Macdonald, May 10 and 17, 1884, MP, vol. 84, pp. 32765–8 and 32779.

8   Middleton to Cambridge, July 16, 1884, Cambridge Papers.

9   *Militia Report*, 1884, pp. xv–xx. See also Middleton to Caron, July 26, 1884, CP, file 4419.

10 *Militia General Orders*, no. 22, December 1, 1882; War Office to Colonial Office, August 5, 1884, CO 42/773, p. 656; Caron to Melgund, November 15, 1884, CP, l.b., p. 321.

11 C. P. Stacey, ed., *Records of the Nile Voyageurs* (Toronto, 1959).

12 Laurie memorandum and notes, March 2, 1885, PAC, Minto Papers, A-130; Lansdowne to Macdonald, September 2, 1884, MP, vol. 84, p. 32903.

13 Macdonald to Tupper, March 12, 1885, in Sir Joseph Pope, *Correspondence of Sir John Macdonald* (Oxford, n.d.), p. 337. See also C. P. Stacey, "John A. Macdonald on Raising Troops in Canada for Imperial Service, 1885," *CHR*, XXXVIII, 1 (March 1957), and "Canada and the Nile Expedition of 1884–85," *ibid.*, XXXIII, 4 (December 1952).

14 Toronto *Daily Mail*, February 20, 1885.

15 Melgund to Otter, March 1, 1885, PAC, Otter Papers; Otter to Melgund, March 5, 1885, Minto Papers, A-130; Macdonald to Melgund, January 10, 1885, *ibid.* See also CO 42/100, pp. 100–3 and 116–18.

16 Walker to Caron, April 8, 1882, RG 9, IIA 1, vol. 600, pp. 360–2; *House of Commons Debates*, February 15, 1882, p. 38.

17 Campbell to Caron, January 12, 1885, CP, file 7710. No order authorizing the commission has been found but its other internal records are in Minto Papers, A-130. The resulting report, "Report on the Defences of Canada, 1886," January 1, 1886, and the documents are in RG 9, IIA 1, vols. 609, 683–92.

18 Campbell to Melgund, March 20, 1885, Minto Papers, A-130.

19 Middleton to Melgund, February 25, 1885, *ibid.*; Middleton to Caron, February 24, 1885, CP, file 5198.

20 C. P. Stacey, "The Military Aspect of Canada's Winning of the West, 1870–1885," *CHR*, XXI, 1 (March 1940).

21 Deputy Minister to DAG, MD 10, November 20, 1876, RG 9, IIA 2, vol. 3, p. 1556; *Militia Report*, 1878, p. xlv.

22 Masson to Macdonald, October 13, 1879, MP, vol. 229, pp. 98673–4; Privy Council minutes, RG 2, 7 a, vol. 18, pp. 404–5, 532–3, 621.

23 Hugh John Macdonald to Macdonald, July 8, 1884, MP, vol. 200, pp. 84653–4.

24 Toronto *Daily Mail*, March 24, 1885.

25 Montreal *Gazette*, March 25, 1885.

26 Dewdney to Macdonald, March 22, 1885, PAC, Dewdney Papers, vol. 3, p. 1103.

27 There are many accounts of the progress of the campaign. See, for example, G. F. G. Stanley, *The Birth of Western Canada* (London, 1936, and rev. ed., Toronto, 1961); C. A. Boulton, *Reminiscences of the North-West Rebellions* (Toronto, 1886). The official reports are in Department of Militia and Defence, *Report Upon the Suppression of the Rebellion in the North-West Territories and Matters Connected Therewith in 1885* (Ottawa, 1886). Middleton's own account, first published in 1893, is reprinted in G. H. Needler, ed., *Suppression of the Rebellion in the North-West Territories of Canada, 1885* (Toronto, 1948).

28 Thomas White to Tupper, April 1, 1885, in C. M. Saunders, ed., *The Life and Letters of the Hon. Sir Charles Tupper, Bart., K.C.M.G.* (London, 1916), vol. II, p. 51. White was editor of the Montreal *Gazette* and a Conservative MP.

29 Macdonald to Middleton, March 29, 1885, MP, vol. 526, l.b. 23, pp. 142-3.

30 Caron's role in the campaign is well documented in the record of messages exchanged between militia headquarters and the field (CP, vol. 199).

31 Middleton to Caron, March 27, 1885, *ibid.*, p. 16.

32 Middleton to Caron, April 8 and May 2, 1885, *ibid.*, pp. 264 and 350. Men of the expedition agreed, christening the police "gophers" after the small, burrowing, prairie rodents.

33 Middleton to Caron, March 27, 1885, *ibid.*, pp. 91-2.

34 Middleton to Caron, n.d. [April 3, 1885], *ibid.*, pp. 129-30.

35 On transportation difficulties, see Wrigley to Caron, March 31, 1885, *ibid.*, p. 78; Department of Militia and Defence, *Report of Major General J. W. Laurie Commanding Base and Lines of Communication Upon Matters in Connection with the Suppression of the Rebellion in the North-West Territories in 1885* (Ottawa, 1887), passim.

36 Caron to Montizambert, March 31, 1885, CP, vol. 199, p. 81.

37 Otter to Caron, March 28, 1885, *ibid.*, p. 27; *Illustrated War News*, April 11, 1885.

38 Edward H. Smythe to Caron, April 2, 1885, CP, vol. 199, pp. 133-4.

39 A. H. Todd, "Account of the Activities of the Guards Company of Sharpshooters in the North-West Rebellion of 1885," CFHS file 505.013 (D 8).

40 Douglas to Caron, March 31, 1885, CP, vol. 199, p. 82.

41 Georges Beauregard, *Le 9ème bataillon au nord-ouest, journal d'un militaire* (Quebec, 1886), p. 15. Another vivid contemporary account is in the Toronto *Globe*, April 13, 1885.

42 Department of Militia and Defence, *Report of Lt. Col. W. H. Jackson, Principal Supply, Pay and Transport Officer to the Northwest Forces, and Chairman of the War Claims Commission on Matters in Connection with the Suppression of the Rebellion in the North-West Territories in 1885* (Ottawa, 1887), pp. 5-6.

43 "War Claims Commission Report," *ibid.*, p. 292.

44 Middleton to Caron, April 29, 1885 (confidential), CP, vol. 192, p. 4934.

45 Caron to Middleton, April 3, 1885, CP, vol. 199, p. 138; Middleton to Caron, April 14, 1885, *ibid.*, p. 270.

46 Middleton to Caron, April 1, 1885, *ibid.*, pp. 88-9 and April 8, 1885, *ibid.*, p. 264.

47 *Report Upon the Suppression of the Rebellion*, pp. 45-7.

48 Middleton to Caron, April 27, 1885 (confidential), CP, vol. 192, pp. 4930–3.

49 Lansdowne to Melgund, April 30, 1885, Minto Papers, A-129.

50 Dewdney to Otter, April 26, 1885, Otter Papers.

51 On the same day that Dewdney urged Otter to attack, Middleton telegraphed him to stay in Battleford: Middleton to Otter, April 26, 1885, *ibid.*

52 *Report Upon the Suppression of the Rebellion*, pp. 51–6; Maj.-Gen. T. B. Strange, *Gunner Jingo's Jubilee* (London, 1893), pp. 408 ff.

53 For an assessment of the various explanations, see Stanley, *Birth of Western Canada*, p. 449n.

54 *Illustrated War News*, May 2, 1885. See also Caron to Middleton, June 12, 1885, CP, vol. 199, p. 506.

55 Lansdowne to Macdonald, August 16, 1885, MP, vol. 85, p. 33192; Lansdowne to Derby, May 19, 1885, CO 42/780, pp. 392–3; Lansdowne to Stanley, July 10, 1885, CO 42/781, p. 67; Lansdowne to Stanley, August 5, 1885, *ibid.*, p. 122.

56 For example, see Mrs Strange to Caron, June 2, 1885, CP, vol. 193, pp. 5196–8, with an enclosed letter from her husband.

57 Middleton to Caron, April 29, 1885 (confidential), CP, vol. 192, pp. 4934–6.

58 G. T. Orton to Caron, September 10, 1885, CP, vol. 193, p. 5350.

59 For example, George T. Denison, *Soldiering in Canada* (Toronto, 1900), pp. 283–4.

60 Panet to Otter, December 11, 1885, Otter Papers.

61 Colonial Secretary to Lansdowne, July 27, 1885, copy in MP, vol. 85, p. 33168; Lansdowne to Macdonald, *ibid.*, p. 33194. On the recommendations, see Sir Fred Middleton, *A Parting Address to the People of Canada* (Toronto, 1890), p. 11. Despite Middleton's observations to the contrary, Caron did press for honours for the officers: Caron to Macdonald, January 18, 1887, MP, vol. 201, p. 84843.

62 Hutton Memoirs, chapter IX, British Museum, add. 50012, Hutton Papers, vol. XXXV. Lansdowne suspected Middleton of actually working against Hutton behind his back: Lansdowne to Melgund, February 8, 1886, NLS, Minto Papers, box 172.

63 *House of Commons Debates*, February 25, 1889, pp. 319 ff.

64 Caron to Lt. Col. Rhodes, April 8, 1886, CP, l.b. 15, p. 319; Caron to Mgr. Grandin, March 25, 1887, *ibid.*, vol. 19, pp. 231–2.

65 Caron to Macdonald, December 17, 1885, MP, vol. 200, pp. 84784–7.

66 In 1888–9 militia spending in the two towns reached $197,000, about 14 per cent of the department's expenditure for the financial year: *Report of the Auditor General, 1888–9* (Ottawa, 1889), pp. D-62–91.

67 Caron to Lt. Col. J. B. Forsyth, November 18, 1889, CP, l.b. 31, pp. 116–17.

68 Caron to Lt. Col. J. V. Laurin, April 3, 1886, *ibid.*, l.b. 15, p. 275.

69 Macdonald minute on Caron to Macdonald, February 20, 1888, MP, vol. 200, pp. 84941–2.

70 On Burstall, see CP, file 13506.

71 For example, *Canadian Militia Gazette*, January 1, 1891; G. R. R. Cockburn, MP, to Macdonald, March 8, 1891, MP, vol. 334, p. 151004. See Caron to Col. E. O. Hewett, November 19, 1883, CP, l.b. 6, p. 264, and *ibid.*, file 3233, for his arguments.

72 *Militia Report*, 1889, p. xii. See also CP, files 9210 and 9741, and Macpherson to Caron, August 29, 1885 (private), *ibid.*, vol. 87, p. 6640.

73 *House of Commons Debates*, April 25, 1889, pp. 1545–51. On Canadian-made uniforms, see "Notions of a Noodle," *Canadian Militia Gazette*, November 10, 1885, to June 19, 1886.

74 W. L. Mackenzie King, *Report to the Honourable the Postmaster-General on the Methods Adopted in Canada in the Carrying-out of Government Clothing Contracts* (Ottawa, 1898).

75 W. E. Sanford to Caron, October 13 and 22, 1887, CP, file 9741.

76 Hollis Shorey to Macdonald, October 29, 1887, *ibid.*, file 9643. The *Empire* was the newspaper for which Sanford was trying to raise money.

77 Middleton to Cambridge, March 1, 1889, Cambridge Papers.

78 Middleton to Melgund, February 18, 1886, Minto Papers, A–129.

79 Macdonald to Lansdowne, August 3, 1886, MP, vol. 86, p. 33859.

80 Military Secretary to Middleton, October 7, 1887, CP, file 10596; War Office to Colonial Office, September 15, 1887, CO 42/792, p. 473. R. A. Preston, *Canada and "Imperial Defense"* (Toronto, 1967), pp. 172–4.

81 Tupper to Macdonald, July 27, 1887, CP, file 11401.

82 Middleton to Caron, March 17, 1888, CP, file 10596.

83 "Memoranda of Interviews," August 17, 1886, CP, file 13095.

84 Caron to Macdonald, November 26 and 27, 1887, MP, vol. 201, pp. 84912–20.

85 Holmes to Caron, May 3, 1888, CP, file 12216.

86 Prior to Caron, February 4, 1891, *ibid.*, file 14634.

87 Knutsford to Stanley, May 2, 1889, CO 42/801, pp. 51–4; Stanley to Macdonald, May 13, 1889, MP, vol. 89, pp. 34852–4.

88 Privy Council minutes, August 10, 1889, CO 42/800, pp. 542–5. See also CP, file 13095.

89 Privy Council minutes, January 24, 1888, with Report of the Minister of Militia and Defence, January 23, 1888, RG 7, G–21, vol. 76, no. 165, file 5. See also Preston, *Canada and "Imperial Defense,"* pp. 178–81.

90 There are no surviving records of the meeting. It was probably held on

January 7, 1888 (Macdonald to Caron, January 5, 1888, CP, vol. 194, p. 5777). For what happened, see Middleton to Caron, March 1, 1889, Cambridge Papers.

91 On Cameron's appointment, see R. A. Preston, *Canada's R.M.C.* (Toronto, 1969), pp. 100–4.

92 Middleton to Caron, November 6, 1888, CP, file 11561.

93 Lansdowne to Stanley, November 28, 1885, MP, vol. 85, pp. 33293 ff.

94 Middleton to Caron, February 4, 1890, CP, file 14085.

95 Canada, Parliament, *Sessional Papers*, Appendix (1), "Report of the Select Committee in re Charles Bremner's Furs" (Ottawa, 1890).

96 Toronto *Globe*, July 1, 1890.

97 *House of Commons Debates*, May 12, 1890, pp. 4731–47.

98 See CP, file 12192. The bell had been hung up in the Millbrook fire hall as a trophy. See also Mgr. Grandin to Caron, July 12, 1885, CP, vol. 193, p. 5292.

99 Macdonald to Caron, July 14, 1890, CP, file 14085.

100 Caron to Lt. Col. George Maunsell, September 30, 1890, CP, l.b. 34, p. 55.

101 Sir Richard Cartwright, *Reminiscences* (Toronto, 1912), pp. 260–1.

CHAPTER FIVE

1 Dundas *True Banner*, July 10, 1890.

2 *Canadian Militia Gazette*, May 1, 1890; *House of Commons Debates*, May 5, 1891, p. 106; Toronto *Mail*, June 27, 1891.

3 Caron to Kirkpatrick, July 31, 1890, CP, l.b. 33, p. 236.

4 For example, Caron to Cameron, August 18, 1890, *ibid.*, l.b. 32, pp. 347–52; Tupper to Macdonald, August 23, 1890, *ibid.*, vol. 194, pp. 6233–5.

5 Caron to Strange, August 3, 1890, *ibid.*, l.b. 33, p. 286.

6 Stanley to Macdonald, July 21, 1890, MP, vol. 90, p. 35099.

7 Lorne to Macdonald, July 27, 1890, MP, vol. 90, pp. 35139–42; Connaught to Macdonald, July 27, 1890, *ibid.*, p. 35110. For Macdonald's replies, see Sir Joseph Pope, *Correspondence of Sir John Macdonald* (Oxford, n.d.), pp. 473–5.

8 The correspondence is in MP, vol. 90, pp. 35133–73 passim. See also Stanley to Cambridge, August 5, 1890, RAW, Cambridge Papers.

9 Stanley to Macdonald, July 21, 1890, MP, vol. 90, p. 35101.

10 Herbert to Cambridge, April 19, 1891, Cambridge Papers.

11 *Militia Report*, 1892, p. 5.

12 *House of Commons Debates*, September 25, 1891, p. 6182. See also CP, file 15006.

13 Herbert to Cambridge, July 6, 1891, Cambridge Papers.

14 *House of Commons Debates,* September 25, 1891, p. 6182; April 8, 1892, p. 1178, when Herbert's comments on the extravagance were mentioned by Colonel Kirkpatrick. See also CP, file 14988.

15 Ottawa *Free Press,* January 30, 1891.

16 On Caron's departure, see Herbert to Cambridge, April 11, 1892, Cambridge Papers.

17 *Militia General Orders,* no. 13, July 17, 1891; Herbert to Cambridge, October 4, 1891, Cambridge Papers.

18 Quoted by C. F. Hamilton, "The Canadian Militia: The Beginning of Reform," *Canadian Defence Quarterly,* July 1930, p. 387.

19 *Militia Report,* 1891, p. 10.

20 *Ibid.,* pp. 12–13.

21 *Ibid.,* p. 9.

22 *Ibid.,* p. 3. On the school, see CP, files 10095, 11620, and 12369; Middleton to Powell, December 20, 1889, RG 9, II B 2, vol. 8, file 23.

23 Middleton to Caron, n.d. [August 1889], CP, file 13560. On Worsley, see *ibid.,* files 4976, 5258, 5724, and 7070.

24 "General Herbert's Report on charges against Lieutenant Colonel Murray," April 9, 1891, *ibid.,* file 14324. For Worsley's case, see PAC, Sir John Thompson Papers, vol. 200, p. 25076.

25 Herbert to Cambridge, April 19, 1891, Cambridge Papers.

26 For the grievances of permanent force officers, see "In Spite of all Temptation ..." (anon., n.p., n.d.), in Wilson to Macdonald, February 22, 1889, MP, vol. 329, pp. 148913–16.

27 *Militia Report,* 1893, p. 36.

28 Stanley to Macdonald, March 10, 1891, MP, vol. 90, pp. 35312–15 and 35322–4.

29 Herbert to Cambridge, December 27, 1891, Cambridge Papers.

30 Herbert to Cambridge, April 11, 1892, *ibid.*

31 Stanley to Bowell, February 18, 1892, PAC, Bowell Papers, vol. 10, pp. 4783–97.

32 The basic British proposal is in Knutsford to Stanley, May 2, 1889, CO 42/801, pp. 51–4. See also Canadian Privy Council minutes, August 2, 1892, CO 42/817, p. 187.

33 Herbert to Cambridge, October 4, 1891, and December 24, 1892, Cambridge Papers.

34 Laurie to Bowell, March 12, 1892, Bowell Papers, vol. 10, pp. 4805–7.

35 Herbert to Cambridge, October 30, 1892, Cambridge Papers.

36 Herbert to Cambridge, March 11, 1891, *ibid.*

37 Herbert to Cambridge, December 24, 1892, *ibid.*

38 Stanley to Ripon, December 27, 1892, CO 42/812, pp. 663-9. For British reaction, see CO 42/819, pp. 109-62 passim.

39 Herbert's attitude is apparent in Herbert to Maj. Gen. Chapman, November 20, 1892, CO 42/812, pp. 949-52. See also Maj. G. S. Clarke, minute, June 14, 1892, CO 42/811, p. 688.

40 "Memorandum on the Command in Canada ...," April 2, 1891, MP, vol. 90, pp. 35340-3; Herbert to Cambridge, January 21, 1894, Cambridge Papers.

41 Herbert to Cambridge, January 16, 1895, *ibid.*

42 Herbert to Chapman, November 20, 1892, CO 42/812, pp. 51-2.

43 Herbert to Cambridge, October 30, 1892, Cambridge Papers.

44 Privy Council report, November 27, 1893, CO 42/822, pp. 96-8. For Caron's remarks see *House of Commons Debates*, February 10, 1893, p. 577.

45 On Lake, see J. F. Cummins, "Lieutenant General Sir Percy Lake and Some Chapters of Canadian and Indian Military History," *Canadian Defence Quarterly*, April 1926.

46 J. C. Patterson to General Montgomery Moore, September 12, 1893, CO 42/816, pp. 137-41.

47 *House of Commons Debates*, February 10, 1893, p. 554.

48 *Militia Report*, 1893, p. 95. See also Herbert to Cambridge, July 6, 1893, Cambridge Papers, and Hamilton, "Beginning of Reform," p. 395.

49 See *Canadian Military Gazette*, May 1, 1895, on the problem. Privy Council order, January 20, 1893, reprinted in *Militia Report*, 1893, p. 37.

50 *Canadian Militia Gazette*, October 1, 1891.

51 *House of Commons Debates*, February 10, 1893, p. 549 (Lt. Col. Amyot), for example.

52 *The Odd File* (Capt. C. Greville Harston), *The Militia of Canada* (Toronto, 1892), p. 20. One critic was a displaced brigade major, Lt. Col. James McShane, *The Dominion Militia Past and Present* (Halifax, 1896).

53 Herbert to the Assistant Adjutant General, February 14, 1895 (confidential letterbook), RG 9, II B 2, vol. 599, p. 46.

54 *Militia Report*, 1892, p. 2; *Militia General Orders*, no. 50, August 18, 1893.

55 *Ibid.* (special order), August 11, 1893; Stanley to Ripon, April 18, 1893, and enclosures, CO 42/816, pp. 433-5.

56 *Militia Report*, 1893, pp. 35-7.

57 Herbert to Patterson, July 31, 1894, RG 9, II B 1, vol. 599, pp. 27-31. His reaction was partly due to reports that trade union members had joined the militia and might not serve against strikers: Montreal *Gazette* July 26, 1894.

58 Hamilton, "Beginning of Reform," p. 395.

59 *Canadian Military Gazette*, May 15, 1895.

60 *V.R.I. Magazine*, February 1895.

61 On Hughes, see S. H. S. Hughes, "Sir Sam Hughes and the Problem of Imperialism," *CHAR*, 1950; Brig. Gen. C. F. Winter, *Lieutenant General the Hon. Sam Hughes, K.C.M.G.* (Toronto, 1931).

62 *Canadian Militia Gazette*, February 3, 1887. See also Victoria *Warder*, May 13, 1887.

63 "Memorandum re Militia," n.d., Thompson Papers, p. 21455.

64 Herbert to Cambridge, November 26, 1893, Cambridge Papers.

65 Patterson to Thompson, January 16, 1894, Thompson Papers, vol. 197, p. 24622; Aberdeen to Cambridge, February 13, 1894, Cambridge Papers; John T. Saywell, ed., *The Canadian Journal of Lady Aberdeen* (Toronto, 1960), p. 56.

66 *House of Commons Debates*, June 22, 1894, pp. 4882–4. For Herbert's view, see Herbert to Cambridge, June 21, 1894, Cambridge Papers.

67 The correspondence is in RG 9, II B 1, vol. 599, pp. 22–5. See also RG 9, II H 2, vol. 1, p. 497.

68 *House of Commons Debates*, May 14, 1894, pp. 2733–4. See G. A. Drolet, *Zouaviana* (Montreal, 1898), pp. 410–12, for Herbert's speech.

69 *House of Commons Debates*, July 17, 1894, pp. 6161–76.

70 *Ibid.*, p. 6161.

71 *Ibid.*, pp. 6186–7.

72 Guy R. McLean, "The Canadian Offer of Troops for Hong Kong, 1894," *CHR*, XXXVIII, 4 (December 1957).

73 Herbert to Cambridge, December 8, 1894, Cambridge Papers.

74 Patterson to Aberdeen, January 24, 1895, CO 42/879, pp. 376–9.

75 *House of Commons Debates*, June 6, 1895, pp. 2197–224. For other comments on Herbert, see *Canadian Military Gazette*, February 15, May 15, and June 1, 1895.

76 *House of Commons Debates*, June 5, 1895, p. 2137.

77 Sir Robert Meade memorandum, n.d., CO 42/879, p. 373.

CHAPTER SIX

1 Correspondence on Gascoigne's appointment is in CO 42/830, pp. 482, 611, and 663. On the government, see Maurice Pope, *Public Servant: The Biography of Sir Joseph Pope* (Toronto, 1960), pp. 105–7.

2 Gascoigne to Adjutant General, War Office (Sir Redvers Buller), February 5, 1896, CFHS, WO 32/275A/266/Canada/2. On Gascoigne, see R. A. Preston, *Canada and "Imperial Defense"* (Toronto, 1967), pp. 237–8; Norman Penlington, *Canada and Imperialism, 1896–1899* (Toronto, 1965), pp. 133–4.

3 Gascoigne to Laurier, June 23, 1898, LP, vol. 79B, p. 24432.

4 R. A. Preston, *Canada's R.M.C.* (Toronto, 1969), chap. VI. See also War Office to Colonial Office, April 11, 1889, CO 42/801, p. 463.

5 Department of Militia and Defence, *Reports in Reference to the Royal College for the Year 1895* (Ottawa, 1896).

6 Gascoigne to Dickey, December 2, 1895, and inspection notes, RG 9, IIB 1, vol. 592, pp. 58–9.

7 Penlington, *Imperialism*, p. 37. On the Venezuela crisis, see Kenneth Bourne, *Britain and the Balance of Power in North America, 1815–1908* (London, 1967), pp. 339–40; A. E. Campbell, *Great Britain and the United States, 1895–1903* (London, 1960), pp. 11–47.

8 *Canadian Military Gazette*, August 1, 1896; Hughes to Otter, February 3, 1896, PAC, Otter Papers.

9 Gascoigne to Buller (see above n. 2).

10 For the defence plan, see "Defence of Canada," July 11, 1898, nos. III and IV, Cab. 18/17. For the mobilization instructions, see *Militia General Orders*, April 1, 1896.

11 *Ibid.*, no. 35, April 1896.

12 Aberdeen to Chamberlain, April 29, 1896, CO 42/838, pp. 983–92.

13 The reports on the Queen's Own dispute are in Toronto *Mail & Empire*, April 23, 1896. Hamilton's version is in *ibid.*, April 30, 1896.

14 "Evidence re Fifth Royal Scots of Canada," RG 9, IIB 2, vol. 3, file (9), exhibits 31, 46, and 47.

15 Canada, *Senate Debates*, April 21, 1896, pp. 10–13; *House of Commons Debates*, April 18, 1896, pp. 6679 ff., and April 22, 1896, pp. 7017–27.

16 Gascoigne memorandum, May 9, 1896, BP; Gascoigne to Otter, May 9, 1896, Otter Papers.

17 Lt. Col. Tyrwhitt, MP, to Otter, January 18 and 21, 1896, *ibid.*; *Canadian Military Gazette*, April 1, 1896.

18 Col. Panet to Governor General's Secretary, June 27, 1896, CO 42/839, p. 306. There was also no money to pay the permanent corps: RG 9, IIB 1, vol. 599, p. 55.

19 *V.R.I. Magazine*, June 1896, pp. 65–6. (Minutes of the third meeting of the VRI Club, May 26–7, 1896.)

20 Gascoigne to Laurier, June 26, 1896, LP, vol. 12, p. 4732.

21 O. D. Skelton, *The Life and Letters of Sir Wilfrid Laurier* (Toronto, 1921), vol. II, p. 5.

22 On Borden, see Carman Miller, "The Public Life of Sir Frederick Borden" (MA thesis, Dalhousie University, 1964). If anything, Borden represented the "phalanx of fighting second-raters" whom Laurier generally by-passed in his cabinet making: J. W. Dafoe, *Laurier: A Study in Canadian Politics* (Toronto, 1922), p. 97.

23 *Canadian Military Gazette*, July 15, 1896.

24 Maj. A. D. Snelgrove to Borden, July 14, 1896, BP.

25 Lt. Col. Thomas A. Egan to Borden, n.d. [July 1896], *ibid.*, p. 48.

26 F. Langelier, MP, to Borden, October 17, 1896, *ibid.*, p. 682.

27 Laurier to Borden, June 13, 1897, *ibid.*, p. 1302.

28 J. R. Stratton, MPP, to Borden, November 7, 1896, and departmental minute, *ibid.*, p. 852.

29 *House of Commons Debates*, August 2, 1904, p. 8157. The Conservatives began their counter-attack as soon as they were in opposition. See *ibid.*, September 11, 1896, pp. 1037 ff.

30 *Ibid.*, September 11, 1896, p. 1041.

31 Borden to Hon. A. G. Blair, November 22, 1897, BP, p. 6055.

32 *House of Commons Debates*, July 10, 1899, p. 7091.

33 Borden to Barron, November 28, 1897, *ibid.*, l.b. 4, p. 710. There are harsher views of Borden's partisanship: "To the Minister, politics meant discriminating bluntly against the Conservatives ...": Norman Penlington, "General Hutton and the Problem of Military Imperialism in Canada, 1898–1900," *CHR*, XXIV, 2 (June 1943), p. 161.

34 C. F. Hamilton "The First Stirrings of Reform" (draft history in CFHS file 900.039, p. 211).

35 Fielding to Borden, August 21, 1896, BP, p. 177.

36 *Militia Report*, 1897, pp. 35–41; Kitson to Borden, February 1, 1897, BP, p. 1426; Preston, *Canada's R.M.C.*, chap. VII.

37 Luard to Caron, August 6, 1883, RG 9, IIA 1, vol. 604, p. 661. The British reaction is in WO 33/36/820.

38 Borden to Oliver, February 16, 1898, BP, l.b. 5, p. 308. See also *House of Commons Debates*, September 15, 1896, pp. 1209–10; September 18, 1896, pp. 1479–84; Gascoigne to Desjardins, February 3, 1896, RG 9, IIB 1, vol. 592, pp. 83–4.

39 Borden to Laurier, August 20, 1898, LP, vol. 84, pp. 25888–91.

40 *Militia General Orders*, no. 73, September 1896. For Militia reaction, see

Canadian Military Gazette, October 1 and 15, 1896. On the reasons for the order: Gascoigne to Otter, March 3, 1897, Otter Papers.

41 Toronto *Globe*, November 27, 1896. The Toronto *Telegram* (December 1, 1896) revealed that the Minister also used the occasion to display his talent as an amateur fiddler: "They say that the genial Doctor can attend to Beethoven when necessary, but much to the delight of his warlike audience, he broke out on this occasion in gallops and reels until he made the hair of the pianist almost stand on end."

42 *Canadian Military Gazette*, January 1, 1897.

43 Gascoigne to Worsley, January 30, 1897, BP, p. 1419; Borden to Laurier, January 16, 1897, *ibid.*, l.b. 4, p. 8; *House of Commons Debates,* June 8, 1898, p. 7517.

44 Borden to Laurier, November 29, 1897, BP, l.b. 4, p. 765.

45 Neilson to Borden, January 3, 1897, *ibid.*, p. 1202. See also Secretary, Canadian Medical Association, to Laurier, October 18, 1898, LP, C–760, pp. 27235–6. On the background of the militia medical service, see George Sterling Ryerson, *Looking Backward* (Toronto, 1924), pp. 94–9.

46 For example, *House of Commons Debates*, May 31, 1898, pp. 6574–7.

47 No formal record of the Lakewood meetings has been found. For informal record of the decisions, see Harry Brown to Borden, March 17, 1897, BP, p. 1618; Gascoigne to Borden, March 28, 1897, *ibid.*, p. 1674. On Cartwright's views, see Cartwright to Borden, March 16, 1897, *ibid.*, p. 1612.

48 Gascoigne to Borden, April 9, 1897, RG 9, II B 1, vol. 592, p. 147.

49 Gascoigne to Borden, May 22, 1897, BP, p. 2084.

50 For British reactions to the Canadian contingent, see CO 42/847, pp. 205–16. For an account of the political pressure, see Lake to Borden, May 3, 1897, BP, p. 1916.

51 *Canadian Military Gazette*, June 16, 1897. The official report is in *Militia Report*, 1897, pp. 42–54.

52 Gascoigne to Buller (see above, n. 2).

53 Gascoigne to Borden, March 28, 1897, BP, p. 1674.

54 On Domville, see Penlington, *Imperialism*, p. 163n; Douglas How, *The 8th Hussars* (Sussex, NB, 1964), pp. 39–51; on Domville's offer of troops, CO 42/838, pp. 684–9.

55 Gascoigne to Borden, April 13, 1897, BP, p. 1757, and April 16, 1897, *ibid.*, p. 1780.

56 Domville to Laurier, February 16, 1898, LP, vol. 66, pp. 20811–14.

57 Borden to Gascoigne, July 7, 1897, BP, l.b. 4, p. 607. On the advice, see *ibid.*, pp. 1562–73.

58 Lt. Col. Gerald Kitson to Hutton, October 2, 1897, British Museum; Hutton Papers, add. 50096, p. 161.

59 *Ibid.*, December 1, 1897; Borden to Lt. Col. J. D. Irving, December 1, 1897, BP, l.b. 4, p. 810.

60 *Canadian Military Gazette*, January 15, 1897.

61 Gascoigne to Otter, March 10, 1897, Otter Papers.

62 Gascoigne to Borden, April 9, 1897, BP, p. 1737.

63 Gascoigne to Aberdeen, November 10, 1897, RG 7, G–21, vol. 79, file 166.

64 Borden to Gascoigne, November 9, 1897, BP, p. 640.

65 Montreal *Star*, November 18, 1897.

66 The correspondence is in the RG 7, G–21, vol. 79, file 166. See also *Canadian Military Gazette*, January 5, 1898, and Borden to F. L. Beique, QC, March 22, 1898, BP, l.b. 5, p. 949.

67 Gascoigne to Aberdeen, November 15, 1897, RG 7, G–21, vol. 79, file 166.

68 War Office to Colonial Office, June 25, 1896, and minutes, CO 42/845, pp. 96–8. See also CO 42/850, p. 305.

69 Laurier to Aberdeen, March 9, 1898, PAC, Aberdeen Papers, vol. 3, pp. 1013–14.

70 Gascoigne to Erskine, April 19, 1898, RG 7, G–21, vol. 79, file 166.

71 *Canadian Military Gazette*, May 5, 1898; Aberdeen to Laurier, April 22, 1898, Aberdeen Papers, vol. 3, p. 1043.

72 *Canadian Military Gazette*, May 17, 1898.

73 *House of Commons Debates*, May 5, 1898, pp. 4932–45.

74 *Ibid.*, May 30, 1898, pp. 6320–1; Gascoigne to Erskine, May 22, 1898, RG 7, G–21, vol. 79, file 166.

75 *Militia Report*, 1897, p. 23; Gascoigne to Commander-in-Chief (Lord Wolseley), December 3, 1896, RG 9, IIB 1, vol. 592, pp. 120–5; Gascoigne to Borden, March 9, 1897, BP, p. 1568.

76 *V.R.I. Magazine*, March 1896, p. 262.

77 For American plans to invade Canada, see Capt. C. B. Levita to Lake, November 1, 1898, WO 106/40/B1/7; Bourne, *Britain and the Balance of Power*, pp. 319–24. In the absence of a General Staff in Washington in the period and of surviving military plans, an unexplored source of American military thinking about war with Canada is the professional journals. See 1st Lt. Thos. M. Woodruff, "Our Northern Frontier," *Journal of the Military Service Institute of the United States*, March 1888; 1st Lt. D. A. Shenk, "Our Northern Frontier," *ibid.*, November 1890, with a commentary, *ibid.*, January 1891. The ablest article is by 1st Lt. Arthur L. Wagner, "The Military Geography of Canada," *ibid.*, May 1892.

78 On the committee, see Zara Shakow, "The Defence Committee: A Fore-runner of the Committee of Imperial Defence," *CHR*, xxxvi, 1 (March 1955).

79 "Defence of Canada," April 23, 1896, wo 106/40/b1/5. Foster's reports have not been found. They are summarized in Maj. W. R. Robertson, "Memorandum on the Defence of Canada," March 15, 1901, wo 106/40/b1/7. See also Preston, *Canada and "Imperial Defense,"* pp. 235–6.

80 Minute by Edward Wingfield on James Slater to Colonial Secretary, December 26, 1892, co 42/813, p. 756.

81 Colonial Defence Committee memorandum, March 27, 1896, co 537/476, pp. 6–7.

82 Maurice Ollivier, *The Colonial and Imperial Conferences from 1887 to 1937* (Ottawa, 1954), vol. I, pp. 132–5; Preston, *Canada and "Imperial Defense,"* pp. 241–3.

83 Montgomery Moore to Aberdeen, November 3, 1897, Aberdeen Papers, vol. 3, p. 1532.

84 Montgomery Moore to Laurier, November 3, 1897, *ibid.*, pp. 1532–4, and in co 537/478, pp. 9–10.

85 Gascoigne to Borden, February 7, 1898, *ibid.*, pp. 6–7.

86 Privy Council report, February 28, 1898, co 537/479, p. 2. See also Aberdeen to Laurier, February 5, 1898, LP, c-754, pp. 20391–2.

87 Colonial Office to Admiralty and to War Office, March 11, 1898, co 537/477, pp. 6–9.

88 Privy Council minute, October 18, 1898, co 42/858, p. 723.

89 Chamberlain to Aberdeen, July 29, 1898, co 42/865, p. 263, and especially Sir John Ardagh, "Defence of Canada," December 14, 1897, wo 106/40/b1/5.

CHAPTER SEVEN

1 Aberdeen to Colonial Office, November 13, 1897, co 42/849, p. 462; War Office to Colonial Office, May 31, 1898, co 42/865, p. 171. See also Gascoigne to Aberdeen, November 15, 1897, RG 7, G-21, vol. 79, file 166.

2 On Hutton's background, see his draft memoirs, in British Museum, add. 50012. The section relating to Canada is copied in HP, pp. 1714–74.

3 On Hutton in Australia, see Warren Perry, "Military Reforms of General Sir Edward Hutton in New South Wales, 1893–1896," *Australian Quarterly*, December 1956. See also Norman Penlington, "General Hutton and the

Problem of Military Imperialism in Canada, 1898–1900," p. 158; *CHR*, XXIV, no. 2 (June 1943). R. A. Preston, *Canada and "Imperial Defense"* (Toronto, 1967), p. 250n.; and *Canadian Military Gazette,* July 21, 1898.

4 *Ibid.,* June 25, 1891.

5 E. T. H. Hutton, "A Co-operative System for the Defence of the Empire," reprinted in *Selected Papers of the Canadian Military Institute,* vol. VIII, 1897–8.

6 Memorandum of interview with Lord Wolseley, July 29, 1898, HP, p. 4.

7 Memorandum of interview with Joseph Chamberlain, August 8, 1898, *ibid.,* pp. 259–62.

8 Wolseley interview, *ibid.,* p. 4.

9 Memorandum of interview with Lord Lansdowne, August 3, 1898, *ibid.,* pp. 26–9; Memorandum of interview with Edward Wingfield, August 10, 1898, *ibid.,* pp. 955–7; and Chamberlain interview, *ibid.,* pp. 960–1.

10 H. P. Gundy, "Sir Wilfrid Laurier and Lord Minto," *CHAR*, 1952, pp. 28–9.

11 Seymour to Hutton, July 25, 1898, HP, pp. 174–5.

12 Hutton to Minto, September 3, 1898, PAC, Minto Papers, vol. 17, p. 3. On his reception, see Hutton memoirs, p. 1720.

13 *Canadian Military Gazette,* November 1, 1898. On the tour, see HP, pp. 147–50.

14 Hutton to Borden, October 7, 1898, RG 9, IIB I, vol. 599, p. 84.

15 Hutton to Borden, October 7, 1898, CO 42/868, pp. 574–5.

16 *Canadian Military Gazette,* January 2, 1899.

17 "Address to D.O.C. s, Commanding Officers and Adjutants," September–October 1898, HP, pp. 1051–63.

18 Hutton memoirs, p. 1722.

19 *Militia General Orders,* no. 12, 1898. See Desmond Morton, "French Canada and the Canadian Militia," *Histoire Sociale,* p. 3.

20 Hutton to Minto, November 20, 1898, Minto Papers, vol. 15, p. 8.

21 "Instructions to Members of the 1898 Defence Committee," Section B, Cab. 11/27.

22 Reports no. 1 and 2 of the Committee of Canadian Defence, 1898, Cab. 11/27. Parts 1 and 2 are also in CFHS, WO 32/275A/266/Canada/99.

23 For Part 3, see President, Defence Committee of Canada, to the Secretary of State for War, November 30, 1898, WO 32/6366 (in CFHS, WO 32/275A/266/Canada/79).

24 Leach to War Office, November 17, 1898, CO 42/865, pp. 369–70.

25 *Ibid.,* minute, p. 367.

26 Hutton to Coleridge Grove, January 9, 1899, HP, pp. 33–7.

27 Hutton's views (May 30, 1899) are bound with Report no. 1 (see n. 22), and also in Hutton to Maj. Nathan, January 9, 1899, HP, p. 1048.

28 *Militia Report*, 1898, pp. 31–42; "Memoirs," HP, pp. 1729–30.

29 On Hutton's surprise, see Hutton to Bevan Edwards, February 12, 1899, HP, pp. 461–3.

30 Galt *Daily Reporter,* March 29, 1899.

31 Toronto *World,* March 30, 1899.

32 "Bystander" in Montreal *News,* April 7, 1899; Toronto *Saturday Night,* April 15, 1899.

33 Tupper to Hutton, April 4, 1899, HP, p. 517; Toronto *Globe,* April 11, 1899.

34 Hutton to Harrison, April 7, 1899, HP, pp. 95–104. The British were by no means completely happy with Hutton's strategem. See minutes to "War with the United States," WO 106/40/B1/7.

35 On the Officers' Association, see *Canadian Military Gazette,* April 2 and July 19, 1898. On Hutton's negotiations, see Hutton Papers, pp. 1259–1443 passim. See also *United Service Magazine,* May 1897, for the United Service Club, and *Report of the Officers' Association of the Militia of Canada,* no. 2, 1899 (CFHS library).

36 Hutton to Grove, January 9, 1899, HP, p. 35.

37 Hutton to Lt. Col. Minden Cole, January 4, 1899, *ibid.,* pp. 447–8.

38 Montreal *Gazette,* February 13, 1899.

39 Toronto *Globe,* March 4, 1899.

40 On the camps, see *Militia Report,* 1899, pp. 19–20. On reaction, see London *Advertiser,* June 10, 1899; Toronto *Globe,* June 5–17, 1899; Montreal *Herald,* July 3, 1899; *Le Soleil,* July 7–8, 1899; *La Patrie,* June 26, 1899.

41 Report of the Defence Committee, part 2, pp. 80–2.

42 On Foster's appointment, see Privy Council report, August 18, 1898, CO 42/858, p. 553; War Office to Colonial Office, September 27, 1898, CO 42/856, p. 324.

43 Borden to Hutton, November 2, 1898, HP, p. 236; Hutton to Borden November 21, 1898, *ibid.,* p. 237; Sir Richard Cartwright to Borden, December 16, 1898, *ibid.,* p. 238; Borden to Hutton, January 30, 1899, BP, l.b. 8, p. 634.

44 Hutton to General Sir Evelyn Wood, May 14, 1899, HP, pp. 59–61.

45 Hutton to Major F. G. Stone, March 31, 1899, *ibid.,* l.b. 24, p. 1340; Hutton to Stone, May 1, 1899, *ibid.,* p. 1405. For examples of criticism, see Toronto *Mail & Empire,* May 13, 1899.

46 Hutton to Ardagh, November 21, 1898, HP, pp. 88–9. (Ardagh was Director of Military Intelligence.)

47 Hutton to Borden, October 7, 1898, RG 9, II B 1, vol. 599, pp. 84–5. On the
    Australian experience, see Perry, "Military Reforms of Hutton," pp. 5–6.

48 Borden to Gascoigne, November 20, 1896, BP, l.b. 2, p. 458.

49 Hutton to Capt. J. C. Clauson, April 24, 1899, HP, p. 1085. On Macdonald's
    criticisms, see Militia Report, 1896, pp. 1–2; 1897, pp. 1–2.

50 Hutton to Maj. Nathan, January 9, 1899, HP, p. 1044.

51 Montreal Gazette, November 21–2, 1898; Ottawa Citizen, November 28,
    1898. On Talbot's appointment, see Borden to Tarte, BP, l.b. 5, p. 768. On
    the affair, see Borden to Evans, November 16, 1898, ibid., l.b. 7, p. 835;
    Hutton to Borden, November 4, 1898, HP, l.b. 24, p. 1227.

52 Hutton to Borden, February 20, 1899, ibid., p. 1297.

53 Borden to Hutton, April 26, 1899, BP, l.b. 9, p. 721.

54 Borden to Laurier, August 20, 1898, LP, C-758, p. 25890.

55 Borden to Pinault, November 23, 1898, BP, l.b. 7, p. 971. On the incident with
    Panet, see Pinault to Laurier, July 9, 1898, LP, C-758, pp. 24932–3; Canadian
    Military Gazette, August 16, 1898.

56 Militia General Orders, no. 90, October 1897. On the effects, see Canadian
    Military Gazette, November 3, 1897; House of Commons Debates, April
    27, 1899, pp. 2183–4.

57 On the Domville affair, see HP, pp. 1414–32; Borden to Domville, March 6,
    1899, BP, l.b. 8, p. 1003; Norman Penlington, Canada and Imperialism,
    1896–1899 (Toronto, 1965), p. 163n.

58 Borden to Hutton, May 29, 1899, BP, l.b. 10, p. 178.

59 Hutton to Borden, May 31, 1899, HP, pp. 904–15.

60 Minto to Laurier, June 7, 1899, LP, C-766, pp. 34269–77. See also Minto
    Papers, A-130, pp. 111–15.

61 Hutton to Minto, June 18, 1899, ibid., vol. 15, p. 28.

62 Hutton to Buller, June 18, 1899, HP, p. 77. (Buller was then Adjutant
    General of the British Army.)

63 Penlington, Imperialism, pp. 162–7.

64 Hutton to Borden, August 4, 1899, HP, p. 1477.

65 Mulock to Borden, December 9, 1899, BP, p. 6181.

66 Borden arranged for Hughes's brother to be transferred to the command of
    another battalion and made other arrangements to get Sam the command
    of the 45th: Col. Cotton to Adjutant General, May 14, 1897, BP, p. 2020.

67 Hughes to Hutton, November 29, 1898, with Hughes to Montizambert,
    November 29, 1898, HP, pp. 1101–18.

68 Toronto Globe, August 30, 1899.

69 The correspondence is in HP, pp. 663–98.

70 On the scheme to "repatriate" the 100th Regiment, see CFHS, WO 32/427/20/100/ files 17–30, and Lt. Col. F. E. Whitton, *The History of the Prince of Wales Leinster Regiment (Royal Canadians)* (Aldershot, n.d.), pp. 123–30. On Hutton's views, see Hutton to Borden, February 11, 1899, CO 42/868, pp. 169–72.

71 Seymour to Hutton, June 3, 1899, HP, pp. 263–4. On the incident, see *ibid.*, pp. 275–9.

72 Seymour to Hutton, July 5, 1899, *ibid.*, p. 288. The justification was Lyttelton to Seymour, May 14, 1899 and ff., CFHS, WO 32/815/058/2525. On Seymour's state of mind, see Minto to Lansdowne, August 9, 1899, Minto Papers, A-130, p. 147.

73 For their correspondence, see HP, pp. 263–290A.

74 Dufferin to Cambridge, December 11, 1874, RAW, Cambridge Papers.

75 For Seymour's attitude, see Seymour to Hutton, April 13, 1899, HP, pp. 183–4, and May 24, 1899, *ibid.*, p. 191. See also Minto to Seymour, Minto Papers, A-130, p. 78.

76 Minto to Seymour, August 3, 1899, *ibid.*, pp. 141–4; Minto to Lansdowne, August 30, 1899, *ibid.*, pp. 165–9.

77 War Office to Colonial Office, October 31, 1899, CO 42/873, p. 455. (The War Office did insist that the confidential reports should pass through Halifax.) For the effect on their later careers, see Hutton to Minto, November 17, 1901, Minto Papers, vol. 15, p. 62; Foster to Minto, June 3, 1901, NLS, Minto Papers, box 205, case 6, packet 1.

78 Hutton had agreed to serve for three instead of the usual five-year term. See HP, pp. 42–7, and Hutton to Borden, November 8, 1898, CO 42/869, p. 371. One example of the antagonism developing between the two men is Borden to Hutton, August 16, 1899, BP, l.b. 11, p. 34: "I venture to suggest that it is unnecessary to remind me so frequently of the impropriety of members of the Militia or others entering into direct correspondence with me about Militia matters. My view of this differs materially from yours."

79 *House of Commons Debates*, July 31, 1899, pp. 8992–8; Chamberlain to Minto, July 3, 1899, Minto Papers, vol. 15, pp. 40–2.

80 Hutton to Chamberlain, July 28, 1899, HP, pp. 973–9; Hutton to Minto, September 3, 1899, Minto Papers, vol. 15, pp. 107–8. See also *ibid.*, pp. 100–5.

81 Borden to Laurier, September 4, 1899, LP, vol. 124, pp. 37194–6.

82 Memorandum on a conversation with Laurier, March 27, 1899, CO 537–483, pp. 8–9. The issue arose from a scheme concocted by Seymour and Admiral Sir John Fisher to seize the French islands of St. Pierre and Miquelon in the

event of war with France over the Fashoda crisis. See wo 32/6367.

83 Laurier to Minto, July 30, 1899, Minto Papers, vol. 7, p. 100; Minto to
Chamberlain, September 23, 1899, *ibid.*, A-130, pp. 181–2.

84 Hughes to Chamberlain, July 24, 1899, co 42/874, pp. 632–3; Hughes to
Chamberlain (personal), July 24, 1899, *ibid.*, pp. 634–5; Hughes to Otter,
September 25, 1899, pac, Otter Papers.

85 Minto to Laurier, August 14, 1899, lp, c-768, pp. 36477–82; Minto to
Hutton, August 10, 1899, Minto Papers, A-130, pp. 149–50.

86 The correspondence is in hp, pp. 1132–77, and "Copies of Correspondence ...
etc.," in Canada, Parliament, *Sessional Papers*, 1900, no. 77.

87 "Memoirs," hp, p. 1745.

88 *Ibid.*, pp. 1746–7.

89 *Canadian Military Gazette*, October 3, 1899; Toronto *Globe*, October 4,
1899. See also Laurier to Tarte, October 4, 1899, cited in Robert Rumilly,
Histoire de Québec (Montreal, n.d.), vol. ix, pp. 121–2.

90 Hutton to Borden, October 10, 1899, hp (British Museum, add. 50083). On
the campaign, see Penlington, *Imperialism*, pp. 183–260.

91 On the cabinet suspicions, see Minto to Chamberlain, October 13, 1899, co
42/869, p. 389; Minto to Chamberlain, October 14, 1899, Minto Papers,
A-130, pp. 203–7; and *ibid.*, vol. 15, pp. 114–17.

92 Hutton to Foster, October 14, 1899, Minto Papers, vol. 15, p. 82. For
Hughes's view, see Hughes to Otter, October 1, 1899, Otter Papers; Hughes
to Laurier, copy to Richard Scott, October 23, 1899, pac, Scott Papers, vol.
14, pp. 1647–54.

93 Hutton to Minto, October 27, 1899, Minto Papers, vol. 15, p. 88; Hughes to
Hutton, October 27, 1899, hp, p. 1126. See also Mrs Hughes to Laurier,
November 1, 1899, lp, c-770, pp. 38523–8.

94 Hutton to Lt. Gen. Forestier Walker, n.d. [November 1899], hp, p. 1674.

95 Hutton to Minto, February 2, 1900, Minto Papers, vol. 18, pt. 2, pp. 42–3;
Minto to Laurier, November 8, 1899, lp, c-770, pp. 38759–62.

96 Minto to Roberts, December 31, 1899, Minto Papers, A-130, pp. 276–7.

97 Minto to Chamberlain, January 7, 1900, *ibid.*, pp. 284–7.

98 Borden to Hutton, December 18, 1899, bp, l.b. 12, p. 126; "Memoirs," hp,
pp. 1761–3.

99 Hutton to Minto, February 2, 1900, Minto Papers, vol. 18, pt. 2, pp. 44–9.
See also Hutton to Kitson, January 11, 1900, hp, pp. 1644–5.

100 Minto to Chamberlain, January 18, 1900, Minto Papers, A-130, pp. 295–300.

101 The original memorandum from Minto was torn up by Laurier with an
apology for having shown it to the cabinet (Memorandum of conversation,

February 7, 1900, *ibid.*, vol. 18, pt. 2, p. 8). The cabinet memorandum is in *ibid.*, vol. 18, pp. 17–38.

102 Beckles Willson, *The Life of Lord Strathcona and Mount Royal* (London, 1915), pp. 518–21; Hutton to Sir Edward Clouston, n.d. [January 1900], HP, p. 557.

103 Borden to Hutton, January 23, 1900, HP, l.b. 12, p. 465.

104 "Memo 'A' prepared and checked with Mr. Ferguson, Q.C.," February 2, 1900, HP, pp. 889–901.

105 "Reasons for General Hutton having decided not to submit a statement etc. ... ," *ibid.*, pp. 880–8 (written on the voyage to South Africa, March 7–9, 1900).

106 Hughes to Hutton, August 26, 1899, in *Sessional Papers*, no. 77, p. 26.

107 Ottawa *Citizen*, January 30, 1900. For reaction, see Toronto *Evening Telegram*, January 11, 1900; Toronto *Globe*, January 20, 1900.

108 Hutton to Minto, January 16, 1900, Minto Papers, A-130, l.b. 1, p. 302; Borden to Laurier, February 3, 1900, *ibid.*, vol. 18, pt. 2, pp. 21–2.

109 *Militia Orders*, no. 16(1), January 20, 1900; no. 21(1), January 26, 1900; Foster to Lt. Col. W. W. White, January 29, 1900, and February 1, 1900, Minto Papers, vol. 18, pt. 2, pp. 26–7.

110 *House of Commons Debates*, April 3, 1900, pp. 3100–1. See also Dr James Stirton to Borden, December 8, 1900, BP, p. 6176.

111 Minto Papers, vol. 18, pt. 2, pp. 24–8.

112 Hutton to Minto, February 3, 1900, *ibid.*, p. 3.

113 Minto to Laurier, February 4, 1900, LP, C-772, pp. 41963–71; Minto to Laurier, February 6, 1900, *ibid.*, C-773, pp. 42073–6.

114 Laurier proposed resignation on January 17. Minto to Chamberlain, January 18, 1900, Minto Papers, A-130, p. 299. The British view is in Colonial Office to War Office, February 2, 1900, CO 42/875, p. 204, and minutes.

115 Minto to Hutton, February 7, 1900, Minto Papers, A-130, p. 320.

116 *House of Commons Debates*, February 13, 1900, pp. 323–49. Laurier's version of what happened is in Laurier to Chamberlain, February 22, 1900, LP, C-771, pp. 40100–5.

117 Ottawa *Free Press*, February 14, 1900; Ottawa *Citizen*, February 15, 1900. See also draft reply to George E. Foster, February 12, 1900, HP, pp. 154–5.

118 Ottawa *Citizen*, February 15–16, 1900; Theodore Roosevelt to Hutton, February 13, 1900, HP, p. 160.

119 Otter to Hutton, March 28, 1900, *ibid.*, p. 167.

120 For example, Minto to Chamberlain, February 7, 1900, Minto Papers, A-130, p. 315.

121 Hutton to Sir Evelyn Wood, February 11, 1900, British Museum, Hutton
     Papers, add. 50086, p. 221.
122 Borden to Lt. Gen. J. W. Laurie, MP, March 5, 1900, BP.

CHAPTER EIGHT

 1 Minto to Chamberlain, February 7, 1900, PAC, Minto Papers, A-130, pp.
    312–13.
 2 *House of Commons Debates*, February 13, 1900, pp. 323–49. See also Mon-
    treal *Star*, February 12 and 16, 1900; Toronto *Mail & Empire*, February
    16–22, 1900; Montreal *Gazette*, February 13, 1900; Hamilton *Spectator*,
    February 13, 1900. One Liberal minister regarded Hutton's farewell speeches
    as a breach of an undertaking: R. R. Dobell to Hutton, February 15, 1900,
    HP, p. 635.
 3 Toronto *Evening Telegram*, March 26, 1900. The correspondence is in
    Sessional Papers, no. 77 (1900). See also *House of Commons Debates*, Feb-
    ruary 19, 1900, pp. 564–605.
 4 *Ibid.*, April 3, 1900, pp. 3102–4.
 5 Chamberlain to Strathcona, February 13, 1900, in Beckles Willson, *The Life
    of Lord Strathcona and Mount Royal* (London, 1915), p. 525. On Hutton's
    reception, see Hutton to Minto, February 27 and March 2, 1900, Minto
    Papers, vol. 15, pp. 4, 40–1. See also Chamberlain minute, CO 42/875, p. 247.
 6 Laurier to Chamberlain, February 22, 1900, LP, C-771, pp. 40100–5.
 7 Laurier to Strathcona, February 22, 1900, *ibid.*, C-773, pp. 42337–41.
 8 Chamberlain to Minto, April 17, 1900, CO 42/875, pp. 551–4.
 9 Borden memorandum, n.d., CO 42/876, pp. 166–9.
10 Privy Council minute, June 9, 1900, *ibid.*, pp. 161–2.
11 Minto to Chamberlain, June 11, 1900, *ibid.*, pp. 158–60.
12 *House of Commons Debates*, February 13, 1900, pp. 339–40.
13 *Ibid.*, p. 333.
14 Minto to Chamberlain, March 26, 1900, CO 42/875, pp. 678–9.
15 War Office to Colonial Office, April 5, 1900, CO 42/879, p. 338; Chamberlain
    to Minto, April 9, 1900, *ibid.*, p. 339.
16 Kitson to Minto, February 18, 1900, NLS, Minto Papers, box 213, packet 2.
17 Laurier to Minto, April 8, 1900, *ibid.*, box 209, case B; Laurier to Lansdowne,
    April 9, 1900, LP, C-775, pp. 44941–4; Lansdowne to Laurier, April 24,
    1900, *ibid.*, pp. 44938–40. The suggestion came from Borden: Borden to
    Laurier, March 20, 1900, *ibid.*, C-774, p. 43605.

18 Minto to Laurier, May 8, 1900, *ibid.*, c-775, pp. 45366–72.

19 Charles Harington, *Plumer of Messines* (London, 1935), p. 6. On O'Grady Haly, see *Canadian Military Gazette*, August 7, 1900.

20 Hutton to Minto, July 19, 1900, Minto Papers, vol. 16, p. 52.

21 Foster to Hutton, August 12, 1900, HP, p. 755.

22 O'Grady Haly to Borden, April 9, 1902, Minto Papers, vol. 8, p. 123.

23 *Militia Report*, 1900, pp. 35–7.

24 Borden to O'Grady Haly, February 18, 1900, BP, l.b. 16, pp. 1126–7.

25 Borden to O'Grady Haly (date unintelligible, probably March 1901), *ibid.*, p. 640.

26 On the scandal, see *Canadian Military Gazette*, April 3, 1900; *House of Commons Debates*, June 6, 1900, pp. 6790–887; Carman Miller, "The Public Life of Sir Frederick Borden" (MA thesis, Dalhousie University, 1964), pp. 116–22.

27 Hutton to Minto, June 2, 1900, Minto Papers, vol. 16, pp. 37–40; Minto to Laurier, July 17, 1900, LP, c-777, pp. 47539–41. The Conservatives were embarrassed by their own attacks on Borden's son. See, for example, *House of Commons Debates*, June 20, 1900, pp. 7892–3.

28 On Borden's sense of grievance, see Minto Papers, vol. 8, pp. 47–62. See also Hutton to Minto, May 28, 1901, CFHS, file 934.009 (D 533).

29 Quoted by W. Sanford Evans, *The Canadian Contingents and Canadian Imperialism* (London, 1901), p. 320.

30 For the effect of the war on Canadian nationalism, see R. A. Preston, *Canada and "Imperial Defense"* (Toronto, 1967), pp. 276–7; C. P. Stacey, "Nationality: The Experience of Canada," *CHAR*, 1967.

31 Foster to Hutton, August 12, 1900, HP, pp. 755–9.

32 Borden to O'Grady Haly, March 21, 1901, BP, l.b. 17, p. 742. Hutton, in fact, had a low opinion of Foster: see Hutton to Minto, April 23, 1900, Minto Papers, vol. 16, p. 18.

33 Borden to Laurier, December 17, 1900, LP, c-781, pp. 51690–3.

34 Foster to Hutton, n.d. [December 1900], HP, pp. 760–2; Minto to Brodrick, January 12, 1901, CO 42/886, pp. 220–1; Governor General to Colonial Office, February 5, 1901, CO 42/881, p. 393.

35 Minto to Laurier, January 5, 1901, LP, c-781, pp. 52242–6; Minutes to Governor General to Colonial Office, January 7, 1901, CO 42/881, pp. 37–8. (Aylmer succeeded his father as the 8th Baron in 1900.)

36 Governor General to Colonial Office, February 5, 1901, CO 42/881, p. 393. On Foster, see Foster to Minto, March 21, 1901, NLS, Minto Papers, box 210, case c.

37 Sir Montague Ommanney minute to Minto to Chamberlain June 6, 1900,
    CO 42/876, pp. 126–30. The matter greatly concerned both Minto and the
    British military authorities, fearful lest a Canadian officer should have the
    right to command British soldiers in action. See War Office to Colonial
    Office, May 11, 1900, CO 42/879, pp. 377–8, and August 31, 1900, *ibid.*,
    p. 510. See also Minto to Laurier, May 18, 1900, LP, C-776, pp. 45698–704,
    and May 22, 1900, pp. 45683–6. See also CFHS, WO 32/058/2600 ff.

38 Privy Council report, March 30, 1899, CO 42/858, pp. 356; Minto to
    Chamberlain, April 5, 1899, *ibid.*, pp. 350–4.

39 Minutes to Privy Council report, April 15, 1902, CO 42/892, pp. 524–8. See
    also War Office to Colonial Office, July 3, 1901, CO 42/886, pp. 406–7, and
    Borden's memorandum, n.d., LP, vol. 771, p. 219266.

40 Maurice Ollivier, *The Colonial and Imperial Conferences from 1887 to
    1937* (Ottawa, 1954), vol. I, pp. 179–81. On Borden's attendance, see
    Preston, *Canada and "Imperial Defense,"* p. 293. But see also Borden to
    Laurier, July 2, 1902, LP, C-794, pp. 66302–5.

41 Ollivier, *Imperial Conferences*, pp. 208–9.

42 *Ibid.*, pp. 179–80. On the Ross rifle, see Col. A. F. Duguid, *"Official History
    of the Canadian Forces in the Great War, 1914–1919,"* General Series,
    vol. I, *Chronology, Appendices and Maps* (Ottawa, 1938), appendix iii,
    pp. 75 ff.

43 *Ibid.*, p. 77; O'Grady Haly to Deputy Minister, May 1, 1902, RG 9, II B 1,
    vol. 600, pp. 63–8.

44 O'Grady Haly to Borden, May 9, 1901, *ibid.*, vol. 599, pp. 527–35; *Canadian
    Military Gazette*, July 2, 1901.

45 *Ibid.*, March 5, 1901; April 2, 1901. See also Adjutant General to DOCs
    (circular), April 9, 1901, RG 9, II B 1, vol. 599, p. 548.

46 Borden to Minto, March 24, 1902, Minto Papers, vol. 8, p. 112.

47 Minto to Roberts, August 8, 1901, NLS, Minto Papers, l.b. 2.

48 O'Grady Haly to Minto, June 25, 1902, *ibid.*, box 205, case 6.

CHAPTER NINE

1 Lord Dundonald, *My Army Life* (London, 1926), pp. 1–186. See also Brian
   Bond, "Doctrine and Training in the British Cavalry," in Michael Howard,
   ed., *The Theory and Practice of War* (London, 1965), p. 108.

2 Kitson to Minto, January 6 and August 6, 1901, NLS, Minto Papers, box 213,
   case 2.

3 Minto to Roberts, October 11, 1901, *ibid.*, l.b. 3.

4 Hutton to Minto, October 11, 1901, *ibid.*, vol. 17, p. 49.

5 Kitson to Minto, December 2, 1901, *ibid.*, box 213, case 2. For another view, later shared by Minto himself, see Sir Hubert Gough, *Soldiering On* (London, 1954), p. 70. See also Lord Birdwood, *Khaki and Gown* (London, 1941), p. 99.

6 Minto to Laurier, February 5, 1902, LP, C-791, pp. 62459–64.

7 Brantford *Courier*, August 29, 1902.

8 Dundonald to Minto, April 13, 1902, NLS, Minto Papers, box 213, case 2.

9 Dundonald, *Army Life*, p. 191 (the only apparent source for this regularly repeated quotation).

10 *Ibid.*, p. 186.

11 On the problems of the militia, see *Militia Report*, 1900, pp. 35–7; 1901, pp. 23, 31; *House of Commons Debates*, April 10, 1902, pp. 2498–534; *Canadian Military Gazette*, 1901–3, passim. The "Special Correspondent" was apparently Lt. Col. Andrew Thompson, Liberal MP for Haldimand. See *House of Commons Debates*, June 30, 1903.

12 O'Grady Haly to Borden, March 6, 1901, RG 9, II B 1, vol. 599, pp. 520–2.

13 Toronto *Globe*, September 2, 1902.

14 *Ibid.*; Toronto *Mail & Empire*, September 2, 1902.

15 Complaints from Minto about some of Hughes's letters which had appeared in Canadian papers crossed with complaints from South Africa. See Minto to Chamberlain, June 18, 1900, CO 42/876, pp. 191–2; War Office to Roberts, June 19, 1900, CO 42/879, pp. 434–5. See also Hughes to Chamberlain, July 16, 1901, *ibid.*, pp. 438–9; *The Times*, June 2, 1900. On the "Turpin" letters, see *House of Commons Debates*, June 24, 1900, pp. 5500–18.

16 Minto to Ommanney, July 1, 1903, CO 42/895, pp. 522–6.

17 Dundonald to Roberts, April 27, 1903, Douglas Library, Queen's University, Kingston, Dundonald Papers (microfilm).

18 Dundonald, *Army Life*, pp. 191–2; Dundonald to Borden, November 12, 1902, and March 19, 1903, RG 9, II B 1, vol. 600, pp. 196–203, 286–89.

19 Toronto *Globe*, November 20, 1902.

20 Undated draft for the unpublished Part II of the 1902 Militia Department report, Dundonald Papers, section B.

21 Dundonald to Col. E. A. Altham, March 6, 1903, CO 42/895, pp. 64–75. See also Dundonald Papers, section F.

22 Hutton to Minto, August 18, 1900, PAC, Minto Papers, vol. 16, pp. 53–5; Borden to Minto, April 21, 1902, *ibid.*, vol. 8, p. 122.

23 Borden to Dundonald, January 31, February 21 and 23, 1903, Dundonald

Papers, section F, pp. 1–4. The changes are noted on the typescript of the draft in this section.

24 Montreal *Herald*, March 20, 1903; Dundonald, *Army Life*, p. 212. Dundonald's estimate of the capital cost of his recommendations came to $11,594,950, with an added annual maintenance cost of $2,791,087. Militia expenditure in 1902 had been $2,914,997. See "Estimate of Cost of Recommendations of General Officer Commanding in December, 1902," Dundonald Papers, section F.

25 *House of Commons Debates*, May 29, 1903, p. 3763.

26 Hamilton *Herald*, April 24, 1903; Hamilton *Times*, April 24, 1903.

27 *House of Commons Debates*, May 5, 1903, p. 2403.

28 *Ibid.*, p. 2406.

29 *Ibid.*, p. 2421.

30 "On reports of difficulties and proposed resignation," Dundonald Papers, section B.

31 Toronto *News*, June 17, 1903.

32 *Militia Report*, 1903, pp. 7–10, 39–40; *House of Commons Debates*, October 8, 1903, pp. 13387–93.

33 Privy Council minute, October 29, 1903, in *Militia Report*, 1903, pp. 8–10.

34 Governor General to Colonial Office, April 13, 1903, CO 42/892, p. 489.

35 Seymour to War Office, May 31, 1900, CFHS, WO 32/815/058/2525. For the balance of the lengthy correspondence, see *ibid.*, files 2414, 2424, and 2526.

36 War Office to Colonial Office, May 8, 1901, CO 42/886, p. 329; Roberts to Minto, May 28, 1901, NLS, Minto Papers, box 213, case 2.

37 Minto to Chamberlain, May 28, 1903, CO 42/892, pp. 649–60.

38 Minto to Chamberlain, May 28, 1903, *ibid.*, pp. 654–9, and Minto to Chamberlain (private), April 15, 1903, CO 42/895, pp. 86–8. On the pressure, see Lt. Col. James Peters to Minto, July 26 and August 28, 1900, NLS, Minto Papers, box 205, case 6, packet 7.

39 Dundonald memorandum (secret), n.d., CO 42/893, pp. 57–61.

40 Chamberlain minute on Minto to Chamberlain, April 15, 1903, CO 42/895, p. 61.

41 Anderson minute on Minto to Chamberlain, April 15, 1903, CO 42/895, p. 59. See also "Command and Efficiency of the Militia," Colonial Defence Committee, n.d., Cab. 11/27.

42 Chamberlain minute to Minto to Chamberlain, April 15, 1903, CO 42/895, p. 61.

43 Minutes of the 25th Meeting of the Committee of Imperial Defence,

December 4, 1903, Cab. 38/3/79; Governor General to Colonial Office, November 13, 1903, CO 42/893, p. 171.

44 Minutes of the 26th Meeting of the Committee of Imperial Defence, December 11, 1903, Cab. 38/3/82. See also Preston, *Canada and "Imperial Defense,"* p. 318–20.

45 Minto to Lyttelton, January 22, 1904, with clippings from Victoria *Colonist* and Montreal *Witness*, CO 42/896, p. 104.

46 Dundonald to Sir William Nicholson, November 25, 1903, CO 42/896, pp. 63–73.

47 Borden to Minto, March 1, 1904, PAC, Minto Papers, vol. 9, p. 42, and in CO 42/896, p. 301. See also War Office to Colonial Office, December 22, 1903, and minutes, CO 42/895, pp. 212–14. See also CO 42/896, p. 8.

48 *House of Commons Debates*, March 22, 1904, p. 262.

49 *Ibid.*, July 11, 1904, pp. 5435–53. Lord Minto also offered strenuous objection to some features of the revised bill: see Minto to Laurier, March 17, 1904, LP, C-809, pp. 83470–84; Minto to Lyttelton, March 21, 1904, CO 42/896, pp. 376–7, and *ibid.*, pp. 373–4 and 396.

50 *House of Commons Debates*, March 17, 1904, pp. 208–9; March 22, 1904, pp. 294–6; March 25, 1904, pp. 479–81.

51 *Ibid.*, March 22, 1904, pp. 291.

52 *Ibid.*, pp. 293–5.

53 Borden to Minto, April 15, 1904, Minto Papers, vol. 9, pp. 66–8.

54 Parsons to Governor General's Military Secretary, March 16, 1904, CO 42/896, pp. 437–42.

55 Minto to Lyttelton, April 11, 1904, *ibid.*, pp. 471–3.

56 Dundonald, *Army Life*, pp. 237–44. On the General's feeling of grievance and persecution, see *ibid.*, pp. 226–8.

57 Dundonald's draft report for 1903 with related correspondence in Dundonald Papers, section F.

58 On the affair, Pinault to Dundonald, May 19, 1904, and other correspondence, Dundonald Papers, section A; *Militia General Orders*, no. 75, May 1904. For an account of the local politics involved, see Toronto *News*, June 14, 1904, and Montreal *Herald*, June 14, 1904. On Whitley's politics, see E. Goff Penny, MP, to Borden, August 19, 1896, BP, p. 260, and Whitley to Borden, August 20, 1896, *ibid.*, p. 270.

59 Dundonald, *Army Life*, pp. 259–63; Montreal *Gazette*, June 9, 1904.

60 Toronto *Globe*, June 9 and 11, 1904.

61 Dundonald to Borden, June 8, 1904, Minto Papers, vol. 9, p. 74.

62 *House of Commons Debates*, June 10, 1904, pp. 4581–663. Laurier's inter-

vention is at p. 4620. See also O. D. Skelton, *The Life and Letters of Sir Wilfrid Laurier* (Toronto, 1921), vol. II, p. 300.

63 Cited in Frank H. Underhill, "Lord Minto on His Governor Generalship," *CHR*, XL, 2 (June 1959), p. 123.

64 Minto to St John Brodrick, April 11, 1903, NLS, Minto Papers, box 210, case C.

65 Minto draft memorandum, n.d., *ibid.*, p. 2.

66 Maude to Dundonald, June 16, 1904, in Dundonald, *Army Life*, p. 266. See also C. E. Callwell, *Life of Sir Stanley Maude* (London, 1920), p. 84. On Minto, see Minto to Laurier, June 10, 1904, LP, C-812, pp. 86571–4; memoranda on meetings with Dundonald on June 10 and 11, 1904, CO 537/491, pp. 13–17; Minto to Lyttelton (confidential), June 13, 1904, CO 537/487.

67 *Canadian Military Gazette*, June 28, 1904; Toronto *News*, June 18, 1904.

68 *House of Commons Debates*, June 23, 1904, pp. 5423 ff. For descriptions, see Toronto *Globe*, June 24, 1904; Toronto *News*, June 23, 1904.

69 *House of Commons Debates*, June 24, 1904, p. 5544.

70 *Canadian Military Gazette*, July 12, 1904; Dundonald, *Army Life*, pp. 266–80.

71 Great Britain, *House of Commons Debates*, C. 138, Fourth Session, July 19, 1904, pp. 482–97. For British press comment, see *Nineteenth Century and After*, July 1904, pp. 160–1; *Saturday Review*, June 18, 1904, pp. 770, 772–3; The *Spectator*, June 18, 1904. See also *Broad Arrow*, July 16, 1904, p. 674; *Army and Navy Gazette*, June 18, 1904.

72 Toronto *Globe*, June 24, 1904; Hutton to Minto, June 21, 1904, Minto Papers, vol. 17, p. 63. Hutton was simultaneously having difficulties with the Australian government: see Sir George Clarke to Minto, September 21, 1904, NLS, Minto Papers, box 210, case C.

73 Dundonald, *Army Life*, p. 283. See also Dundonald Papers section A.

74 Dundonald, *Army Life*, pp. 288–9; Ottawa *Citizen*, July 26, 1904; Maude to Minto, July 27, 1900, NLS, Minto Papers, box 213.

75 Laurier to S. H. Janes, October 7, 1904, LP, C-816, p. 90381.

CHAPTER TEN

1 *House of Commons Debates*, July 11, 1904, p. 6367.

2 *Ibid.*, pp. 6367–9. In the bill there was still provision for the appointment of

a "Colonel in the Militia or in His Majesty's Regular Army as Major General commanding the Militia" (4 Edw. VII, c. 23, s. 20).

3 *Militia Report,* 1903, pp. 35–6.

4 *House of Commons Debates,* July 20, 1904, p. 6383; August 1, 1904, pp. 8155, 8185.

5 War Office to Colonial Office, July 25, 1904, CO 42/899, p. 265; War Office to Colonial Office, August 2, 1904, *ibid.,* p. 270. See also CO 42/900, p. 94.

6 J. F. Cummins, "Lieutenant General Sir Percy Lake and Some Chapters of Canadian and Indian Military History," *Canadian Defence Quarterly,* April 1926, pp. 247–50; Minto to Lyttelton, July 9, 1904, CO 42/897, pp. 25–6; War Office to Colonial Office, August 25, 1904, CO 42/899, p. 283.

7 Minto to Borden, November 21, 1904, PAC, Minto Papers, vol. 8, p. 148.

8 Otter to Secretary of the Militia Council, March 5, 1908, CFHS, WO 32/909/091/2396. See also PAC, Otter Papers.

9 On the Hughes-Mackenzie dispute, see "Memorandum re General Mackenzie," PAC, R. L. Borden Papers, OC 55, pp. 741A ff. (and in CO 537/498).

10 Kenneth Bourne, *Britain and the Balance of Power in North America, 1815–1908* (London, 1967), chap. 10.

11 "The Defence of Canada," February 24, 1905, Cab. 38/8/13; "Remarks by the General Staff on the Admiralty Memorandum," Cab. 38/8/24; Admiralty reply, n.d., Cab. 38/9/36; Memorandum by the General Staff, December 13, 1904, Cab. 38/6/121; Minutes of the 73rd Meeting of the Committee of Imperial Defence, June 28, 1905, Cab. 38/9/52.

12 Minto to Lyttelton, June 18, 1904, CO 42/896, pp. 704–9; Minto memorandum, December 29, 1904, Cab. 38/6/125.

13 Minutes of the 73rd Meeting of the CID. On the British motives, see "The Defence of Halifax and Esquimalt," March 31, 1905, Cab. 38/830. The Canadians had discovered the truth by September 1905. See Borden to Laurier, September 20, 1905 and CID letter, "Strategic Conditions of Esquimalt," May 4, 1905, LP, vol. 381, pp. 101368–72.

14 *House of Commons Debates,* July 11, 1904, p. 6367.

15 *Ibid.,* May 5, 1903, p. 2405.

16 G. E. Buckle, ed., *The Letters of Queen Victoria, 1886–1901* (London, 1931), vol. II, p. 502.

17 Draft memorandum, NLS, Minto Papers, box 213, p. 3.

18 Minto to Parkin, September 26, 1904, in Frank H. Underhill, "Lord Minto on His Governor Generalship," *CHR,* XL, 2 (June 1959), p. 123.

A BIBLIOGRAPHICAL NOTE

Since this study attempts to fill a gap in the history of Canadian political development, it does not claim to supplant other works in the field. Of these the most substantial is Professor Preston's *Canada and "Imperial Defense"* (Toronto and Durham, 1967). The author has been in contact with Professor Preston for many of the past ten years and has gratefully absorbed his advice and suggestions. Another book, which covers part of the period in impressively painstaking detail is Professor Penlington's *Canada and Imperialism, 1896–1899* (Toronto, 1965), while Professor Stanley's *Canada's Soldiers* (rev. ed., Toronto, 1961) provides a convenient synthesis of the period. A number of valuable books have recently appeared in company with Professor Preston's work, examining the problems of British defence policy in North America in the nineteenth century. These include Kenneth Bourne's *Britain and the Balance of Power in North America* (London, 1967); Donald S. Gordon, *The Dominion Partnership in Imperial Defence* (Baltimore, 1965); and J. Mackay Hitsman, *Safeguarding Canada, 1763–1871* (Toronto, 1968). However, these, like Professor Stacey's older *Canada and the British Army, 1846–1871* (rev. ed., Toronto, 1963), do not deal with the political situation in Canada and its intimate relationship to the Dominion's military policy.

The main body of material – to the inevitable satisfaction of an historian – must be found among the primary sources. These are relatively full. Private papers can be found for most of the main protagonists. In the formation of militia policy there were four main sets of antagonists: the Ministers of Militia and their Generals and the Governors General and their Prime Ministers. For the Prime Ministers, the collections in the Public Archives of Canada are particularly complete and well-indexed for Sir John A. Macdonald and Sir Wilfrid Laurier. Governors General are less satisfactorily represented and the records of the Military Secretary suffer from a gap between 1878 and 1901. The Minto Papers, copied by the Public Archives of Canada, need to be supplemented from the originals in the National Library of Scotland to be a satisfactory record of that Governor General's military contribution.

Among Ministers of Militia, two of the three most important are represented by large bodies of material, inadequately catalogued so far and mingling personal, business, and departmental affairs. The Caron Papers include thousands of files for the period 1883–91 and forty letterbooks covering his full period in the Militia Department. The Borden Papers in the Nova Scotia Archives at Halifax are comparably rich sources although the bulk of the documents only cover the period from 1896 to 1900. There are letterbooks for a much longer period but many of them have suffered severe water damage. The third important minister, Sir George Etienne Cartier, left only a few volumes on militia patronage and less influential ministers are very slightly represented indeed. Only two General Officers Commanding were found to have substantial and accessible private papers. The Hutton Papers in the British Museum were valuable although obviously pre-selected and ordered for autobiographical purposes. The same limitations apply even more forcefully to the Dundonald Papers. For other generals no surviving papers were found. Lord Treowen's papers were dispersed or burned at his death in 1937. On the other hand, there is valuable material for the earlier period in the Duke of Cambridge's papers in the Royal Archives, Windsor Castle. One development of this study has been to add many of the surviving papers of Sir William Otter to the collections in the Public Archives of Canada.

Private papers are supplemented by a mass of surviving documents in the records of the Department of Militia and Defence, also deposited in the Public Archives of Canada. Unfortunately, little of it relates to the senior officials of the department or to questions of policy. Documents in the Colonial Office, War Office, and Cabinet inventories of the Public Record Office in London have also been necessary for this study. Many of them have been copied and are deposited in the Public Archives in Ottawa or in the Canadian Forces Historical Section. The Carnarvon Papers in the Public Record Office contain some valuable items which were not reprinted by de Kiewiet and Underhill in their collection of the Dufferin-Carnarvon correspondence.

Among the printed records, the annual reports of the Militia Department, the debates in the Canadian Parliament, and contemporary newspapers were obviously essential. The libraries of the Department of National Defence and of the Royal Canadian Military Institute were able to provide access to their collections of rare contemporary pamphlets on militia policy. Others were found in private collections and, particularly for the North-West Rebellion, in the Toronto Reference Library.

Index

This book

was designed by

ANTJE LINGNER

under the direction of

ALLAN FLEMING

and was printed by

University of

Toronto

Press